ELEGY FOR THE DALES

NIDDERDALE

ELEGY FOR THE DALES

NIDDERDALE

RICHARD MUIR

The History Press

TO FADING FACES
AND ECHOING VOICES
OF THE DAYS OF
SIMPLE DECENCY

First published 2010

The History Press
The Mill, Brimscombe Port
Stroud, Gloucestershire, GL5 2QG
www.thehistorypress.co.uk

British Library Cataloguing in Publication Data.
A catalogue record for this book is available from the British Library.

ISBN 978 0 7524 4782 7

Typesetting and origination by The History Press
Printed in Great Britain
Manufacturing managed by Jellyfish Print Solutions Ltd

Contents

Foreword   7

Introduction: The Valley of Ghosts   9

1   The Valley Beckons   (10000 BC – 4000 BC)   15

2   A Leafy Place   (c.4000 BC – c. 1000 BC)   31

3   Weakness in Numbers   (c. 1000 BC – AD 43)   53

4   A Sound of Marching   (AD 43 – AD 410)   69

5   A Nation is Born   (AD 410 – c. 1000)   79

6   The Red River   (c. 1000 – c. 1100)   103

7   The Swelling Bud   (c. 1100 – c. 1300)   119

8   Where Disasters Collide   (1348 – 1380)   153

9   Filling the Spaces   (1380 – 1536)   169

10   The Safety of Shadows   (1536 – c. 1700)   187

11   Two Steps to Today   (1700 – c. 1850)   209

12   The Last Grains of Sand   (1850 – present)   229

References   253

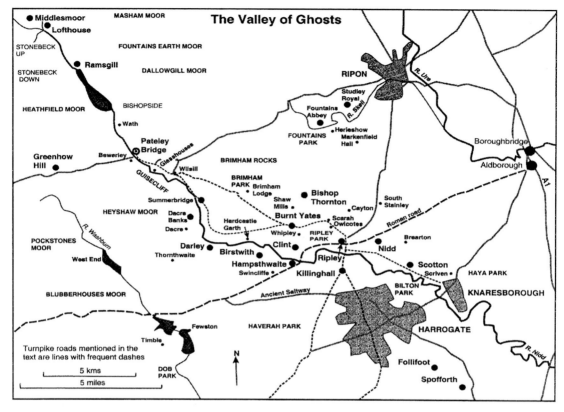

The Valley of Ghosts

Middlesmoor • Lofthouse • MASHAM MOOR • FOUNTAINS EARTH MOOR • STONEBECK UP • STONEBECK DOWN • Ramsgill • DALLOWGILL MOOR • RIPON • R. Ure • Studley Royal • R. Skell • HEATHFIELD MOOR • BISHOPSIDE • Fountains Abbey • FOUNTAINS PARK • Herleshow • Markenfield Hall • Boroughbridge • Aldborough • A1 • Wath • Pateley Bridge • Glasshouses • Bewerley • Wilsill • BRIMHAM ROCKS • Greenhow Hill • GUISECLIFF • BRIMHAM PARK • Brimham Lodge • Shaw Mills • Bishop Thornton • Cayton • South Stainley • Roman road • Summerbridge • HEYSHAW MOOR • Dacre Banks • Dacre • Hardcastle Garth • Burnt Yates • Whipley • Scarah • Owlcotes • RIPLEY PARK • Brearton • POCKSTONES MOOR • R. Washburn • Darley • Thornthwaite • Birstwith • Clint • Nidd • West End • Hampsthwaite • Swincliffe • Ripley • Killinghall • Scotton • Scriven • HAYA PARK • KNARESBOROUGH • BLUBBERHOUSES MOOR • Ancient Saltway • BILTON PARK • HARROGATE • R. Nidd • Fewston • Timble • HAVERAH PARK • Follifoot • Spofforth • DOB PARK

Turnpike roads mentioned in the text are lines with frequent dashes

5 kms
5 miles

N

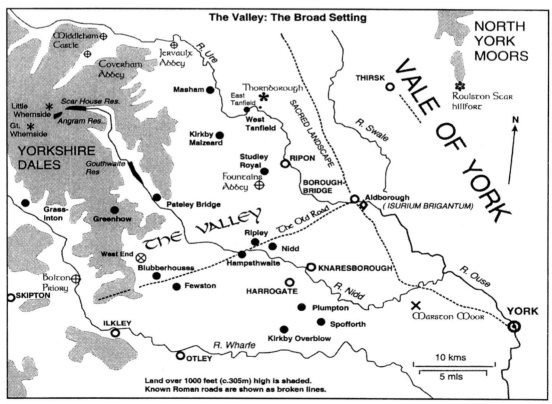

The Valley: The Broad Setting

NORTH YORK MOORS • Middleham Castle • Jervaulx Abbey • R. Ure • Coverham Abbey • THIRSK • Roulston Scar hillfort • Masham • Thornborough • East Tanfield • VALE OF YORK • Little Whemside • Scar House Res. • West Tanfield • R. Swale • Gt. Whemside • Angram Res. • SACRED LANDSCAPE • YORKSHIRE DALES • Kirkby Malzeard • Studley Royal • RIPON • Gouthwaite Res. • Fountains Abbey • BOROUGH BRIDGE • Aldborough (ISURIUM BRIGANTUM) • Grass-inton • Greenhow • Pateley Bridge • THE VALLEY • The Old Road • Ripley • Nidd • R. Ouse • West End • Hampsthwaite • KNARESBOROUGH • Bolton Priory • Blubberhouses • Fewston • HARROGATE • R. Nidd • YORK • SKIPTON • ILKLEY • Plumpton • Marston Moor • Spofforth • Kirkby Overblow • R. Wharfe • OTLEY

N

Land over 1000 feet (c.305m) high is shaded.
Known Roman roads are shown as broken lines.

10 kms
5 mls

FOREWORD

This is not a local history book. Rather, it is an attempt to *evoke* history: it seeks to use historical and archaeological information to recreate not just the facts, but also the feelings and the colours of the past.

My book has a surprising origin – or at least, it surprises me. I found myself with a mass of my own research material on Nidderdale that concerned topics such as village evolution, trees and woodlands, grouse moors, deer parks, route-ways and deserted settlements. Most of it had already been published in academic journals, but I thought that it might be good to bring it all together and make it available in book form: a history of the Nidderdale landscape. This required sponsorship, and while sponsors tend to be keen to promote themselves, sponsorship for research in landscape history and archaeology in North Yorkshire is extremely hard to find. Having failed to attract such a sponsor, I began to think about a different form of presentation, one that would stress the human qualities of the generations of Valley people.

I began to write in this way and was soon surprised to discover that I was writing with more passion and self-involvement than I had done for years. It was then that I realised that it was the epitaph for my wonderful Valley people that was just bursting to come out. So this is what I have written.

For most periods covered by this book, history (i.e. written records) is almost absent or does not exist and the evidence is of an archaeological nature. Where real people with well-documented histories exist, I have mentioned them. In the imaginative sections, I have created characters who, in their attitudes and lifestyles, will be very close to the real individuals of their times. I have thought it extremely important to recreate, too, the environments in which they lived. We, today, live in settings that, more often than not, impose stresses upon us. The old Valley people will have derived great comfort from lives spent in wonderful, vibrant settings that will have soothed life's stings like an all-enveloping dock leaf.

Writing this book has made me conscious of the immensity of recent cultural losses and the great degree to which people and land were bonded together. Dales-born, I have been fortunate to live both in Ireland and the North East of Scotland. In these countries, rural communities are respected and still partly intact and their members derive immense mental strength from the ties between personal identity and place. They know who they are. The work has also reminded me of how much I have lost. When I returned to my boyhood home in Nidderdale in 1985, I found that the local tongue and its speakers had largely disappeared, while I struggled to recall the old words and ways of saying them. In the course of writing this book I have lost count of the times that I have been amazed by the ease with which a rich cultural heritage and some wonderful countryside (both of these having been centuries in the making) were simply discarded, evicted, devalued and forgotten. Doubtless, before very long there will be a Visitor Centre with a huge car park in the Valley. In that centre there may be fading photographs of communities in the harvest field or village hall. Perhaps there will be scratchy recordings of how Dales people talked and, meanwhile, the last of the real ones will wander around like dinosaurs, at home but completely lost.

Given that Nidderdale is still a fascinating place, it seemed essential to produce an illustrated work. However, I soon became conscious of the fact that clinical conventional photographs taken in 2005 would sit uneasily with a book that sought, imaginatively, to evoke past lives and landscapes. Then, I recalled dabbling with infra-red photography in the 1980s. This monochrome film, with an extra heat-sensitive layer and used with a red filter, has the strange quality of sensing the radiation from living things: leaves, grass, faces and so on, and rendering their images brightly, in pale greys and white. It photographs life, though the effect is somewhat ghostly and unsettling. I believe that it is very well-suited for a project like *Elegy for the Dales*. The pictures displayed combine my low-tech 35mm film technology and high-tech digital negative scanning.

In a way, this book is the latest chapter in a very long story that began with me taking my sheepdogs for walks from about age eleven onwards (though poaching might be a more succinct description of the activity). I started to struggle to understand why my then so lovely homeland between Ripley and Darley was formed in the way it was. Where did the lanes, the walls and the homesteads come from? This is a report on the state of the enquiries so far.

INTRODUCTION

THE VALLEY OF GHOSTS

The old man stepped stiffly down on to the pitted surface of the road. A cry had stabbed through the stillness of evening. Were the royal Foresters out with nets and dogs poaching their master's deer again? Best keep out of their way. He was just counting himself lucky to live outside the Forest edge when he saw something glinting in a crevice in the crumbling road. With fingers like scarred hedgerow twigs he fumbled to pick it up. A minute coin: he struggled to focus his eyes on it, failed and tucked it carefully into his purse.

Five centuries earlier, a benighted traveller had lost the silver coin while journeying on the road that even then was thought ancient. The old man would not have understood his language or even the concept that language, ways of lives and landscapes evolve. He knew nothing of Anglo-Saxons or Romans and history for him was not at all about change or 'progress'. Instead, it was about tradition and had much to do with the importance that antiquity conferred on a line and its property. It existed for as far back as one could recite the names of one's ancestors. Beyond that, things did not really matter. Nothing changed very much – and then you got back to those people that the clerks talked about, like Adam and Abraham. And you didn't really need to know much about them, so long as you went to church every Sunday. Yet this indifference did not signify an empty mind, for he could recite the uses of every hedgerow plant, build a house from the resources of his township and predict rain hours before it came. He believed in keeping his mind free for the things that mattered.

He gazed across and then up the Valley as twilight subsided into darkness. In the gaps between the black stripes that were tree trunks, pinpoints of light from distant dwellings could be seen, but the groves, the 'hollins', where holly was grown as winter feed for starving beasts, blotted out any lights, like dark clouds masking a starry sky. The air smelled different from the way it had smelled when he was young. Then, it forever bore the tang of wood-smoke. People were pushing outwards, reducing the woodland like sheep converging on a clover patch. Then, the births exceeded the dying and so hunger pushed households into the margins. The Pestilence had put an end to all that. His shoulders slumped as he turned to look at the mound of mud, wattle and rotting rafters that had been his neighbours' home. Five families had lived in straggle of narrow dwellings strung out along the old Roman road, but now there was just him. He thought of how they would sit at the roadside, their bowls of oatmeal on their knees and some bread in their hands, talking about the farm work and hopeful that an interesting stranger might emerge from the shadows on the bend. Two strangers made for a memorable evening.

Now he had forgotten why he had gone outdoors. A blackness such as we never see today sank heavily on the Valley, magnifying silence. Cattle slept; roe deer barged furtively through thickets and then owls of several types and ages erupted from different quarters to orchestrate the darkness. Stooping below the peat fug that hung in the roof space, the old man shifted his straw-sack bed closer to the embers on his hearth stone. Waiting for the chills to seep out and sleep to fill their place, he tuned his ear to the owls. Those were the Knaresborough tawnys, and those the owls of Hampsthwaite – and that the Ripley barn owl: he knew just where it raised its young. The hoots and screeches were resounding and reverberating in 100 side chambers in the Valley, each more distant than the one before, to make Nidderdale one resonating cathedral of owls.

'Nidderdale': what a strange name. Why did some names mean something and others ape the mutterings of a madman? Had you told him that 1,000 years earlier, British people had used the word 'Nidd' to signify a river that was brilliant or sparkling and that perhaps half as long ago Old Danish speakers had named this place a valley or 'dale', he would have given the notions little time. Danes were vaguely remembered in folklore in much the same way as devils or goblins, but everyone knew that the Dalesfolk had been here forever, since Abraham and those other people. Nothing changed much. It had not even occurred to him that were Abraham himself to appear from around the bend he would speak anything other than the Middle English dialect of northern England.

During the next six centuries, things changed a great deal. At the end of the twentieth century, I found the old man's house. It was a shelf or platform on the northern side of the track. It was about the length and breadth of one of the little buses that took me to the grammar school each day, arriving predictably and in defiance of my prayers that it might break down before reaching Birstwith.

The house stood perhaps a couple of feet above the level of the Roman road that had linked the empire's Pennine forts with the little administrative centre at Aldborough, a track that would already have been scuffed and ground into the countryside by the old man's day. Sometimes the route is slightly winding, so perhaps the Romans had adopted a native trackway. The old man's house was on a slight curve at the foot of a shallow slope where the Roman kerbstones can still be seen, its long axis parallel to the roadside in typical medieval fashion. Now large trees stand at its ends. A few more dwellings were strung along the side of the ascending road, while on the bend a 'better' house in an enclosure was set back from the road. This was a loose, roadside hamlet of a kind very common in the Dale, but the sort of place that seems, often, to have been unable to recover from the successive onslaughts of the Black Death.

The name of that hamlet has been lost. However, it lay in a little cell of land called 'Godwinscales', and of this we do know the story. The old Scandinavian word 'scales' often seems to denote a pasture grazed by livestock in the summer, while 'Godwin' was a real person: a semi-historical one. His granddaughter, Avice, was entirely historical and records show she lived at the start of the thirteenth century. We know Godwin partly through his granddaughter, but he must have been quite some man, for he gave his name to his district and to a little bridging place. He was also remembered in a great boundary oak: Godwin's Oak. It lived into the eighteenth century, and the remains of it could still be seen in 1767. How strange to die in obscurity yet leave a locality, a beck crossing and a tree as one's monuments!

For countless generations, the people of the Valley lived like skin scales on the body of their countryside. They were sloughed away and fell, but the countryside lived on, largely indifferent to their arrival and departure. Yet without any one of them, it would not quite have been the same.

Their collective marks were deeply etched into the landscape. It was their artefact, so that just as the potter may leave his fingerprint on a vessel, so each countryman and woman left some trace. They tended the beasts that grazed the meadows green and free of alder seedlings. They trimmed and laid the hedges and kept them dense and healthy, and they padded along paths until they became tracks, and then roads. Pots, once fired, are immutable. Well or badly made, the potter has no scope for second thoughts or chances. Countryside is a much more plastic artefact. Wood pastures can become open grazings or coppiced woods. Palings can become hedgerows and the hedgerows can be replaced by walls. And fine countryside can be rendered as bleak as a prairie. It all depends on the makers and custodians of the scene. Countryside is a comment on its makers, so only the greedy can fashion landscapes of greed.

The couple on the track may possibly know they are on a Roman road, but none of the ramblers passing realise that the dwellings of a deserted medieval hamlet line the roadside at the bend.

This is a tale of a Valley and its ghosts. The Valley: a window on ancient ritual; a zone of transition between the civilised and unstable parts of Roman Britain; a scene of slaughter; a hunting reserve of medieval kings; and a place of little ponds and goits at the dawn of the Industrial Age – this was never much more than a backwater and yet it was placed to witness events of national importance. In its backwater guise it was allowed, at least until recently, to develop its own personality without too many forceful impositions.

The narrative is underpinned by objective historical research, mainly my own work as a professional landscape historian/archaeologist. The makers of countryside were very largely people who, if they appear in the historical record at all, do so but fleetingly, as witnesses to charters, offenders in manor courts or tenants on a rental. The great canvas that is England is the work of countless very largely anonymous hands. Our distance from these forbears is increasing at an ever-accelerating rate. The technological divide might almost seem to make the differences between ourselves and our forbears differences of kind rather than of degree. Even so, those of us who remember the Valley as it was in the 1950s or even 1960s can feel excluded and usurped by what has happened since, and yet still stand quite close to those ancestral ghosts. We can remember a world in which people did not just arrive and grab control of a setting. Rather, we were part of it. We settled gently in the folds of its great slumbering body. Dawn was its way of greeting us, and dusk, its invitation to slumber. We knew the name of every sike, path, bank, bluff and outcrop. The badger, linnet, redstart, woodcock and cowslip were our neighbours. We knew where they lived and when to find them.

The Valley is stalked by their ghosts, layer upon layer of them. Almost 500 generations of them, very largely composed of people who lived nearly every minute of their lives in a recess of the Valley and knew it in profound detail. Sometimes, we can almost feel suffocated by their presence. They can seem just a couple of steps behind as we tread the old pack-horse lane. If they can mutter or murmur they do so in Old Welsh, Latin, Old English, Old Danish, Old Norse, Middle English, Elizabethan English and several ancient tongues we do not even know about. Where the rambler of today places his cleated boot, hobnailed ones from Mr Stott the Birstwith cobbler have trod before. Clogs of alder cut from the banks of the Nidd, deerskin boots tied with rawhide thongs, bare heels as hard as elm, the hoofs of some friar's donkey, the pads of the wolf and the bear – all have also trod. Perhaps it is the weight of all these ghosts that make the Valley seem heavy and soulful when the wind has dropped and the birds have gone to roost. What can they think when they see their language dying and their old homeland becoming tattered and gnawed by greed? Will there come a time when we can tell the grey, accusing ranks that, despite it all, we cared too?

CHAPTER 1

THE VALLEY BECKONS

(10000 BC – 4000 BC)

We know that our land was populated for thousands of years before the dawn of history. We know that these prehistoric people wrought immense changes in their setting. And yet, almost everything about them remains mysterious. It is unlikely that they were schooled in a society that, like ours, judged its members by their ability to 'make a mark'. So perhaps it is the influence of modern values that makes us feel it rather tragic to depart a lifetime and soon vanish without leaving a single legible entry in the ledgers of history? We probably haven't gained in intelligence in the last 25,000 years; we have simply shifted the balance of knowledge around. People living in the Valley at the close of the Old Stone Age may have known less than 100 other people and knew next to nothing of the world beyond their corner of Yorkshire. However, the people that they did know they will have known very well, and they will have had a whole vocabulary of words associated with every part, habit and degree of the reindeer as well as a religion that explained everything on heaven and earth to their total satisfaction. Probably, they did not care to be remembered as individuals – it was their contribution to the survival of the community that mattered.

History is not about greatness but about failure. Even those thought to be great will be reassessed, devalued, and later reappraised, before being edged aside to make way for those on whom greatness was more recently conferred. Most of us have sought to make our mark. In this we are doomed to fail. Memories of the good non-league cricketer will perish even before the score-books moulder away. The just employer will be forgotten soon after the takeover of the firm. The good house painter will live to see his work crack and peel, while the inspirational teacher will discover the tight limits of adulation as soon as he or she needs support in a crisis. All our little quests for immortality yield much less than we hope for, or expect. But, as I have suggested, how sad it must be to have prepared the way for others and yet vanish absolutely, utterly, and with no recognisable trace from the memories of humans. This was the fate of most of our ancestors. The huge majority of our human forbears were prehistoric, which is to say they lived before the habit of recording history reached their homelands. Travel back just 500 years before the Roman army dragged history into our Valley in the first century AD and not only do we not know anything about any of the individuals living there and none of their names, but even their language is uncertain. They were transforming an already ancient countryside, making strong marks upon it, yet there is nothing at which we can point and say, 'There is their work'. Time has layered it over and covered it across. Move forward almost 1,000 years to the closing days of Saxon England: the foundations of the modern landscape are now mostly in place, yet we do not know the names of enough Valley people of the time to make up a cricket team. We know something of their mark, but little of their names. It is a position rather like one of thinking, 'We think some Americans may have made the first powered flight, but we do not know who they were, where it happened, or exactly when'.

From our position of ignorance it is easy, indeed comforting, to assume that the most ancient of settlers were ignorant. Unlikely. If the various apparent parallels between the lives of Native American and prehistoric British communities are not illusions then it is probable that these distant ancestors could have taught us a great deal. Perhaps they could tell us about the dominion of community over individuality and of how even the communities of humans are simply facets of the great unity that is creation. In other words, they might have taught us to respect our environment rather than, ultimately, to die from its abuse. They might have shared a vision of an earth that should not be violated and would suffer if it were. Even so, it would be folly to imagine that ancient people always lived in harmony with their settings. Archaeology reveals the graves of those who died in the struggles for territory, the dwellings abandoned in worn-out frontier lands, the streams choked with eroding plough soil, the plague pits, sewers and fouled wells.

In modern times, humans have acquired a taste for talking or reading about history. But we have never, ever, *listened* to its lessons. Perhaps as recently as 1970, we might have learned enough in time to set a new course for the world. Now we insatiably consume, breed, build, arm and produce; we gas the beautiful planet that must be our only home and soon, it seems, our graveyard. It was sometimes said of beautiful aircraft, like the Spitfire, that if they looked right, then they were right. Equally, it can be said of landscape or countryside that if it looks sick, then sick it is. We need to *listen*. The visual media treat archaeology like treasure hunting and archaeologists like dotty exhibitionists (too often, they confirm the stereotype). Far more valuable than any treasure it might unearth are the lessons serious archaeology conveys about why civilisations and communities and villages perished, and what we can learn from their fates.

It began more brightly. One day, some day (for we cannot know quite when) before the last great glaciation, a new creature stepped warily into the Valley. Humans had arrived. Probably rather grubby, tanned and matted but by now white-skinned, they will have represented a very early stage in our own, *Homo sapiens*, line. Behind them stretched generation upon generation, leading back across time and deep into Africa, perhaps to a single mother of all humankind. Arriving in the Valley as a small group of brothers, mothers and cousins, they had followed the nervous herds of horse and deer through an Eden that was cool in climate yet (to our eyes) almost African in its fauna. Straight-tusked elephant, lion, hyena and hippo all had their places in the floodplains and thickets of Nidderdale. After many centuries of feeding, fleeing, killing and being killed, the animals would drift away to the south, leaving very few traces behind. The early humans, still little more than an afterthought in Eden, would vanish and not return. Evidence of their presence there in truly distant times is yet to be traced in the Valley. Perhaps it never will be, but if it is, then flint 'handaxes' shaped like huge flattened eggs with glass-sharp edges are the most likely find – they were the multi-purpose tools of their day.

The musty smell of approaching snow was smelled ever more frequently, until no noses remained to smell it. Snow-dusted and with nostrils like steam valves, life retreated as the snow gathered ever deeper in the upland hollows. There it stacked and piled, cliff high, until tongues of rock and dirt-stained ice nosed down where once the river had flowed. The Valley lost its identity as smooth, rounded whiteness masked its grooves and bulges. Only the lost young eagle or flocks of frightened migrants blown off course would see the ice-gorged Valley in all its whiteness for a very long time.

In these times of pristine sterility, there would be phases when the grip of the ice sheets slackened and the game nosed nervously northwards. Herds might branch away from the old trails and reindeer eyes would see thawing landscapes that no reindeer eyes had glimpsed for thousands of years. Perhaps, too, there were times when the humans joined with the wolves to trail the antlered herds into the northern wildernesses. If so, they were not much like the first humans to have set foot in the Valley, for, standing closer on the gene map to our ape cousins, these Neanderthal people represented a fascinating yet ultimately doomed sidetrack of humanity. If the capacity of their skulls is an indicator of their brain power, it was not stupidity that sealed their fate – their brains tended to be as large or larger than our own. The fact that they were finely adapted to survive in glacial environments could have played a part. Their huge and bulbous noses helped to filter out the cold; their thickset builds reduced heat loss while exceeding the muscularity of any modern Olympic competitor; and their massive limbs must have given them near-inexhaustible powers of endurance. However, when the climate eased and streams of new, thoroughly modern humans flowed out of Africa these Neanderthalers (named after a German valley where their remains were first discovered) gradually vanished. Perhaps, when faced by competitors, they fell victim to their own conservatism and inflexibility: a reluctance to discover new skills or explore new places? It was the ability to adapt to new settings, from the Polar shores to the hot desert margins, which gave fully modern humanity our spectacular success. Equally, may it not be a refusal to face the challenges of our successes: an over-populated and polluted world that will seal our fate?

Did the Neanderthalers ever set foot in the Valley? Quite possibly, but like all before them and many to follow, they did not leave not a mark on the face of their setting that we can identify. Neanderthalers had no idea that, over many thousands of years, ice came and went. They could never have imagined that, eventually, it might go forever. Go it did: about 12,500 years ago, mammoth, woolly rhinoceros and moose wandering in the thawing lands of northern England found that healthy mates were ever harder to find. By around 12,000 years ago, the ice that had plugged the Valley and plastered the uplands was in retreat and time in Europe was fast running out for the giant deer, rhinoceros and cave bear. The land was awakening. The ice re-advanced, briefly and harshly, before shrinking back to the valley-head hollows: the places from whence it had come so many thousands of years before.

Like midnight's vandals, the latest Age of Ice had left behind scenes of mindless devastation. The Valley was littered with expanses of sands, and silts flushed out of the dying ice by bucking streams of meltwater. These swarming torrents had gouged channels in the hillsides as they searched blindly for ways past the masses of dirty, declining ice that blocked their paths downstream. The grits and grains in the frenzied waters scoured the rock like liquid sandpaper. In the upper Valley, blister-shaped hills were moulded from ice-bound debris by the wasting ice. In days when apt, evocative phrases were not judged an affront to scholarship, these flocks of mounds came to be known as 'basket of eggs topography'. And that is how they seem today, especially when viewed from the air. While the river, reborn from the ice, wove an unstable course among the dumps of rocks and clays, sands and gravels that spattered its old floodplain, short-lived lakes formed in the valley bottom. Before too long, most would be breached and drained by the twining river, a few surviving the centuries to be slowly consumed by rushes and alder that crept in from the margins like a scab around a wound. Meanwhile, the Valley was coming to life.

The landscape was changing and so, too, was the soundscape. The silence of winter during the long glacial chapter had been breached only by the explosive crack, unheard by any ear, when the stresses of freezing and thawing split another rock fragment from a scar. Down and down it would make its rattling way to rest in the scree that littered the glacier's edge. In the glacial summers, not much was heard but the faint dripping and trickling of water when summer was at its height. An easing of the year-long winters was marked by new sounds: the piping, trilling and mewing of moor fowl and waders, firstly brief visitors and then birds returning to breed among the stone litter and reindeer moss. Soon, the relative silence of the millennia was shattered by the thunderous din of meltwater. For centuries, torrents hurtled out of the ice tunnels, gushed across the glaciers and sprang out of the leaky edges of the ice sheets until it might have seemed that all the water in the universe had teemed, pell-mell, across the face of Yorkshire. After that, the sounds dropped to conventional levels as the Valley settled to the chatter and swirl of the reborn river and becks. Then, life added more of its myriad sounds to those of the inert physical forces. Wildfowl appeared, wheeling over the lakes, then plummeted feet first into the waters. Eggs trapped in the scales of their legs sank in the water and turned into fish or bugs. Specks and spores drifted in the breeze; seeds of life travelled in fur and feathers. Buzzing and whirring, screeching and warbling, baying and howling announced that the Valley was alive again.

Following many uneventful millennia, everything would soon be happening very quickly. At first, the stripped and barren slopes were textured by the angular frost-shattered scree, scarred boulders shed by the ice, slithery clay dumps, gravel beds and bare soils of slippery shale. Wherever one looked, the only colour below the skyline was a shade of grey: yellow-grey clay, pale limestone grey, greenish grit-stone grey and the brown-greys of the shingle in the beds of the streams. Beneath the periodic blueness of the sky, the land was seldom more than a touch removed from the monochrome. But soon, the slopes became colonised by lichens, tussocky sedges and grasses, dwarf alpine plants and wormwood – and then they were dotted with arctic willows, dwarf birch and juniper in an ever-thickening stipple of shrubs. The hardiest plants were doomed: it was their role to feed the soil until it could nourish those plants destined to replace them.

As the slopes went from grey to green, the herbivores came drifting in to enjoy the new setting: reindeer, enormous red deer, the aurochs (a terrifying form of wild cattle) and stocky little horses. Quietly they appeared and then came on, shyly tasting the air as they advanced further to the north and west than they had ever

Dwarf birch was one of the first trees to return after the last Ice Age and birch is common in woods on the steep Valley sides.

been before. There would have been other creatures, too, that seem more bizarre in the context of the Dales, like the saiga antelope, the pika, a short-eared but otherwise rabbit-like rodent and perhaps even wolverine and spotted hyena. The air fizzed with bugs that bred in the stagnant meanders abandoned by the footloose river, making the herbivores kick and twitch and move off to the drier places. Each year brought new species of birds into the Valley. Firstly, there were the wildfowl and the arctic migrants, but as the community of plants became more diverse, so, too, did that of the birds. Whole populations of wildlife that had found ice-refuge on the northern flanks of the Alps were now populating the Valley. Linger in the shadows, and one might have seen wolves loping with deceptive indifference after elk, bears jostling to scoop out salmon or the sparring of giant bulls. Quite soon, the low-growing hardy shrubs were shaded out of existence by the tree birch and Scots pine clusters. Grass and reed clumps carpeted the land between, and small rodents and predators performed dances of death in tunnels among the tussocks. Death was back so life was back: life was everywhere.

Fully modern humans returned with the great herds that nibbled their ways across the limitless pastures of sedges and reindeer moss. The first Dalesfolk of our lineage came from Africa. So, too, did everybody else. The arrival in Europe of modern humans was associated with a most remarkable social occurrence: change. For thousands upon thousands of years, human life and technology had hardly changed at all. Now, people developed a range of advanced tools and thereby equipped themselves to hunt many more species and in a variety of different ways. New talents erupted and in caves on the continent, beautifully observed animals were painted, perhaps by artists in trance-induced states of consciousness. Spear-throwers of bone or antler magnified the throwing power of the human arm. The people were potent hunters; bows and arrows had been in use for a few thousand years before the waning of the ice, but as the ice receded, the shaping and employment of tiny flints involved new expertise almost comparable to that of the watchmaker.

In the Valley and its surrounding uplands, a place that had been a sterile, ice-bound desert seemed set to become a paradise such as humans might dream of. There was a pure, shimmering river with trout, grayling and migratory sea trout and salmon. There were hollows in the valley flanks where the red deer and reindeer might huddle from winter's bite. Pastures were sprinkled with horses and cattle; there were bison to kill and bears to worship. Soon, a dream is all that there would be. Had the climate stayed in that halfway house between the polar and the temperate, only a sustained over-killing of the animal stocks could have slammed the gates of this Eden. As it was, it continued to warm and the beneficiary of this was … the tree. More precisely, it was the deciduous hardwood: trees like the alder, birch, oak, elm and ash, which pressed into the places where the Scots pines and birches stood, robbed their seedlings of light and nutrients and eventually, banished the pines to the Lake District and the Scottish lands, beyond.

Scarcely had humans assimilated the valley into the great seasonal circuit that was 'home' to people who had no home, than the whole basis of their life was undermined. Dozens of generations had passed as they learned to convert the hunting and scavenging of their African origins into a way of life that could sustain them in the frigid plains around the icy core of the northern continent. They had learned to stalk where there were no trees, to stampede mammoth over cliffs and to make house frames from their tusks and bones, to disguise and to mimic their prey and to fashion warm garments from their pelts. They knew how far

For a while, Scots pine woods will have dominated the Valley scene.

a woolly rhino could see and when it could catch their scent, where to spear a bison and how to usurp a cave bear.

They could look out from knolls and cave mouths across expanses where nothing larger than a bilberry plant might grow and see the herds of horses and deer ranging in numbers that seemed greater than the pebbles in a stream. As they looked at these slowly shifting masses of impending food and warmth, they may well have imagined that they were divinely favoured, the chosen ones of whatever divinity they revered. And then, the whole culture, finely tuned and carefully tailored for survival on the tundra margins of a glaciated continent, collapsed and had to be rebuilt. There was no allowance for trees in their manner of living. Trees masked the hunters' view and trapped the more extravagantly antlered of the deer. They fragmented the herds and gave too much advantage to the wolves. But mainly, they displaced the pasture.

However, it is now beginning to seem that the change was not as immediate or as total as was imagined. We were taught of the primeval 'wildwood' – expanses of woodland that were breached only by the tallest summits and narrowly cut by ribbons of riverside marsh. Regional folk myths claim that even as recently as the medieval period, squirrels could traverse large portions of counties without ever setting foot on the ground. Now, it appears that the wilderness had a more park-like character. Boars, bison, cattle and horses would browse the edges of woodland and their rooting, trampling and grazing would enlarge the clearings that were opened when great trees fell. Meanwhile, fungal attacks and other diseases would kill local communities of trees to create some more open areas. In such ways, the woods were forever opening and healing to produce a greater diversity of habitats than the wildwood alone could ever have sustained.

There is more to the story than this, for some soil layers dating from 6,000 to 9,000 years ago contain charcoal. Forest fires very rarely take hold in deciduous Forest, so we seem to be encountering deliberate burning by humans. This might have been done to increase grazing resources by enlarging existing clearings and to create hunting areas deprived of cover. The woodland being difficult to burn, it may be that trees were first killed by removing a ring of bark from around their trunks, and then set on fire. Whatever the details, the drifting smoke haze signalled that for the first time in the Valley, humans had ceased to be simple members of its animal population and had begun, significantly and deliberately, to change and re-shape their setting. It might be argued that the beaver then living on the Nidd, whose timber dams made the river bulge and check, were doing the same. The beaver, however, were not initiators but rather, they were innately programmed to do what they did. There was, too, a limit to what they could change – a river could contain only so many dams. The human initiatives were open-ended; there were no limits or controls to the direction or destiny of change. The species that owed its success as much to its versatility as to its mental superiority could be many things in many different places.

While upland moors formed naturally in Norway and, probably, in Scotland, in our dales they were greatly influenced by human activity. It is likely that before the trees had been able fully to return to the high fells, humans had converted the uplands into open hunting ranges. With the high rainfall and snowfall incurred as the clouded plateaux intercepted the air currents from the Atlantic, the ground was often soaked. But with no trees to suck the moisture from the soil and with few bacteria in the sepia mush to decompose dead plant material, a blanket of wet, black, acidic peat soon cloaked the interfluves. In this way, the first important human contribution to the landscape of the valley may have been its heather moors.

In the time of the hunter gatherers, deciduous trees invaded the pine woods and scenes like this mixed wood of pines and hardwoods will have been seen.

When we go up there today, the keen freshness of the upland air, the vast, seemingly desolate panoramas and the general absence of others of our crowded kind inspire us to imagine that here is a true wilderness: a pristine reminder of how pure and carefree the world once was. Really, the moorland is probably as much a human artefact as Bradford or Briggate. It was begun almost 10,000 years ago, maintained by commoners, shepherds and bracken burners for untold centuries, and now it depends on the periodic 'swaling' or localised burning to produce the fresh growth that the grouse nibble. It was burning that created the grouse moors and swaling that dapple-patterns them with blotches marking the different years of burning. Should we turn our backs on the heather moor for too long, the bracken, sedge and rank grasses would encroach, with the rowan and birch not far behind.

Today's rambler might scuff his boot amongst the gritty sands that leach out from under the peat or flip over a stone where the adders bask. There, almost invisible among the grains of quartz, there just might be a pearly flake of flint. It must have moved many miles to get there, travelling against the directions of river and ice movement. There is flint away to the east, and we know that in the next age (the Neolithic or New Stone Age), people on the beaches gathered nodules fallen from flint seams in the chalk cliffs near Flamborough Head. They shaped them into axes for export far inland. Flint was so valuable to people like the makers of the moors. No other rock apart from obsidian, which is not found here, could be struck, pressed or rapped to produce, in a predictable way, blades sharp as a sliver of glass.

When our moor-makers reorganised their lives to cope with the advancing woodland, they developed new toolkits. The heavy axes shaped from cores of flint and the blades like cutthroat razors lost favour to new tools, axes redesigned for cutting trees, barbed arrowheads that would lodge in the body of a bird and other implements for grubbing out tubers, or for harpooning fish, while an amazing delicacy and refinement were achieved in the working of minute flakes of flint. Blades no bigger than the fingernails of infants were made. Using animal and vegetable glues, these must have been bonded to shafts and used to point and barb missiles, to make serrated knives or, perhaps, as cutting teeth in graters for preparing the edible roots, fungi and shoots that offered new dietary opportunities. And so the pearly flake beneath the rambler's boot might come from a barbed missile lodged in a wounded deer, from a hasty shot that missed a blackcock or from a knife used to cut some rush bedding or grass seed heads. Or maybe someone had sat upon a nearby boulder, a protective pad of thick hide on his thigh, as he pressed the edge of a blade of flint with a blunt point of bone and watched a flake fly away, gliding on the air like a petal of stone.

As the climate improved, oak advanced up the slopes to cover most of the dale.

To begin an (ultimately impossible) attempt to enter the minds of these people we would need to empty much from our own minds. Firstly, we would need to abandon all our ideas about 'home'. Home was not a single place, brimming with powerful emotional associations of security and insularity. Home, such as it was, was wherever the people went. In the course of a year, there would be several homes. There were the fuggy, scooped-out refuges from cruel frost, roofed like tents with boughs and skins. There were the halfway houses on the wooded slopes that became 'homes' in spring and autumn, and there were flimsy summer shelters amongst the thyme on the open uplands, tents that any unseasonal gale might bear away. From what we know from other scenes of life in this, the Middle Stone Age, small communities survived by wintering in the sheltered valleys or on the shorelines and progressed up through woodlands of the valley slopes to pass the summer hunting on the open ranges of the high fells and upland plateaux.

Large territories are needed to support human hunting groups and our valley may have been home to only three or four of them. In winter, they may all have met together to find partners, exchange information and perform the rituals needed to ensure that game was plentiful when the hunting year was reborn. It was a time for meeting and mixing but it was also a hard time for the hunter. Stores of hazelnuts and dried berries gathered in the autumn were nibbled by the families as they huddled, steaming in their winter quarters. Other refugees from the freezing fells, the red deer, slipped shyly among the trees, trapped between the blizzards of the fell tops and the fearful stench of humans by the riverside. Fish, almost torpid in the deeper pools, helped to sustain the people, though some families may have quit the Dales to winter on the faraway coast, where mussels, crustaceans, stranded whales and other flotsam of the strandline provided a more reliable food store.

When the short, cold and hungry days ended, the elation must have been profound. Freed from their winter huts, the families will have worked their ways slowly through the wooded valley flanks, where everything was fresh and bursting with renewed energy. There were nests to pillage and animals to chase, but not quite the assemblage of fauna that we see in the woods and waterways of the Dale today. The roe deer, fox, otter and badger were there, but the pheasant may have been a Roman introduction, while both the rabbit and the fallow deer were Norman importations (though the rabbit was known to have lived in the Cheddar Gorge around 12,000 years ago and the fallow deer was also a former resident, though perhaps more distantly so). The mammoth probably disappeared from Europe around 12,000 years ago, before all the ice had gone. From the close of the Ice Age the animals now associated with colder climates, like the lemming, lynx, bison, arctic hare and arctic fox gradually declined and the giant deer was extinct around 10,500 year ago. With its immense antlers it could never have survived in woodland.

Reindeer probably lingered a fair while longer (perhaps even into the Iron Age in Scotland), and as the people fanned out on the upland ranges in mid-May they will have found the newborn reindeer easy prey, their long bones being split to release the fat-rich marrow. Other animals declined in the face of human predation. Beaver may have vanished from the Dale in Saxon times, with the bear perhaps lasting almost as long. Wolves, which carried a bounty from some medieval monasteries, were only evicted during the Middle Ages (when Gilbert de Gaunt, who died in 1241, granted great pastures in Swaledale to the monks of Rievaulx Abbey, he also gave them the right to kill wolves there). Boar also vanished in the medieval period, while after its close, the red deer, now greatly reduced in stature and the victim of poaching wars between the gentry, vanished from the open fells and valley winter refuges. The pine martin, known in Nidderdale as the 'fomud', survived in Nidderdale until modern times and was recorded on High Ash Head Moor in 1870.

Alder swamp cloaked the Valley bottoms, though these alders at Birstwith were probably planted to stabilise an artificially straightened river channel and, perhaps, to provide timber for clog-makers.

Brimham Rocks will have provided excellent vantage points for huntsmen.

This was about the time that the grey squirrel was introduced from North America, and while there are differences of opinion about this squirrel's virtues, nobody can doubt the carnage wrought in the Nidd and its riverside life by the mink, which escaped from a Scottish fur farm as soon as they were introduced, in 1938.

Emerging from the birch woods into the freshness of the upland plateaux, the sisters, uncles, cousins and parents of a Valley clan might clamber and leap on the great gritstone pinnacles at Brimham Rocks, surely a great landmark ritual focus and vantage point for all prehistoric peoples. From the highest formation they could look north-westwards towards the source of the river that glinted among the alders far below. As they looked, to their right were the heather moors, smudged at their margins by smoke from the receding woodland. To their left, the panorama embraced the Valley, with its floodplain bordered by reed swamp and alder carr and its 'banks' or slopes pattered in green by woods of oak, hazel, holly, elm, lime and ash. Every habitat and every nook of the Valley produced food for the people. Gazing across the setting, they did not see beauty in the way that a connoisseur of art and scenery would see it. For them, beauty was born from the blending of sensations from both the eye and the stomach. The splendour of the river was partly composed from flashing rapids and rippled currents that became mirrors as water glided over the deeps. But it was partly based, too, on an awareness of trout to be tickled and toasted in embers and eels to be speared and crunched. In the woods, the loveliness derived from leaves that shimmered in the sun, and also from an anticipation of honey from the nests of wild bees and fungus prised from a trunk, from the thud of a well-aimed arrow in the ribcage of a deer and the certainty that fat tubers lay hidden beneath the woodland floor.

Beauty lay in both the eye and the stomach of the beholder and a scene was as good as it tasted. It was not to be enjoyed alone, and a solitary existence would have been regarded as a form of living death. Neither was the setting something remote that could be pillaged and then discarded. Individuals, the people would have told us, only have identity as part of a community, and the community itself is part and parcel of the world that it inhabits. Success was gauged by one's contribution to the life of the community rather than by how many of its members one could intimidate or enslave.

Distinctions between the human and the natural did not exist: everything was, in a way, a part of everything else. Within creation, divisions between the living and the inanimate were uncertain. Foxes were alive and so were trees, but the river and the rocks at Brimham were also alive – if, perhaps, in a rather different way. Presiding over it all was a Creator, a Creator who would be affronted and saddened if one tiny component of creation, like humans, should deface and destroy any other part of it. If a place, setting or resource was abused and defiled, then the Creator felt the pain and the shock waves ran through creation so that everything in its oneness was stressed and impoverished. We do not know what religious beliefs people of the Middle Stone Age possessed. However, their lives had many points of overlap with those of the woodland Indians encountered by the first European settlers in North America, whose religious beliefs were much as I have just described. Perhaps the last 7,000 years or so have witnessed a march of ill-named 'progress' during which humans have forgotten all they once knew about the oneness of creation? Little time remains for it to be recalled.

Their skin darkened and still glowing from the last of summer's sunshine, the people drifted down from the high grazings. The ducks and geese were yet to leave. The woods were festooned with fungi and the tangled brambles of the burnt-over ground and the fruit trees of the woodland edge proffered sweetness in several forms. Nuts were gathered as survival rations for the winter ahead. For perhaps 120 successive generations people came down from the summer ranges to their sheltering places in the valley bottoms with their survival pouches stuffed with hazelnuts. With 3,000 years of experience to draw upon, their lives were as finely tailored to exploiting their wooded setting as those of the tundra hunters had been long ago. This time, when change came to challenge tradition, it arrived less as a challenge and more as an opportunity.

CHAPTER 2

A LEAFY PLACE

(c. 4000 BC – *c.* 1000 BC)

The Valley was now a leafy place. At the head of the slopes there were the shimmering, silver-green birches and darker rowan. Below them, the ash, oak and elm stood over the underwood trees: hazel, holly, gean, bird cherry, crab and many others. Almost everywhere one went, life was lived to the rustle of leaves and the rattling of twigs. Pollen clouds veiled the breezes and for every creature that stood and walked there were many more that perched; 1,000 versions of birdsong vied for attention. The Valley countryside that we see today was still largely unformed. As yet, the only pieces of its scenic jigsaw firmly in place were the heather moors on the upland margins. The landscape was taking shape from the top, downwards. The Valley people had begun to set the course that their setting would take, but these people were still fairly few and not intrusive. One might walk along the Valley for a whole morning without seeing any of them, though some of them would certainly see you.

✳✳✳✳✳✳✳✳✳✳✳✳✳✳✳✳✳✳✳✳✳✳

We have travelled back 6,000 years, to an instant in prehistory when the women of the Valley seemed to have been producing only sons. This is why he left, with a pouch of bone and antler points and barbs and a bundle of the best quality fox, marten and beaver belts: heading south-east to find a wife. 'Get someone with a good set of teeth to chew the hides and make them supple', called his father, when his mother was out of earshot. 'If she's got no teeth, strong gums will do.' Two years passed and it was assumed that the boy must have married into some other clan or else have been killed. Then he

In the New Stone Age, the Valley will still have been a leafy place, and at first people spent most of their time in the dappled shade of oak, elm and ash.

returned, leading more than just a wife. She was rather slight, but sinewy, like someone who constantly bustles. She was leading a most peculiar creature; it looked like a miniature and heavily sedated aurochs. Fibrous bags full of grain were slung over its mottled back and there was no doubt that the animal at its side was some sort of calf. Five even more outlandish little animals tugged nervously at their halters. 'Finch nests on legs', was how one onlooker described them. Had he been able to afford them, the lad would have brought back more sheep, and wives. The relatives, salivating in happy anticipation, imagined that he had walked his own homecoming feast back on the hoof, but they were disappointed. Yet the notion of domestication should not have seemed too bizarre, for the deer on the fell sides were already more herded than hunted.

She did not seem to know how to sit for a few hours and, well … just sit. These hunting people were accustomed to long treks, culminating in moments of violent exertion, followed by long, restful hours lounging, telling tales, listing the names of relatives distant and deceased, and poking the embers with sticks. The most experienced of them could poke the embers in the most impressively thoughtful and calculating manner, yet keep their heads free of almost any trespassing thoughts.

Moreover, nobody could understand a single word that she uttered, so perhaps she was saying curses or casting spells? Soon, it was rumoured that she was a devil or a shaman of the darker sort. They kept out of her way. Her husband, however, had a clearer idea of how these things worked, for he had seen the most incredible sights in the chalk Wolds that lay four days away to the east.

He was about to start implementing some changes when she went down with a rasping cough. It did not last long, but a few days later, he was far, far sicker than she had been, the victim of a searing fever. They all said he would die, but she kept bathing his head with cold beck water and made a thin, glutinous broth from the seed grain in the bags. He lived. Within a month, half of the community died of the strange virus from the Wolds, and then it returned to cull the community twice more. The survivors said she was to blame as, in a way, she was, but they couldn't quite explain how she had brought it all about.

The mortality had opened up the territory and there were fewer conflicting interests to hinder the search for good land. Farmland. She led him downstream and showed him the light soils of a sandy river terrace: loose soils so easily shaken from the roots of the clumps of grass. They were sweetened by a little local blue limestone, cast up long ago by the ploughing snout of a glacier. The land faced south and stood above the limits of flooding. There was no better place for that first plot, the one that would be the nucleus for the changes that would eventually transform the whole valley. Ash trees were felled and heaped upon the ground; it was a while before the branches were dry enough to catch light. They fashioned unwieldy, fire-hardened spades from split boughs, hacked out shrubs with antler picks and dug the ground over. Once a drying breeze had loosened the soil, the cow was harnessed to a curved bough and led back and forth to create a tilth and to work in the rich wood ash. Curious eyes peered from the shadows. The laughter in the thickets was unrestrained when the bough or 'ard' lurched from the ground, towing the ploughman in a stumbling dash over the tussocks behind the startled beast. Seeds were sown; a spiky wheat and a spikier barley and a strong wattle paling was set up to keep out the deer. As the woman stood guard over the ripening grain, the man would lead his little flock up to the steep, free-draining grazings among the rocks. Looking down he could see, far below, the grain ripening and darkening in their plot and the soft new stems growing through the grass stubble in the riverside meadow.

He did not like the unremitting toil of the farming life, a life where every minute seemed packed with pressing chores that jostled for attention. Still, his face had filled out and he was losing that drawn look seen in people who experience starvation in at least one season of the year. He missed the intense concentration of the chase and the way the tension would suddenly explode into violence and then disperse. He missed the sharing of spoils at the campfire, the lolling and bragging. He missed the old storyteller and his childhood pals, too, and those still alive missed him. They were frightened of his wife, but sometimes they would materialise at the edge of the wood and then they would lean together on the fence posts, chatting. A couple of times they came into the strange house of posts, wattle and wheat straw, but they distrusted its rigidity and the walls which did not shudder and sag like those of real dwellings. They found the whole business of being inside what could well be a trap manufactured by someone who might very easily be a witch rather stressful. The convert to farming understood all this, but was determined, eventually, to unite his friends and family.

One morning, she heard a ruckus in the woods overlooking the wheat plots. She grabbed a stick to shake at the deer that must, once again, be trying to barge through the fence. The anguished rattle of the jay and the bickering magpies drew her into the wood. Her eyes did not adjust quickly enough to the gloom and when her irises had opened she found herself facing an aurochs. Rather like a fighting bull, but very much bigger, it had been lured from a distant fastness by the smell of the milk cow. The old Valley women would have backed away slowly, avoiding any sideways movement that would register more strongly in the eye of the bull, until they could grab a branch and scramble up out of reach. There they would sit, unabashedly braiding their hair and searching for ticks, until the loathsome beast was gone. She was not a Valley woman and so she just froze. She had scarcely sensed its powerful smell before she was airborne.

When they found the body, she had been gored and then knelt on by the aurochs until her black hair, grass cape and woollen skirt were all matted together in a pulp. Her husband, more grief-stricken than he cared to admit, reverted to tradition and wandered around the woods seeking advice from the bear spirits in the different quarters of the wilderness. They seemed to say that she was not of these places and should be buried in the bare farm ground that she knew best. A little shelter or shrine could be built over the grave and, if he wished, he could leave a gift and sit outside. If she was happy there, she would stay and her ghost-spirit would not wander. That would be best, as she had caused enough trouble already. If he would stab a knife into the ground at the entrance to the shrine, that would be even better – it would help her to know her place was inside. It was right that he should visit her, she would welcome him, but he should realise that her true spirit had already been born somewhere else. Maybe in a fish, a wolf, elk or human, or even in a bear. And so he found it good to spend some time at the end of the day by the little tent of boughs, reporting on what had been done, how the farm was growing and what was still to do.

Farming in isolation was a daunting task. More and more he recruited his friends, the huntsmen, to help with the planting and weeding before they left, jostling, teasing and singing, for the hunting grounds. Though they pleaded ignorance of such women's work, they had been gathering fat hen and grass seeds for generations. It was the steady, unremitting rhythm of farm work that really upset them. One moment they were reaching out almost in unison to grasp their ears of wheat, then sawing them free with their wooden sickles edged with flints. But a moment later, one would straighten, stretch, and start joking and soon they would all flop down among the dusty straw. Next they would have departed on a spontaneous quest for honey or have followed a baying hound. They were the children that we, in our innermost souls, want to be and have forgotten how to be.

Two unusually baneful winters brought people to the farmer's house, firstly to beg for a little milk or gruel, then, their eyes downcast and their moccasins brushing the dirt, to ask for help in setting up their own farmsteads. With several households now engaged in farming and many lessons needing to be learned, he turned to his brothers-in-law, far away in the Wolds. He returned with a trio of experienced but land-hungry farmers, their families, and some livestock that were desperately needed to diversify the Valley gene pool. Hooked over their shoulders, the strangers had axes, two of greyish Lakeland tuff and one of Flamborough flint, with slightly splayed blades a full three fingers wide. They were ground and polished and shone with a silkier lustre than any river cobble. Their hafts were made from thick poles and the axe heads were bound to short side stems springing from these poles, so that they were somewhat angled back towards the axe-man. Used with a wristy, chopping action rather than being swung like a sledge-hammer, these axes were highly effective. They rang around the Valley woods, each with their own pitch and tone.

Eventually, the hunters were the strangers. Unreconstructed and intransigent, one heard stories about them over the hearthstones. Women warned their children not to talk to strangers in the woods. They might whisk you away for a life of savagery, daub you in rancid bear fat and dress you all in itchy fur. To the extent that the hunters became demonised it was because people heard their whistles, clicks and false owl hoots far above and beyond the Valley and something inside them ached for all the spontaneity and freedom that they had surrendered. The hunters began to symbolise all the delightful fecklessness that had been sacrificed in return for lives that were more ordered, less relaxed but considerably safer. Short lives of blazing colours were no more. The hunters embodied the spirit of innocence and when the last of them went, so, too, did Eden. Nobody noticed as its gates slowly closed. They never did re-open.

A young golden eagle launched itself from a high crag in the Langdales. This was the place from whence the strangers' axes had come and the bird was escaping the rapping and clatter from the people smashing stone on the scree, below. It sank down the face of the Pike until its hungry, bowed wings filled with air; it glided, scanning the landscape, and then it began a languid wing beat that bore it skywards. On this, its maiden flight of discovery, it soared high over the Dales. As it arced southwards, it saw the brightening mauve of the heather moors. Then, the landscape turned a dark olive and the slender silver thread of a river was seen stitched across the alder swamp. A few more strong strokes of its wings and little patches of wheat plots, meadows and pastures came into view, like bright archipelagos in the dark woodland sea. Yet gliding further to the south and east, the eagle saw these gold and emerald areas swell and merge. It could see beyond the sombre woods, peat fen, alder carr and farm plots of the great Vale to the bright, bulging Wolds, where chalky rubble frosted the fields. There, the woods were now the islands, lapped all around and nibbled by farmland, like beef cubes in a bag of maggots. Little was left for an eagle there. In a flight of over 100 miles and scarcely three hours, the great bird had seen a couple of millennia of the landscape's history unfolding.

✳✳✳✳✳✳✳✳✳✳✳✳✳✳✳✳✳✳✳✳✳✳✳

As one generation succeeded another, people gained in security but lost in spirituality. The shaman and the bear cults seemed less relevant now. There were scant compelling reasons to dress up as deer. The traditional belief that, by acting out a successful hunt one could actually determine the outcome of a real chase, seemed ever less convincing, less relevant. Deer were now as much a nuisance as anything else, things to be discouraged rather than sought. At the turning of each year's tides the Valley people were gathering at Brimham in ever-increasing numbers. What had begun as impulsive and unco-ordinated gatherings took on more serious tones. After drinking some cloudy barley ale and eating the right fungus the world took on a crazy and magical character, with the grotesquely elongated shadows dancing across the rocks like a tortured pageant from El Greco. Faces streaked and dotted with charcoal or ochre looked otherworldly in the dancing light of flames. Dancers lost their identity and surrendered their throbbing bodies to the spirits. Yet afterwards, they sensed that something was lacking. They were far better aware than the people of today that self-indulgence only magnifies any emptiness of the spirit. Ceremony was a part of the spiritual world and the spiritual world should be providing answers to all the most fundamental questions. As yet, the ceremonial and ritual were but one step elevated from a booze-up or orgy. A new intensity of focus would be needed if something better than the bear cults were to be found.

Hunting people can recite their immediate ancestors, but they may not live with them. Often uncertain of the father's identity, in a footloose world they may trace their lineage through their mother's people. Their quarry are not tied to a family home or sepulchre, so neither can they be. The farming life binds people to a place, a farmstead, and around this place the spirits of their forbears drift and watch. People in the Valley remembered the strange woman from the Wolds who, by dying, proved herself human. They thought of the little shrine over her grave and the visits that continued for the length of her husband's life. Was there something in this that they had missed? It was not hunting magic they needed any more, so farewell to the shaman and diviners, with their tatty feathers, distant eyes, their rancid hides and rattling bones.

What was needed was a goddess of the earth rather than of the woods: someone to keep the river of fruitfulness flowing steadily from the soil to the bowl and to the spit. And who could be better fitted to intercede on their behalf than the ancestors? Their blood, bones and ashes were spattered and scattered around the Valley homeland, planted in its soil, nourishing its life. With the stimulus of ideas filtering in from the south, the new theology assumed its shape.

The Valley was shared between a few farming communities, each one consisting of combinations of inter-relative natives and the incomers and innovators who had married into the long-established Valley lineages. Now, each community became fascinated with its ancestry. The indigenous people had been rather scorned for their traditional outlooks, but now their star rose, for it was they who could provide the deeply-rooted forbears. Bodies were now being exposed to the magpies and kites, or else left to decay in little timber houses for the dead. On the level tops of the great grit formations at Brimham, above the reach of wolves and foxes, there were macabre scenes as crows and kites ripped the last wind-dried flesh from the bones of corpses. Then the clean bones were gathered together and hoarded in tombs, often just natural clefts in the rocks, later to be brought out, displayed and employed in rituals.

These ancestral bones were like the deeds to territory, the proofs of ownership. No interloper could produce the bones of forbears who were born and had died in the Valley. The bones were also certificates of insurance, for they attested to guardian spirits who would keep the lands secure for the living of their lineage. In days when population was swelling and the landless might swarm in, it was good to have such guardians on station, glowering blindly from their tombs. Few other societies have been so ingenious in finding vital work for their dead to do.

The landscape was still dominated by woodland but, here and there, the farming territories were pressing close together. At first, the farming life had brought a narrowing of perspectives and a tightening of the ties to a single place. Later, as the people became more numerous and their demands more varied, there was a broadening of contacts. Salt, better pots and less brittle axes began to pulse between the regions, like blood around a body. The more that people were exposed to the utility and quality of these things, the more that they wanted to buy. Trade took some people to places not visited by Valley people since the long-forgotten days of their hunting forbears. Travel informed them about the configuration, neighbours and contents of

Brimham Rocks, with its big skies, weird rock formations and vast panoramas might have been made as a venue for rituals.

their region. The opportunity for trading came in the early summer, when the crops were sown and the cattle were driven up through the moors to the flower-spangled pastures of the high fells and plateaux. Here, in the keen, thyme-scented air, there were no boundaries to guard or secrets to store and contacts with strangers were welcomed. Arrangements with neighbours or others from further afield were agreed at high meeting places on communal boundaries. Once up there on the common, one could take to a lofty trackway and travel for 100 miles and more without setting foot in an exclusive homeland or affronting an ancestor. The uplands offered liberation from the stifling territoriality that gripped the valleys and plains.

Herdsmen from different clan lands could combine their herds for protection against wolves. A week of leisurely ambling in stimulatingly unfamiliar company could take them from one side of the Pennine plateaux to the other. Youngsters, brought along by their fathers for their first seasons on the upland pastures, could see the summits of Ingleborough and Pen-y-ghent, flat-topped like the capstones on tombs, soaring up above the upland plains. Could anything in the whole of creation stand so tall? By day, one could watch the short-eared owls swooping and tumbling over the lairs of the hare and grouse, while at night, the northern breeze brought a special clarity to the blazing firmament and the whole of Heaven was like one great diamond chandelier. Then the wolves would start to moan and yelp like tortured souls, the distant deer would stamp, the cattle would shift and judder and it was time to toss another bleached root from the dead forest on the peat fire. Who now grows up so well?

If one followed the cattle trails north-westwards for a few days, the peaks of Lakeland came into view. They were not like the Pennines, not stepped at the edges and flat above like a poorly stacked pile of doorsteps. Their dragon-tooth profiles were ominous and intimidating, even from afar, and showed that their rocks were quite different from the level beds of limestone, shale and grit in the Dales. Travellers, tanned by the upland wind, told of a chain of ridges and peaks where one light grey summit jutted straight upwards like a septic thumb. That was where the stone for the finest axes came from: a rough, steep and sometimes ugly range with rocks that were a mass of tiny volcanic crystals. This was not an eye-catching rock, like the showy greenstone traded up from The Lizard or some speckled stones from Wales. But it lent itself, like hardly any other, to being ground and polished to give a sharp, smooth and true cutting edge. Many stone or flint axes would chip and splinter, but these would slice. Such was the fame of this rock that axes from Pike o' Stickle travelled the trade routes in great numbers down to Wessex, the power centre of late Stone Age England.

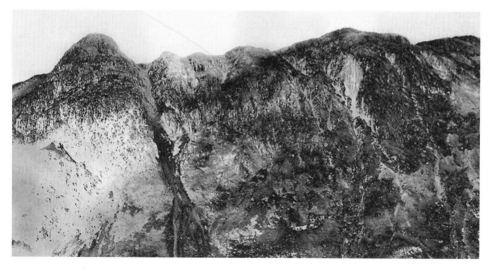

Pike O' Stickle, the domed peak on the right, was the most important of the axe factories in the Langdales.

The great stone circle of Keswick Carles or Castlerigg is likely to have served as a marketplace for the Lakeland axe trade.

The people who knew the upland trade routes explained that one did not have to brave the sickening exposure on the saw-toothed ridges or the dark woods in the claustrophobic ice-gouged valleys in order to lay hands on the axes. The mountain people quarried the rock, roughed our axes on the shifting, clattering scree below the quarry face and sent them off on pack ponies to the coast. There, they were ground and polished on the sands and then returned. On certain festive days, the Lakelanders would then bring them to a most amazing place – a great ring marked out by thirty-eight enormous boulders. It was some 90 paces across, as large as a compound or paddock. Ten stones formed a super-holy rectangle against the inner face of the circle and two huge stones flanked an entrance to the sacred interior that led in from the north. Arrive there with your surplus cattle on the right day and you could barter for the axes. The traders sat on mats at the edge of the feasting and gaming ground, with their wares set out on the grass before them; they were within the sacred confines, so all deals were divinely endorsed.

Herdsmen from the Dales had seen arrangements of stones, chest high and but a few stones to the cluster, but no stone setting there could compare with this staggering temple and meeting place. On their first visits, they might be so bemused by the majesty of the circle set in the Lakeland's northern fells that their bartering skills were undermined. More cattle could be led away than were needed to strike a deal. Later, when the Langdale axes were being used to chop, wedge apart and splinter trees, onlookers might ask if the axe-bringer had really seen the magical mountain that had given up the stone? 'Yes…well, almost', could be the reply. Only the mountain people knew precisely where the secret mountain lay, but the axes had been bought from the very hands of those bandy legged slope striders. Our narrator might have added, impressively, that somewhere in Lakeland, a cow from this very clan had been sacrificed to ensure that the mountain could carry on producing the truest of axe stones.

As this, the New Stone Age drew towards its close; the Valley was still a leafy place, but less so than before. There were far more people than at the start of the Age, but less innocence or impulsiveness. Numbers, prosperity and growth produced their own kinds of pressure. There was an appetite for change rather than revulsion towards it, for the experiences of change were still slight. With a more secure food supply, survival had less immediacy, and this freed minds to look for answers and meanings. But as production, contacts and potential wealth increased, so, too, did the concentration of power. The future of the little clan of cousins seemed uncertain in a world of bigger ambitions, more inspirational priests and more ambitious leaders. There had been a time when not many ideas got into the Valley and very few indeed got out. Those days, days when the known world consisted of just a small number of neighbouring clans, were over. Increasingly, people were looking to eastern lands for inspiration, guidance and example.

Quite why it was decided that the Ure (rather than, say, the Nidd) was a supremely holy river we may never know. However, there is no doubt that as the Stone Age slipped away, those who orchestrated the spiritual existences of people had discovered that, though most rivers flowed, the Ure burned with a liquid, flowing sanctity. Could one not see how the holiness radiated out across its valley as the blessed Ure twined and coiled like some snake emerging from the bowels of Mother Earth? People who had heard this explained could no longer gaze inertly at all the divine power. They must respond to it, glorify it and channel it. The sheep and the frogs could not do this: only humans had the power to answer the river spirit and articulate its pure energy into focussed meanings. This was their destiny. (Perhaps the Swale, too, was thought holy, for the greatest abundance of religious sites lay around its junction with the Ure. It was as though two great streams, one of oxygen and one of magnesium, had united in a blinding eruption of sacred energy.)

So as the sphere of attention widened and spilled out of the Valley, it was not the axe-makers to the north-west who commanded attention, but the vale of the sacred rivers, to the east. Well before the end of the Stone Age, a ceremonial avenue or 'cursus', around a mile in length and on a north-east to south-west orientation, was constructed there. It was bounded by ditches that were set about

33 paces apart. This must have become a focus for rituals that took place at important landmarks in the year, though whether the processions were held in daytime,
or else led towards heavenly bodies or constellations, we do not know. Elsewhere,
such avenues tend to kink slightly, so the celestial orientation argument is greatly
weakened. In any event, this ritual walkway was not some esoteric local invention.
The downlands and vales of England were patterned by these avenues; they were
part of a national/international religious currency and they embodied immense
amounts of physical toil.

The expansion of belief and power was apparent in the Valley when sub-chiefs
and priests from the vale of the Ure arrived to enlist labourers equipped with
antler picks and wicker earth-carrying baskets to work on the cursus. A work
camp had been set up and the local farmers had been mobilised to feed the strangers; some had packed their daughters off to live with relatives for so long as the
men were there. For month after month, year on year, lines of diggers and earth
shifters could be seen, excavating ditches and building banks before moving on to
begin work on the next section of earthworks bounding the sacred avenue. When
the work was eventually complete, the Valley people found themselves drawn
into the congregation that lined the flanking banks as the priests walked by. They
saw the headmen processing behind, some of them with the new copper axes,
more marks of status than tools, which glittered more brightly than any autumn
leaf. Societies were merging, and though a few faces from the Valley could be seen
in the retinue, most were strangers. People were encountering the notion that
one could share loyalties with others that one did not even know.

Eventually, there were lapses in the timetable of ritual. They increased: ceremonial became less relevant and harder to recall. Old people who understood died
and took the meanings of things to their graves. The ditches of the great cursus
became silted and tanglesome as cattle trespassed on the holy ground. However,
the early phase had been like a brief spouting of the sacred flame. Its quiescence
preceded an eruption of sanctity that burst with a blinding flash of such a kind
as the North would never see again. The force of this blast propelled the country
where Dales, Vale and Moors came together from a position on the outer margins
of human awareness into a central position in the realms of spiritual significance.

The idea was not original, for in the south-west people had been building
henges for some time. The notion of creating a monument to a scale that would
surpass anything attempted between Wessex and Scotland's Northern Isles was
quite unique. A henge is a great, circular sacred space that is defined by its surrounding ditch. The ditch separated the sacred and the profane The upcast from
the ditch formed a circular outer bank, and this made be an excellent, elevated
place for members of the congregation to gather to watch the rituals performed

The sacred Ure near the Devil's Arrows.

within the holy circle. In this way, one might relate the henge to a church with a circular chancel surrounded by a raised, ring-like nave.

Thornborough does not have one henge, but three, and these were set in line with the central one having its southern entrance over the old cursus, as though to inhale its older sanctity. However, if the orientation of the old cursus was important, the henges did not respect it and were roughly aligned with the Ure. Each henge had a diameter of more than 260 paces and their banks stood almost twice the height of a woman. The henges at Thornborough were unusual in that their banks were separated from the inner ditches by a broad 'berm' of level ground, about 13 paces wide, while there was also a ditch just outside the banks, but of a less tidy construction. Each henge was more normal in having the conventional 'double banana' form, with two opposed entrances. At Thornborough, these entrances were all aligned so that one might walk straight through the trio of circles without breaking step.

The fact that there were *three* aligned henges is not unique; there are three aligned henges at Knowlton in Dorset and four at Priddy in Somerset and the largest of the Knowlton henges is very slightly larger than the Thornborough circles. This fact of multiple occurrence undermines the very tempting analogy between henges and cathedrals, for a diocese only needs one cathedral, not a clutch of them. And so we must wonder whether the different henges were for use at different seasons/festivals; whether they served different clans or districts of a territory; or whether they were for different castes or degrees of people?

One factor about the Thornborough circles underlined their southern origins on the one hand, and their regional identity on the other. The well established religious foci of England lay on the chalk downlands of Wessex, and in other chalk countrysides, like the southern downs and Yorkshire Wolds. Such settings had always appealed to the early farming communities. When henges and cursus were constructed in these places, the newly dug chalk of the banks and ditches shone brilliantly white, at least until lime-loving vegetation regained a foothold. But in the valley of the Ure there was no chalk, so that the impact of whiteness might be lost. However, a few miles downstream on the Ure there are gypsum deposits, and relays of conscripted workers must have carried countless basket loads of the crystals back to Thornborough. There, the gypsum was spread across their banks to give the huge earthworks a sparkling icing of white.

Leading prehistorians have described the locality of the super-henge trio as being the most important ritual site in northern Britain, or even in the whole country. Ten Stonehenges could be accommodated in each of the henges. The super-henges probably reached the peak of their celebrity around 5,000 years ago, when they may have been the supreme religious focus for the whole North of England. The antiquity of worship here went back at least another five centuries, to the time of the cursus, and perhaps for further centuries, too. This was not just the site of a single, showpiece monument. Instead, a whole region was devoted to the dead and their links with the living – a great complex of ritual creations covered dozens of square miles and had the sacred Ure as its spine. To the north, and referencing the sanctity of the Swale, laid the Scorton cursus, destroyed in modern times by quarrying of gravel.

Long after the celebrity of Thornborough had begun to wane and religion to change, people were still aware of the holiness of the place, and wanted to be buried there. Those of sufficient status or purity had had their barrows cast up there, or the urns with their charred bones buried there. Later still, people were buried in the flanks of the old barrows, tapping into the sacred energy of the ancient tumuli. Mysterious chains of pits, alignments still not properly understood, traverse the area from earlier phases of worship. If the line formed by the super-henges is extended for about 3½ miles (5.6km) south-eastwards it intersects another, perhaps earlier, henge, near Nunwick. Then 2½ miles (around 4km) further to the south-east is the Hutton Moor henge, and beyond this, the Cana henge. From the last centuries of the Stone Age to the earlier ones of the Bronze Age, societies intensely motivated by religion produced a vast and intricate assemblage of gigantic ritual monuments on a site that became studded with a profusion of tombs.

✳✳✳✳✳✳✳✳✳✳✳✳✳✳✳✳✳✳✳✳✳✳✳

By the time that the head of the clan died, her status had grown so great that she qualified as the first member of a Valley community to rest in that holiest of places. The radiant sanctity of the rivers would illuminate her spirit and she would last forever, intervening at times of danger to protect her people.

She came from the local line of chieftains and was preferred when each of the male claimants had seemed, in some way or another, deficient. The choice had been a good one. Touchy issues about rights to wild honey in common woods and the pursuit of game into neighbouring territories had been resolved, deftly and justly. Her reputation as a negotiator and conciliator had spread and she was summoned to give counsel at some of the greatest assemblies in the land. She had done the most that any leader could do; not only had she kept her clan and kin out of trouble, she had also, on the whole, kept them alive.

But now she was dead. There was no prescriptive formula to govern the funeral rites, and several practices co-existed. She might be placed, crouched on her side, beneath a domed barrow in a stone box or 'cist', with a pottery beaker containing an alcoholic drink to warm her dead limbs. She could be placed on planks in a burial pit, or even cremated and her charred bones buried in an urn. The gods were relaxed about these things.

In fact, she wished to be buried in a coffin, and so one of the most revered of the young oaks in a sacred grove was felled. Then the trunk was split by a line of stone wedges, hammered in sequence until planks broke free. In life, she had been much influenced by the rituals adopted by the people living across the great Vale in the North York Moors. When she was vexed by problems of politics or perplexed by theological doubts, she would clamber up to the high ground by Brimham and watch the specks of light twinkling from camp fires miles away on the steep edge of the Moors. She said that seeing these eastern lights ignited new ideas in her own mind. With her earthly life now ending, she followed the customs of the eastern territories and opted for burial with a food vessel.

The clay for this vessel (rather like a miniature jardinière in shape) was shaped between thumb and fingers and then a crude herringbone decoration was applied by impressing the soft clay with a barbed flint arrowhead before it was fired. This vessel would contain a ritual meal to sustain the lady's spirit as she negotiated the hazardous transition between the world of the living and that of the dead. Nobody quite knew what lay in wait there or what tests would confront the spirit before it could proceed.

The cortege left the Valley at sunrise, the rough coffin draped with strong-smelling flowers being shouldered by relays of bearers. They took the track along the northern flank of the Nidd and crossed the Ripley Beck at Scarah. Then they arced away from the river until the morainic knoll of Yarmer Head signalled that they should then turn due north. Within three hours they could see the merged courses of the Skell and Laver crossing their path, and beyond, pin-pricks of glinting light from the steely Ure as it twined, serpent-like, across its floodplain. Fording the holy river would not be easy. They would need to explain their mission and placate the great spirit before defiling the water with their dusty feet and shins. While the adults rehearsed their plan, the youngsters were allowed to lope away for a couple of hours to see the incredible stone row that had recently been erected. In historical times, the construction would be regarded as beyond human capability, and thus be judged as bolts hurled at Boroughbridge by the Devil, apparently on a day when his aim left a little to be desired.

Four gigantic, pillar-like slabs of Millstone Grit had been selected, with Plumpton Rocks or Knaresborough being the sources. The tallest of the Devil's Arrows stands more than 22ft (6.9m) above the ground and there may be a further 7 or more feet buried in the ground. Having had the great pillars man-hauled across country for more than 6 miles – probably on rollers, perhaps sometimes on beds of straw – the men of power had demonstrated to one and all their formidable abilities to organise and/ or to coerce. The stones were erected in a line. (This was not a dead straight line, to the much later consternation of the apostles of astro-archaeology. What we see must have been what was intended, for since they could shift these phenomenal pillars across 6 or more miles of rough country the ancients were surely capable of erecting them in exactly the places they chose.) Their presence again underlined the significance of the sacred river, for the alignment runs towards (or from) the Ure, with a short and broad member of the quartet seeming to announce the presence of the river and the other stones increase in height as they lead away from it. One stone was destined to be taken down and used in the prosaic purpose of bridge-making, while more than 5,000 years of exposure have caused the tips of the upright stones to become fluted as channels for rainwater.

The sun was well past its zenith when the priests took charge. The coffin was set down and the footsore bearers, with the agreement of the water spirits, bathed away their dust-caked sweat in the sacred waters. Returning purified, they looked out across the landscape of the dead. The great white banks of the henges rose high, each henge like some gigantic bridal circlet of May blossom, tossed carelessly on the ground after the wedding. All around, the land was strewn with barrows: domed tombs that blistered the land surface as though a force of gigantic moles had been frenetically at work. Footpaths and processional ways wove among the monuments, puffs of dust drifting from the places where the turf had worked away. Kites, attracted by the funereal scents, soared above in fruitless anticipation. The Valley people were lucky to live in quite easy reach of the monument. The task for funeral bearers from far-off clans increased in unpleasantness with every mile. Strewn around the margins of the ritual area and into the Ladybridge locality were the encampments of those who had travelled for days to reach the great circle, and pits dug for discarded pots and other debris told of countless previous visits.

Her grave was ready: the coffin pit had been coated in gypsum and the earth for the barrow was mounded all around. And so she was placed in what they all regarded as the holiest setting on earth, a place that bubbled, lava-like, in white-hot, river-borne sanctity. The loosely fitting lid was lifted and the priest inserted the food vessel and its sanctified contents. A tiny curved knife of flint, recently re-sharpened, was added too. Was this to allow her spirit to cut the last ties with the mortal world? Then the mound of the barrow was heaped over the grave and one more dome of death was added to the growing flock. Bronze Age society had acquired an establishment. Beneath these domes were the priests, the chieftains, the power-brokers – and perhaps the thinkers, too – those who had produced what was perhaps the largest, most elaborate and most intense concentration of sacred monuments the world had ever seen.

✳✳✳✳✳✳✳✳✳✳✳✳✳✳✳✳✳✳✳✳✳✳✳✳

Around 800 years after the super-henges were built at Thornborough, work began on the earliest stone pyramids in Egypt.

What did it all mean? Was it a political attempt by the clans of what would one day become North Yorkshire to assert their political and theological importance? Were they demonstrating their equality with the rich trading culture of Wessex? Is this why they took monuments from the southern downlands and reinterpreted them on a grander scale? The geography seems important too, for the great monuments stood at the junction between uplands and plain, at a place of encounter between contrasting lifestyles and values. Whatever the political or social motives of the founders may have been, let us not forget that the religion of the lower Ure created a momentum of its own. It generated spiritualism of such a dynamic intensity that its flame burned for perhaps as long as that of Christianity has – and it did so without recourse to any media for broadcasting faith and without there being an ability to record gospels or theology. The monuments must represent far more than man-hours of toil extracted from a frightened and enslaved labour force. No tyrant or dynasty of tyrants could have held armies of diggers and draggers in thrall for so long. The endurance of the monuments testifies to the popularity of the beliefs.

And what now? Parts of this unique landscape have been degraded or destroyed and other parts are threatened. Were some of those people who gave Yorkshire perhaps its greatest era of glorious achievement to read these words, they might think that an immensely potent rival belief had made a cataclysmic arrival. Or perhaps they would imagine that the very forces of nature had turned against them. They could probably never comprehend the overriding dominion of something as low and debasing as the profit motive. How could we explain that a millennium of fantastic achievement is being threatened for a trivial commodity with one of the lowest bulk-to-value ratios known to commerce, something that can be found in scores of other places, something we buy by the cubic yard and see set in grey mortar displayed in the ugliest of buildings? Gravel.

Were we able to hold a referendum in Yorkshire to discover whether ordinary people would prefer to retain what English Heritage regards as the most important site between Stonehenge and the Orkneys, or whether they would rather see it carted away in gravel trucks, the answer is easy to predict. Hundreds upon hundreds of us have signed petitions, pleading for the protection of our northern birthright. Meanwhile, those institutions that should have protected Yorkshire's heritage as a matter of duty are directing efforts to attracting tourists, for this is good for business. Would it not be better to protect the heritage first and then invite visitors to share in its celebrations?

And so, the centuries rolled on. The axes of copper hammered as the forge gave way to far superior implements cast from the new alloy, bronze. Now, the

This gritstone pillar is an isolated member of the Devil's Arrows (the two other surviving members are shown on page 60).

secretive bronze smiths, wandering the high roads with their bellows and their bags of broken bronze goods for re-casting, rivalled the mystique of the priests. Perhaps they were often one and the same. The assault on the woods on the valley sides became more purposeful. Once opened, the clearings were less likely to be allowed to close again and heal after a few years of cultivation. The leafy landscape of the Stone Age had taken on a dappled look. On the upland plateaux, the heather moors were mottled with patches of newly burnt ground, of fresh young heather and of duller, older stems. The wandering flocks drifted across the heather moors like murky clouds in a sky of mauve. Lower down, the woods no longer dominated the landscape and were fragmented into patches by clearings, some new, some permanent and some abandoned. The cleared ground stretched up and across and there were several places where one could go down through fell pasture and moor to the very riverside without passing through a single wood.

The volcanic sanctity of the Ure and its margins had dimmed, but the embers still glowed brightly. Centuries after her death, people of substance and ambition were still being buried in the outer layers of the Valley woman's barrow and in and amongst those others scattered all around. Perhaps people thought that the radiance from the half-remembered religion could still vitalise their souls as fearfully they passed through the unknown into the realm of the dead?

Before the Ure began to spew its energy like the flow of sacred magma, the Valley had been an outpost of a northern backwater on a peripheral island on the dark side of a continent. The eruption had catapulted our small Valley into a position on the very threshold of one of the most revered and celebrated places in the whole world. When the traders in copper, axes or salt entered the Valley, people no longer listened in awe to their tales of the wonders of Wessex, Orkney or the Wolds. Rather, the traders asked them about their homeland. For 1,000 years and more, the Valley basked in renown as a region whose most fleet-footed clansmen could visit the religious heartland of the known world and then return bearing a vessel of the holy river water sealed with a dock leaf, all within the space of a day. More than once, the sacred water was mixed, in hope and awe, with that of their own Nidd, but nothing was catalysed; the miracles did not happen. The Nidd had its own spirit and mission. Perhaps one day it, too, would start to fizz with sanctity. But the most it ever did was turn a host of mill wheels.

It was a little before 1500 BC. The farmer stood at the edge of his field as the droplets pattered from the leaves to form rivulets down the hide draped over his head. He had grubbed out the hawthorn bushes and broken the land back into cultivation – he could still show you how the thorns had scarred his hands. It was the loftiest plot in this part of the Valley, but with the scrub burned and the turf dug in, it should yield a sequence of harvests. Yet the slender stems of the emmer wheat, with their arcing, whiskery heads were beginning to sag and bend. The summer was well advanced and the crop was still soft and green. Soon, patches of mould would appear, and that would be that. The straw would rot and what the animals would not eat would have to be ploughed back into the soil. Something had gone wrong with the climate.

About 400 years later, in 1159 BC, a distant descendant of the baffled farmer struggled to get the same land back to work and he faced a now-familiar challenge. He spat on his thorn-ripped hands. This would be a poor return for all those days spent in hoeing out the wretched charlock. He looked up at the grey, buffeting clouds and cursed the weather, but his anger was rather misplaced. He should have blamed Mount Hekla in Iceland. It had erupted the previous year and vomited so much ash into the stratosphere that the skies throughout the northern hemisphere were darkened. Water gathered around these tiny nuclei, the sun's light was reflected back into space and summers became cool, cloudy and dim. Those living in farming's heartlands could survive, but for those on its edges, especially the north-western margins, the end was near. The British uplands became patterned by abandoned fields and empty dwellings. On all of them, in a layer invisible to the naked eye, lay specks of the Icelandic ash that had sealed their fate. The survivors learned to endure a collapsing climate; it would be helpful to know more about how they did so.

CHAPTER 3

WEAKNESS IN NUMBERS

(*c.* 1000 BC – AD 43)

If 'progress' is about increasing population to the limits that the environment can support, then this was a time of great progress. There were as many people living on the land at the end of the Bronze Age as would be found living there at the close of Anglo-Saxon England, two millennia later. It was also a time of stress and insecurity. It was a time when people discovered that there were things more frightful than the beasts that one might hear, snorting or pawing in some dark thicket. People under stress discovered just how frightening and irrational *other* people under stress could be. In response, they sometimes became frightening, too. The life of innocence in an uncrowded countryside could be no more. Every wilderness now had its claimants and any plans now had to take account of outsiders and what their ambitions might be. The people of this, and countless other valleys had to survive in a world of neighbours, often rivals, who forever pressed in upon their spaces, intruded on their lives and ogled their possessions.

It began so well. The dappled days of brightness had lured people into all those empty places. The Dale was home to lots of confident folk who could wake, duck under the thatch above the doorway, rub their teeth with a twig and gaze over and into the awakening Valley. Soon, little twists of smoke would start filtering out of the thatch-cone roofs and ovens of the homes, way below. But you, an uplander, were up above. The air was fresher and you could see what was happening in the big vistas. The Valley was your toy farm, warmed into life by the slanting sun-rays. They prodded the ground like pokers, stirring the communal embers back into life. Distant dogs wheeled distant flocks, tiny milkmaids with skirts sodden and heavy with dew shooed the cows up hill paths to the pastures, while pewits arced like fighting kites. Areas of countryside were rapidly filling up, but you were less hemmed in or controlled up here. The upland farm, with its stone-walled paddocks, well-manured crop plots and sheep pens, was a world of its own: there was plenty of pasture between your world of work and those of other people. You might look down on a scatter of farmsteads, but turn around and green banks, open moor and fell were all that you saw.

A few blessed generations of farmers watched from their privileged perches as the Valley landscape filled in. Then it happened very quickly. Within days of the eruption, the sky had noticeably darkened, and within weeks the change in climate was established – not profound, but important in the sensitive uplands. Just a few days of sunshine could be the difference between storage pits and jars full of golden grain, each seed as plump as a bullfinch, and unripe crops driven flat by deluges in September.

Far aloft with the dust that was blasted into the firmament by Mt Hekla went masses of sulphur, and this returned as acid rain. In the Valley, much more than in the neighbouring limestone Dales, it was particularly toxic to the already acid soils – and the higher that you went, the more acid they would tend to be. Crops suffered and livestock became crippled by fluorosis. In ancient farming there were sometimes bad years, and these, you had to endure. It was the clustering of bad years that caused problems, so that sickly people with ailing stock who were weakened by food shortage found themselves lacking the resilience to face the next season of harvest failures, and the next. And so the uplanders will have hoped to survive the first and second years of mouldy grain, collapsing beasts and rotting fodder. The third, fourth and fifth years after the eruption will have been the ones that dragged them down.

The Valley people saw them trudging by, family by family, skinny dogs and hobbling sheep. Sometimes they had a small cart carrying the ard, the now-idle quern stones for milling grain and the posts from their house. The posts proclaimed a hope that they could be used to build a new house somewhere else; in an overcrowded countryside an unclaimed space would be hard to find. After a few bad summers, the failed farming families almost formed a procession as they retreated down the Valley. Many of the holdings that had been farmed for generations by the uplanders of the Bronze Age would never again be anything more than rough hill pasture or grouse moor. History would show that these were part of a far longer procession of victims of an uncaring and revengeful environment. Their tradition would be taken up by the Irish famine victims of the 1840s; the Okies, Arkies and Texans who fled the Dustbowl on the Great Plains in the Depression years; and today's refugees from an expanding Sahara desert. In one respect, at

In the first half of the Bronze Age, settlements colonised the higher ground. Archaeological evidence from the gritstone country does not register well in air photography, but a site like the one from which this photograph was taken, a south-facing shelf overlooking the Valley, would have been a popular choice. The view is across Pateley Bridge towards upper Nidderdale.

least, the Bronze Age uplanders had an advantage: there were no tabloid editors to exploit insecurities and to orchestrate campaigns of hatred against those guilty of poverty, misfortune and being slightly different: guilty of seeking to save their lives by migrating.

In other respects, the uplanders were less fortunate. America's Dustbowl refugees had California as their goal and promised land, while the starving Irish who survived the potato famine could choose between various New World destinations and England. There was no promised land beckoning the uplanders. The Valley had almost filled with people, and while a few refugees might return to their families living on the lower ground, this created pressure to produce more from the existing holding. The corset of land hunger could no longer be let out a few notches. Further to the east, the Vale of York was a little more promising. There, there were settlements and cultivated land on the better drained soils and the slightly higher ground provided by mounds of glacial sands was valued. There were also damp hollows where swamps formed and peat was laid down and heaths – lowland moors – standing on hungry, acidic sands. In such settings there were marshy commons where cattle could graze, there were wildfowl breeding in abundance, and countless fishing places. A few dozen families might be accommodated in the wastes of the great Vale, but not so many more. Once established in the 'moorish' country, perhaps the refugees became fiercely independent, secretive and disrespectful of authority, like wetland people such as the Cajuns or the 'diddicoys' and Fen tigers of East Anglia of more recent times.

When fate thrust the failed uplanders into the settled communities of the heartlands, society came under stress. Have-nots are always feared by those who sense their desperation and see it as a threat. Frightened people may turn to the protection of warlords and other 'godfathers' of the twilight world. Warlords, as figures of fear, beget other warlords, and so they pass fear around society. Fear infects wherever it goes. Once, the men of any household, armed with staffs and cudgels, could be a force in most local skirmishes. Now, however, the ability to fight with any real effect was restricted to an elite of armed warriors. They were armed with bronze rapiers that could cut through a staff or sever a club-wielder's hand in one blow. Their spears were tipped with lethal points of cast bronze, so they could fight at a distance. They had bronze daggers and round shields of wood and leather for close combat, and some had bronze-studded leather helmets. With power and fear went glamour: the warriors were decked-out in expensive goods, with armlets, bracelets and 'torcs' or neck rings of bronze or even gold. Some of them had small horses with jangling harnesses linked by bronze fittings and, on the plains, some rode to battle on war carts.

These armed men had created a caste with a creed that regarded tokens of wealth and might as symbols of courage and high birth, yet each trinket and blade was bought of fear and paid for by the toilers in the fields. Some might say that, in risking their lives to defend a community or a locality, they earned the right to be an elite. Others might regard them as the operators of a great protection racket. In either case, the warriors feasted and flourished on the social tensions. The anxieties of the small people became a vehicle that carried the nobles ever further from the workaday world of tillage and harvest. The more they sought to strut and posture, the more that funds for imported pins and wristlets from France or swords and axes from Germany had to be extracted from those who did work.

Communities were being stretched; the social classes were increasing in number and the gaps between them were widening. As the class system became attenuated, the size of territories was increasing. In the days of the Stone Age clans, community was composed of great uncles, cousins and in-laws, and most people in the clan were related, however distantly. Leaders were few, modest and familiar and there was hardly anyone who did not spend most of the time at manual work. But as the leaders became grander and the territories merged through conquest or marriage, the cement binding the communities became weakened. At first, it seemed preposterous that that one could belong to the same tribe as somebody else and yet never have known them – never even have met them. Super-tribes and super-tyrants: the two marched hand in hand. You felt threatened by a rampaging warlord, so what did you do? Why, you appealed for help to another warrior aristocrat, probably one to whom you were already slightly obligated. He promised to protect you provided you offered tribute … and more tribute … and more. The rationale of the feudal system was born here, rather than in the Norman era.

There was a new tautness to life. Long gone were the days when a carefree youth might return with a wild piglet on a stick and spend the rest of the morning on his back in the sun wondering how long it might take for a butterfly to settle on his nose. There was pressure for space, pressure to extract enough from the ground to feed an over-sized household and pressure to produce a surplus as tribute when the armed men came to call. Societies were squeezed and tribute came out. But there was more than just wealth to be got out of people: they could be squeezed for labour, too. If communities were scared – of enemies or of their own warriors, it did not matter which – then the fear could be converted into labour and the labour could create great constructions. Of these, the most useful were fortresses, for they fortified not only the landscape, but also the status of the warriors: they aggrandised those who had commanded their construction.

Within a few centuries of the migration from the uplands, a new metal, iron, began to circulate. It did not glitter like copper or develop the same lustre or patina as bronze. However, once one mastered the much greedier and more demanding forging techniques it did provide a material for tools and weapons that was harder, more widely abundant and cheaper. To the people at the time it did not seem that a new Age had dawned, but rather that one had acquired a somewhat more effective sickle and a less expensive cauldron. The Dales had rather been by-passed by the bronze technology, with its demands for copper and tin. They were never super-abundant, and in the Valley, they were distinctly lacking. There was lead there, if one could know what to do with it, and there was also iron, some stratified in ironstone, and some obtained from bogs on the moors and heathlands.

✳✳✳✳✳✳✳✳✳✳✳✳✳✳✳✳

Shoeless, the trio were making their ways slowly across the peat marsh. Every pace or so, each man would thrust a rod down into the bog. Invisible in the black, squelching mess beneath their feet there were concretions of bog ore: iron-rich lumps formed by oxidising algae, bacteria or atmospheric action. These bog ore masses were about head-size, and this was a problem. They often formed between stones at the junction between the peat and the glacial boulders and pebbles below. When a rod hit something it might be a stone. However, it might be a head. The bog was not only a place for prospecting and bird nesting; it was also a place of ritual and execution.

✳✳✳✳✳✳✳✳✳✳✳✳✳✳✳✳

The old compulsion for grandiose worship and for the provision of gigantic temples had vanished, but those elements of the old beliefs associated with water and water spirits had evolved and intensified. This was a somewhat greyer and more rain-lashed age. One might have expected, then, that people would have worshiped the sun. However, perhaps the abundance of water and wetlands argued a stronger case for a dialogue with the forces that were actually in charge of events. The water spirits were greedy: the sacrifice of the occasional chicken was not enough. They wanted swords and shields, the most costly of possessions. They also wanted people; ones that had been killed. Rapiers dredged from river beds and corpses from bogs are the defining relics of Iron Age worship.

Those who probed for bog ore concretions in the black, peaty waters occasionally came across the bodies of these victims. Tanned and pickled in the acidic, airless waters, the people were preserved, though their peat-stained hides and features were often obscenely flattened and distorted by pressures from above. Sometimes, the cords with which they had been throttled were still around their necks. Who were these poor people who were wrenched from their communities and slaughtered for imaginary gods? Were they criminals or deviants? Were they unfortunates who were judged inadequate in some way? Might they have been suspected of witchcraft? Could they have been victims of loathsome campaigns to demonise strangers? Or did the communities offer only their best members to their gods? We do not know, but since this was a time when ordinary people were falling ever more deeply under the thrall of leaders, it is hard to imagine that these leaders were not orchestrating the ritualised murders.

The Valley had been a meeting place, a zone of transition, for a very long time. In this, the Iron Age, it once more found itself to be a cultural marchland. Now, it was at the margin of one great tribal territory, Brigantia, and quite close to another, that of the Parisi. Each tribe had a distinct and quite different ethos. Among the fells and dales of the Pennines, old ways could endure. Change could not come sweeping across the landscape like a tidal wave. It might seep slowly up the valleys, but only at a pace that allowed leaders to accept, reject and adapt. This was a conservative region where tradition had the upper hand in any confrontation. The Brigantes, who may possibly have taken their name from that of the Celtic goddess, Brigit, controlled most of the land between the Mersey and the Tweed.

While the Brigantes, probably a confederation of various smaller upland tribes, were rooted in Bronze Age traditions, the Parisi were more progressive and outward-looking. It is sometimes said that they were a branch split from the tribe of the same name that lived on the banks of the Seine (and who gave their name to the French capital). In favour of this argument is their use, in the third and second centuries BC, of unusual rectangular burial enclosures, whose graves are sometimes found to contain dismantled carts/chariots. Such tombs are duplicated in the Seine valley. On the other hand, it is not easy to see how or why part of a tribe could have moved across the sea and through other tribal territories in order to reach east Yorkshire. The lands of the Parisi lay to the north of the Humber, and the tribe's southern neighbours were the Coritani, people of the East Midlands from whom the Parisi may have learned some more advanced ideas.

The Iron Age was a time of turbulence and despotism and there must have been tensions between the Brigantes and the Parisi. With regard to the people of the Valley, the position of their common boundary would have been crucial, though boundaries could shift according to the fortunes of local fealty and war. Under the Romans, the Brigantian lands were governed from *Isurium Brigantum* (Aldborough, near Boroughbridge, close to that great monument of the old religion, the Devil's Arrows). At Roulston Scar, overlooking the notorious Sutton Bank road, there is a gigantic hillfort that overlooks the Vale of York. Our knowledge of the frontiers of Brigantia and the territory of the Parisi is insufficiently exact to ascribe the hillfort to one tribe or another, but inside the fort there are the traces of a square barrow. This, combined with the fact that the fort faces across the Vale towards the Brigantian heartlands in the Pennines, suggests that Roulston Scar was a frontier stronghold of the Parisi (or their immediate precursors) constructed in the Hambleton Hills on the north-western limits of their tribal lands.

The Valley now lay at the margin of one great northern territory and near the threshold of another. For the more nervous inhabitants it might have seemed

The Devil's Arrows and the holy territory beside the Ure were venerated throughout the prehistoric era.

to be in a vice between two great fortresses. Ingleborough, a regional capital of the Brigantes, lay away to the west, hidden by the swells of the intervening topography. The 'foreign' fort, however, was visible whenever people wandered up from the trough of the Valley. Given the eyes of an eagle, one might even have seen the warriors patrolling its ramparts. It is no less visible today: all one needs do is look across the narrowing Vale to the cliff-like face of the North York Moors. The fort of Roulston Scar stands there, directly above the White Horse of Kilburn, the head of which was cut into the ramparts when the horse was made in 1857.

❄❄❄❄❄❄❄❄❄❄❄❄❄❄❄

It was about 400 BC, and sitting at the trackside on the high ground that would one day become Killinghall common, two bored youths gazed north-eastwards towards the steep face of the North York Moors. Though it was rather more than 20 miles away, in the clear morning light it seemed much closer. Near to the skyline, directly above the dusty thread that was the snaking Sutton Bank routeway, there was a bright line of silver-grey, like a hairline crack in a lampshade. It was produced by light reflecting from the fresh, limey stones and subsoil cast up from the excavations at the edge of the tableland of the Moors.

It was late spring, and the boys had some time on their hands between the lambing and the hoeing. They had been breaking the tedium by undertaking a series of dares, each one a little more foolhardy than the last: riding sheep, then cows and bullocks, retrieving cobbles from the bottom of river deeps, sailing downstream on a log – the usual things. Their neighbour's fort (for so it seemed) was a matter for intense speculation. For one thing, agents of the Parisi had been touring the Valley to purchase every cow, sheep, cheese and jar of wheat or barley that they could find. It was clear that there was a large and hungry workforce up at Roulston Scar. For another, the fort was facing directly at them. It controlled a main trade route to the coast and nobody could help but wonder if, one day, an invasion might not be launched down that twisting road and into the valleys that opened on the great Vale?

Having touched the tail of the savage bull that grazed the common, the victorious youth returned, smirking, to his friend, 'Now it is my turn to choose. I dare you to go into the fort at Roulston Scar and bring back a stone'. Silence fell: each was shocked by the magnitude of the rise in the stakes, and neither was ready to concede that things had gone too far.

He set off before daybreak with a lunch bag over his shoulder, setting a score of dogs yapping but easily navigating the dark lanes and tracks that led eastwards into foreign territory. Crossing the Ure near the place were Ripon would grow, he looked upstream and saw meadows and pastures that seemed covered in pimples, like a severe attack of terrestrial goose bumps. The old barrows were overgrown, but the spreads of fresh earth from internments in a couple of mounds showed that some people still revered them, still saw them as gates to the realms of death and resurrection. Then the lane opened on to the Vale and the main coast road. It was still fairly empty and for the first hour the lad met only a trader in Whitby jet and a salt merchant who sat milking his mare for his mid-morning drink.

The lad's pulse began to quicken as he saw the placid track become contorted as it encountered the towering face of the scar. It writhed and it coiled, as though desperately seeking some purchase on the rearing slopes of Sutton Bank. A short life lived in the uplands had not entirely prepared him for the climb and halfway up he sat gasping and rubbing his calves at the trackside. He reminded himself that he was now in a foreign country. The locals still spoke in Celtic dialect, but he must remember to shorten his broad Dales vowels and to speak a little faster. Then the awful thought stuck him: foolishly, he had not prepared a plan for deceiving any guards and watchmen, who were probably now scarcely 100ft above him. As he ran the strap of his bag through his fingers, an idea took shape.

One moment you were trudging, head down, forcing another step from your aching shins. The next moment was like bursting through the surface after a deep dive. Suddenly, it was flat underfoot. Instead of staring at the next tedious stretch of dusty, rock-studded road just a few feet from your nose, there was now a great panorama, packed with scenic details that competed to capture your gaze. In that instant, you became conscious of sounds again: the rapier notes of the pipits and the twisting music of larks, songs that bucked and gurgled like the rapids on the Nidd.

There was also the staccato chatter from teams of pick-wielding workers, and a voice, 'Yes?' The guard was stationed – or at least, leaning on his spear – near the point where the track levelled and calmed after its dramatic ascent. The boy held out his bulging lunch bag and explained that he had brought some lunch for the gang-master as tribute from one of his hamlets. 'Which gang-master?' He could feel panic rising as he claimed that it was 'the easterner'. 'You don't sound like an east coast lad', said the guard. 'Have some goat milk cheese and a lump of bread before I hand it over, he'll never know', urged the boy. As he left and moved among the workmen he felt partly paralysed by the thought that he could have been one mistake away from becoming a sacrificial victim or a slave. At the same time he was intoxicated by thoughts of the tale that he would tell when he got home, most of it true. If, indeed, he got home.

From the other side of the Vale it had seemed that the works were arranged in a line along the top of the scar. From inside it was seen that the earthworks that crested the scar formed just one side of a great, triangular enclosure of some 60 acres (24ha). The lad walked among the excavations and estimated the circumference of the fort to be more than 2,000 paces. The defences took the form of a rampart built like a timber box that was twice the height of a man and packed with rubble. The top of the 'box' formed a walkway, while the posts of the palisade rose above this walkway to head-height. The great ones responsible for designing the fort were observant and very responsive to the nuances of terrain and the opportunities they offered. To the north-east, where the natural topography was less favourable to defence, the rampart was fronted by a straight-sided, flat-bottomed ditch, much deeper than a man, largely excavated from the limestone bedrock and equipped with its own outer post and rubble fortification to steepen the approaches to the trough. In the south-east, the ramparts turned inwards so as to flank and guard both sides of the road leading up from the plain. It was, though the boy could not know it, one of the largest and most imposing hillforts in all England.

Looking around, the lad could see that great swathes of woodland had been cleared from the slopes of the Hambleton Hills and from the upland plateau, above. In their places were landscapes of stumps, textured like stubble on the face of a giant. His eyes had often seen abandoned fields being cleared of thorn scrub and birches, but never the likes of this. The stump-studded ground swept all around the face of the hill formation as beaches follow a shoreline. The building of the box ramparts and palisades had devoured more timber than any forest fire, probably around 3,000 trees. Meanwhile, sufficient earth, subsoil and rock had been picked free and shifted to fill a giant cube that had sides of around 25 paces. The discipline of the work gangs as they picked stone free from the ditches and basketed the rubble away in relays exemplified that this was a very well organised project, though even so it was taking years to accomplish. The labourers themselves did not have the bearings of slaves and seemed, more likely, to be ordinary tribesmen conscripted for the duration of the works. This underlined the high levels of organisation involved: there must be arrangements to feed them all, there must be a temporary village to house them, and people must be taking care of their affairs while they were away from home. Society had moved a long way from the days of the homely little clan and its elders, who were known to one and all.

As he scampered down the scar, hoping to be secure (secure as one could be) with his own people by nightfall, the boy remembered the dare and picked up a stone from the roadside – a stone was a stone, so what? He thought about all he had seen. Mainly, he wondered what the intended purpose of the great fort on Roulston Scar might be. It was plainly engineered in the most thorough and expert of military ways and must be more than just a showpiece. Discomfortingly, it was positioned

on a scar of the Hambleton Hills that faced directly and unmistakably at
Brigantia. Was it a symbolic means of warning the larger confederation
that their smaller neighbours were determined to repel aggression and
were capable of doing so in a most purposeful way? Was it a defensive
frontier outpost on the border most distant from the Parisi capital at
Brough on Humber? Or was it a forward base, a springboard for more
aggressive warfare?

✾✾✾✾✾✾✾✾✾✾✾✾✾✾✾✾✾✾

The hillfort might have been different things at different times. It could pre-
date the Parisi and have been reworked according to changes in their politics
and strategy. It certainly magnified the status of the dynasty that initiated the
great project and saw it through to completion. It was also a most impressive
location for assemblies, both those of local tribes-people and congresses involving emissaries from Brigantia and from Scotland. In the Dark Ages, meetings
were sometimes held on frontiers and boundary hills, and if Roulston Scar was
a frontier post of the Parisi, this practice could have gone back into prehistory.
Strangely, unlike most lesser hillforts, it became forgotten and 'lost'. Fragments
of rampart were recognised in the nineteenth century, some being bulldozed in
the 1960s to extend a runway for gliders. More of the ramparts were recognised
in the last third of the twentieth century, but it was only around the dawn of the
new millennium that a proper picture was recovered.

The Brigantes had defences of their own, though they were more thinly
spread than in other tribal territories. The people of the Pennines knew that
their knowledge of the dales, scars and gorges of their own rugged homeland
was their best defence against invaders. Their great hillfort (for such it seems
to have been) on Ingleborough reflected the odd and enigmatic character of
the confederation. The stone ramparts ring the 2,372ft (around 723m) summit
to form a pear-shaped enclosure and to constitute the loftiest hillfort in all
England. As at Roulston Scar, a phenomenal amount of toil was invested. The
ramparts, of Millstone Grit rubble and scree strones, were around 13ft (around
4m) thick and the great wall was stabilised by slabs that ran through it to divide
it into rubble-filled compartments. Within the ramparts, the circular outlines
of numerous stone buildings can be recognised, yet nobody could have survived a northern winter in such a high and exposed place. Perhaps these were
the temporary homes of shepherds and herdsmen who accompanied their
stock to the summer pastures. Still, the fort would seem a costly setting for so
prosaic a use.

The rubble is the remains of an Iron Age dwelling inside the summit ramparts of Ingleborough.

The Ingleborough fort might have been a venue for tribal councils, though reaching it would have taxed the strength of the older sages. On the other hand, it might have been a distant descendant of the already-ancient henges and thus have been more concerned with ritual than war. It could easily have been several things. It had all the physical attributes of a fort and its weakness in this role may have concerned the difficulties that the surrounding communities would have had in actually reaching the shelter of its ramparts, with their livestock and some form of water supply, before invaders could cut them down. It lay less than 25 miles due west from the head of our Valley, and in the unlikely circumstance that Valley people ever sought refuge there, they would have faced a trek of well over a day, often across very broken terrain.

In any event, the Valley folk had a modest yet still impressive fortification on their doorstep: Bank Slack near Fewston, where the natural topography did not offer a great deal to the military engineer but where a modest promontory was fortified with double ramparts. Whatever its defensive potential, it would have constituted an ideal 'moot' or meeting place for the local sept of the Brigantes. Did the Valley people have a fort of their own to dominate their Dale from within? None is officially recorded, although in 1894 the antiquarian Harry Speight noted the setting of the ruined hall of the Beckwiths in Clint:

The site is a fine prospecting one and may have been the summer station of the early British possessors of this place. There are indications of an earthen rampart on the south, west and north sides of the field, and the ruins of the hall occupy the centre of an ancient entrenchment… (p.399).

The old antiquarians were notoriously gullible where local mythology and speculative early history were concerned. However, they did enjoy the advantage of seeing historic landscapes in much fresher states than we do. If Clint did not have a hillfort, its Iron Age masters should be blamed for missing the opportunity to create a superb stronghold by fortifying a promontory in the manner of Roulston Scar and Bank Slack. Speight was quite correct in praising the commanding character of the site. It still dominates the road winding up from the Valley bottom to the watershed and the place is visible from a remark-

The ruins of the Beckwith's Tudor hall at Clint stand within the traces of a medieval moat. The theme of high status defence might go right back to the Iron Age if this is a hillfort site.

ably large number of other locations in the Valley. However, the ground appears to have been ploughed on a few of occasions; as a result, the moat surrounding the crumbling hall is now but scarcely visible and the ramparts that Speight recorded would be difficult to trace.

The world around our Valley people was changing fast, but where was change heading? The clans of extended families had given way to larger ones of distant relatives. These, in turn, had merged into tribes, and now the old tribes were septs of super-tribes whose chiefs were becoming king-like. Would this expansion and merging of communities continue until Britain was the home of a single nation under one super-king or super-tyrant? Might the people develop their own, intensely Celtic, identity, so that the islands would be renowned throughout the world for the brilliance of their music, the bright-hued genius of their poetry and narrative skills, the breathtaking fluidity of their art and the vainglorious antics of their warriors? They might have.

Some places remained much the same in a world full of change. The house on the shelf that faced south over the river that our Celts called 'Nidd' ('the brilliant or sparkling one') was much like some created centuries earlier, when the Thornborough temples were being made. The circular wall of rocks prised from the ploughland stood but waist high and was broken by the gap of an entrance, one that faced away from the prevailing wind and towards the morning sun. Like all the homes of the time, it was more a roof than a house. The great cone of thatch was carried on a double ring of upright poles, linked together with more pliable rods that formed rafters.

Primitive though they may have seemed, such houses often contained much better materials than would be built into medieval village dwellings, and they could last longer, too. Even so, Iron Age homes were for reclining in: if you stood up you were likely to find your head wreathed in the peaty fug from the turf smouldering in the hearth at the centre of the dwelling. Everyone was partly kippered in peat smoke: everyone smelled of it so nobody noticed. There were no separate rooms, and when darkness fell the members of the family could be found facing each other across the fire, their backs against the wicker facing of the low wall and their feet toasting over the embers. 'Pet' orphaned lambs might shy from the embers, stabbing the earthen floor with their pointed feet. Then hounds and farm dogs would be restrained and pulled closer, to settle snugly in the curve of a human form. Even in sleep they were at work as body-warmers. Flees, ticks and other parasites drifted around in search of their preferred hosts. The storage jars, cauldron, pots, pot hooks and harness cast strange shadows across the earthen floor. Progress meant more clutter. As darkness settled, the owls called across a starry sky that was glimpsed through voids in the swirls departing through the smoke hole, way up above. Bats struggled to decode their echo sensors and flirted with the smoke hole till the peaty wisps drove thoughts of roosting away. Then the storytelling would begin.

Children curled up and gripped their cloaks as they heard, once more, of the frightful man-eating goddess who would bite you clean in half. They learned of the craft of the fox and how he out-witted all the other creatures, and then one yapped on the far fell, a perfect finale to the tale. The attributes of the river goddesses of the Dales – Wharfe, Nidd, Swale and Ure – were reviewed, and then the children recited the bounds of their holding, landmark by landmark, as though this feeble mantra would keep intruders at bay. In the daytime 'progress' and innovation were at work all around, but darkness brought its time warp and the people returned to the days of their distant ancestors and the long-forgotten campfires. Mr Fox and Mistress Hare took over from the warlord and his henchmen. It was Mr Fox who bestrode the land at dusk, his wicked eye glinting from behind the mask of his red tail. He would have their eggs, their pretensions and his revenge – could it ever be otherwise? The children loved the security of a predictable ending. Stories matured as they sank through dozens of successive generations of tellers. The night was as black as in those far-off Stone Age times; the wolf and the nightjar sounded just the same. For a few chilly hours, progress could be set aside, though who knew whom it might claim tomorrow?

The huddled families of the Valley did not know it but progress, if that is what it was, was out there lurking, advancing, soon to beat down their doors. It would come in an unexpected guise.

CHAPTER 4

A SOUND OF MARCHING

(AD 43 – AD 410)

The summer had reached its sultry phase. Dusty leaves seemed to sag in the breathless haze and flies made little beehive patterns around the heads of horses and cattle. The meeting of headmen about harvest arrangements had turned into a session for drinking and gossip, as those in the Celtic-speaking Valley so often seemed to become. This time, there was more of an excuse, for an itinerant smith was visiting. These occasions were always an opportunity to discover what was going on in the wider world.

And so the headmen discovered that an army of Romans from across the sea had landed down south somewhere. They did not know much about the Romans. They appeared to be a powerful tribe, but they did not like crossing the sea. The stories of Julius Caesar and his raids almost a century earlier were still fresh in people's minds. They were retold many times, though without gaining much in accuracy. How lucky he had to been to get away with his skin intact! That would teach the continentals to mess about with the British tribes! The parties agreed that, while the Brigantes were the best fighters, the other British tribes were a great deal tougher than the continental Celts, who had let themselves be subjugated by the Romans. One headman, a loss to the tabloid era, collided with a roof post as he demonstrated how he would deal with any Romans he caught in Nidderdale. The roof shook and dust and cobwebs landed in the black pot holding the brew. Meanwhile, it was widely known that the southern tribes were exporting religious fanatics, fermenting uprisings on the continent and generally antagonising the Romans. Nobody in the Valley was very concerned: it was all going on so very far away.

This time, according to the smith, who seemed to have taken things far too seriously, the invasion was more purposeful. The Valley headmen discussed its implications and decided that on the whole it was probably a good thing, for if the tribes to the south were preoccupied with routing the Romans then they, and the tribes of the Midlands, would be less likely to raid across the Brigantian borders. Somebody raised the point that if the southerners were preoccupied with the Romans then the Midlanders would consider their backs safe and be more inclined to raid in *Brigantia*. However, it was too late for complicated ideas; the ale was good and it seemed to be telling the elders to shun bad thoughts and be cheerful. They were happy to oblige. They were helped by the fact that nobody really knew much about Romans; the great silkie or seal-man of the northern seas was only slightly more mysterious. Little was known about Roman religion or civilization, though it was said that the sails of their Scotland-bound slavers could be seen form the shores of Parisi territory, so not all of them were scared of the sea.

In fact, the Brigantes were themselves stumbling towards a home-grown civilisation, and a few strange foci which seemed to combine the attributes of capitals, towns, parks and forts had appeared. Of these, by far the most impressive would be Stanwick, close to Scotch Corner. Under Aulus Plautius the Roman occupation of Celtic kingdoms soon proved to be much more threatening than Caesar's raids had been . Cartimandua, the queen of the federation of tribes that made up the Brigantes, may have felt that the bonds between the sub-tribes were too loose for effective performance in battle. The ease with which the southern tribes were defeated and their hillforts smashed must also have influenced her. Neither discipline nor heavy artillery were things that the British knew very much about, though they seemed to have been decisive in the Roman victories. And so, even in AD 43, the very year of the Roman landings, she opted for client status under Rome. This did not prevent Ostorius Scapula from intervening against rebels led by Brigantian nobles in AD 48.

Three years later, Cartimandua, now a traitor in the eyes of many Britons, handed Caratacus, a Catuvellaunian insurgent, over to the Romans. This placed her firmly in the camp of the collaborators. Cartimandua had a consort, Venutius of the Carvetii tribe, and his sympathies seem to have been of a more patriotic character. About the time that his Queen was holding Caratacus, Venutius seems to have been remodelling an old enclosure and fort of 27 acres (10.9ha) to become a gigantic capital-cum-fortress, a stupendous 750 acres (304ha) in area.

While the fortress at Stanwick was taking shape, Cartimandua, in the most bizarre fashion, became enmeshed in an affair with her husband's armour bearer. Venutius was divorced, and was thus released to lead the anti-Roman faction amongst the Brigantes into open revolt against Rome. At the same time, it is possible that he was establishing a defensive line of earthworks and fortified camps

A surviving section of rampart and ditch at the British stronghold at Stanwick.

from Sheffield to Doncaster to guard his southern border. Stanwick was the most impressive of Brigantian fortresses, with a rampart about 5m high (around 16½ft) crowned with a 2m (around 6½ft) high drystone wall and fronted by a ditch some 6m (around 20ft) deep. Inside the defences was an inner fort, Tofts Hill, which may have served as a command centre for a part of the far-flung defences, though the fort was so big that several others must have been needed.

However, the military role of Stanwick is questioned. The development of British towns was so young and its products so diverse that models for what was 'typical' cannot exist. Perhaps this was really more a commercial focus with its trading prestige bolstered by its gigantic defences. By AD 75 it had been abandoned, though it is uncertain whether it was ever actually stormed by an invading legion. Some prestigious Roman goods have been found here, but they could have been looted by Venutius from his unfaithful wife, captured in raids or even paid for by the Romans for compliance in some imperial scheme.

What is known is that the insurgency caused by Venutius prompted the Romans to advance and establish their own fortress at York after AD 69. It was apparent that if the conquest of Wales were to be relaunched on a sounder footing than the one disrupted by Boudicca's revolt in Norfolk at the start of the decade, then *Brigantia* would have to be pacified. Though it may not have been realised at the time, this conquest would oblige the conquerors to establish a secure imperial presence to the north of *Brigantia*, paving the way to Hadrian's Wall over fifty years later. Vespasian, renowned for his lightning conquest of southern England, was now the Emperor and he directed a force composed of the IX Legion and auxiliary troops under Petillius Cerialis to conquer the north and to rescue Cartimandua, captured in a renewed uprising among the Brigantes.

The IX Legion marched to York via Lincoln, a river crossing on the Humber and Malton. Established there, they could appraise the character of the communities and topography that they would have to deal with. The lands of the Parisi clearly had considerable agricultural and settlement potential, and on the whole the gentle terrain would be easy to occupy. The Brigantian heartlands to the west were a different matter. Some lead and some meat and hides could be had, but the task here was plainly one of policing the country and crushing any rebellion before it could take root. This would require a string of military bases linked by roads for the rapid deployment of troops. When the region was pacified then its resources could be stripped away, like gold from a dead man's purse.

Isurium Brigantum or Aldborough was established on the *Isura* or Ure. This provincial and administrative capital and commercial centre probably grew from a marching camp established when a weary force ended their day's march and fortified their encampment. Petilius Cerialis was appointed as govenor in AD 71 and during the following years the subjugation of the North continued. Out in the 'bandit country' of the Pennines, a series of strongpoints that were garrisoned. Ilkley, Elslack, Bainbridge, Long Preston and Brough were the forts used in the pacification of the Pennines. These were far from being peaceful postings; the fort at Elslack seems to have been burned in an uprising at some time and the Bainbridge fort, *Virosidum*, seems to have experienced a series of attacks in the second century. Usually, the garrisons and their regular patrols managed to impose peace upon the Brigantian hill country, and to protect the vulnerable flanks of the new roads that supplied the Hadrian's Wall garrisons and armies penetrating into Scotland.

Once again, and not for the last time, the Valley people found themselves to be close spectators of great historical events. Military roads were needed to link the forts together and to the great imperial fortress at York. Such roads very quickly became commercial routeways, too. One of these linked Aldborough to Ilkley or *Olicana*. Since it served as the main road between York and Lancaster until well after the close of the Middle Ages, it seems reasonable to assume that it was used by armies despatched from York to be stationed in towns/forts as far away as Lancaster. It ran right across the Valley and crossed the Nidd at modern Hampsthwaite. It will have been built at an early stage in the conquest and occupation. The first that the Valley people will have know about it may have been when a small party of surveyors and engineers and their guards arrived and began working with their cross staffs and rods to set out the route. (This route could have partly resulting from a cobbling-together of existing tracks.)

Descending into the Valley from Aldborough, a great meander loop on the Nidd forced them to veer slightly to the north, while the descent down the bank below Clint and onto the floodplain was steeper than they would have liked. Then the flood-prone character of the river meadows meant the road had to be causewayed. With the line of the route established, the building work was accomplished by ordinary troopers. Firstly, they built a well-drained and ditch-flanked foundation of rammed sand and gravel, which was raised until it had the typical ridge-like 'agger' form. Then gritstone from local quarries and river cobbles were used to pave or cobble the surface and heavy kerbstones were placed at either side to prevent the centre of the road from spreading.

About a millennium and a half later, in the nineteenth century, quarries were opened in the Valley to export such local stone for use as kerbs and hard surfacing. However, quarried stone was difficult to shape and shift, and right through into the nineteenth century, local people would rob the Old Road for stones to use for this or that. In 1894, Harry Speight wrote, 'Remains of this old thoroughfare are still in evidence here in the shape of pave-stones, some of which are as much as five or six feet long, and a foot and upwards in width. Many of them have been taken up for walling, &c., but many yet remain in situ along the line of Roman march.' Several large kerbstones are still visible, but the pillage of pave stones must have continued after Speight's time.

No sooner were sections of the road complete than Valley people surely began to use them for moving their livestock and carts. It soon became used for the export of lead by wagon and packhorse, for the Romans had wasted no time in opening mines for this valuable roofing or coffin-lining commodity. Two pigs of lead dated from AD 81 or 82 that had somehow been lost at Hayshaw Bank, to the east of the lead mines on Greenhow Hill, have been discovered. Another, dating from AD 98-117, was found near Appletreewick on the way to Wharfedale. The narrow road also provided a remarkable window on activities in the very marchlands of the world's greatest empire. People living its vicinity sometimes witnessed scenes of colour and excitement that could be seen in few other parts of occupied Britain.

Word of the almost interminable winters on the Pennine hill stations and the ferocity of the Brigantian freedom fighters would have explained the grim expressions seen on the faces of soldiers marching from York or Aldborough for their first posting in Ilkley or other upland forts. Some of the worst Roman defeats, before and after the Brigantian campaigns, were inflicted on armies strung-out in defiles or divided at river crossings. When larger formations were approaching the Nidd

Part of the road that the Romans built across the Valley.

they must have sent mounted scouts and skirmishers ahead and have raced sections across the river to guard the flanks of the column as it crossed. Legions and cohorts may have been protected by flanking forces that crossed the river on either side of the main body. However, at times when troops were familiar with their posting and the political climate was relaxed, young officers might have been seen to detach themselves from the cohort to chase the deer in the woods at Clint for a while. The prospect of spit-roast venison in the evening might allow the niceties of military conventions to be forgotten. The crossing on the Nidd must have been a significant landmark on the route between the civil and military parts of the colony. Whether Speight's speculation that there would have been a check point and post house here where passports and travel documents could be scrutinised as well as a stable for changes of mount for imperial messengers, is true, we may never know.

❋❋❋❋❋❋❋❋❋❋❋❋❋❋❋❋

The boys from the hamlet near the river crossing would dash from the farms as soon as they heard the war trumpets bray at the approaches to the ford or saw the light slanting from the burnished bronze breastplates. Within moments, they would be lying side by side in the little hollow at the foot of the roadside hedge. A good century had passed since the coming of the road and its hedges, but there were still gaps between the thorn stems where one could see, yet not be seen. This seemed wiser, for though the Romans encouraged people in the Valley to get on with their business, there was a very harsh side to life. One sometimes saw strings of shackled slaves interspersed with the packhorses and livestock on the road. They might be Brigantian rebels, or perhaps captives that the hill people had sold to the Romans. Anyway, it was best to remain out of sight.

The medieval gatehouse defences at Bootham Bar stand upon the Roman gate that was the last thing of York that departing legions bound for the dangerous north saw.

At first, the boys would just stare at the soldiers as they passed – sometimes stocky Roman troops with their oblong shields, stabbing swords, javelins and proud eagles; more often auxiliaries from different parts of the empire and beyond, all decked out in the most amazing colours and guises. So now, the lads would try to memorise every detail of the passing soldiery and convert them into carved wooden models painted in ochre, madder, charcoal and limewash. Today, they waited with mounting excitement, hearing first the hoofs, then the rattling harness, and next the strange voices.

What they saw as the mercenary Sarmatian cavalry came into view, framed by the gap in the hedge, made their eyes pop out. A Roman writer, Pausanius, had explained that the Sarmatians resembled dragons, adding for those unfortunates who had not glimpsed a dragon that their armour was like a closed pinecone. This was very apt, for the robust armour was composed of interlocking scales made from the split and shaped hooves of mares. It covered not only the cavalrymen, but also their mounts. The horses, from Central Asia, with their neck bands and tails tied to form long whips, were graceful and erect, far different from the workaday local nags. As they watched the troop ride by, the boys struggled to memorise

The bridge at Hampsthwaite stands where Roman troops will cautiously have forded the Nidd.

every single detail; one imagined the criss-cross cuts he would make to represent the scales of armour, but how to recreate those colours with the dull earth and plant pigments to hand? Eventually, some time-elapsed Sarmatian troops would be settled on land near Ribchester, where they could act as reservists. Doubtless they left their contribution in the already diverse gene pool of the Yorkshire Dales.

No less impressive, in their way, were the Nervii infantry, descendants of the Belgic tribesmen who had caused such great trouble to the army of Julius Caesar when he campaigned in the heavily hedged country in the region of modern Belgium. However, the most remarkable local encounter came when the auxiliary Sebussian cavalry went past on their long way to Lancaster. Now it was the boys' grandchildren who heard the hoof clatter and the clank of harness. Then came the voices and the boys stared at each other in disbelief when a rider said quite clearly, 'If we don't get a drink soon, I think I'll fall off!' It was not exactly the Celtic that they were used to, but the meaning was quite clear. The *Sebusani* were Celts from the Loire valley, who would refurbish the basilica and bath-house during their service at Lancaster. They had made an offering to the Celtic river god, Ialanus, when they crossed the Nidd.

****

The Valley was a borderland, as it had been before and would be so often again. To its east spread the Great Vale, pacified, obedient and productive, while to the west the land rose to the insurgent fell country. The troops moving in from Aldborough or York had recently left safety, well-appointed barracks and urban comforts behind. The Valley was the first point on their westward march where they could be in danger of ambush. As they made for the paved ford on the Nidd, they became soldiers again. On the other hand, the cavalry and foot soldiers retiring from the outposts of the Yorkshire Dales were about to leave stress and caution behind for a while. Before descending into the Valley they had glimpsed the smoke-stained sky over York and had seen the distant Vale spread out like a comfortable quilt. As soon as they were safely across the Nidd, a wave of relief surged across the cohort or company, shield arms dropped and the troopers started looking at each other rather than scouring the shrubs and hedgerows as they had been doing for weeks. The decurions and centurions at once became more tolerant of the chatter and banter in the ranks.

The Valley people were aware of their borderland status. They were not relied upon to lead their lives lawfully like their cousins in the Vale. It was plain that the administrators and military did not entirely trust them not to harbour spies or ter-rorists and not to send runners with information about troop movements into the hill country. Occasionally, one heard of youths who had left their Valley homesteads to join the rebels. In reality, the modest prosperity of the Valley gave many people an interest in protecting the peace and the system that had imposed it.

At first, the conquerors or their agents would simply commandeer what they wanted and leave the byre and granaries empty. Later, they paid for what they took, and soon regular markets were in place. Moreover, one could trade at these markets and return, drunk or sober, with very little danger of being robbed. The evening debates were as frequent and no less boozy than before. When the occu-pation question was raised, as it usually was, the elders could see that it was not about issues of freedom versus foreign domination. If it had an ethical dimen-sion, this concerned whether native warrior aristocrats had a greater right to exploit people and impose arbitrary justice than had the invaders. Most country people aspired to little more than to farm and raise their families in peace. For the Britons of the Valley, mistakes or ill-judged acts leading to slavery or execution could happen under either regime. Under native rule one might possibly end up as a sacrifice, while under the Romans the chances of dying as a gladiator or beast fighter might have been about the same. If one thing tipped the balance in the Roman favour it was their ability to get things done. This made for prosperous farming, and this allowed for bigger rural families – increasing the chance of a son surviving to look after one in one's dotage.

Farming became a much more purposeful and remunerative affair. In the old days, the chief or warlord took his tribute, the family consumed what it needed and anything else, you bartered with your neighbours or exchanged with any per-ipatetic craftsman or trader who happened by. Now, the imperial market would gobble up everything you cared to offer. Some went to feed the legions; some vanished and might have ended up in Rome for all one knew. Certainly there were taxes to pay, but it was good to know that you would get a good, secure price for every egg, grain, joint, hide or fleece you had for sale. This encouraged people to break in more land, create new people to work on it, get more out of the old farm land and earn more cash to buy luxuries and pay debts. These motives would lead to the degradation of the environment in the medium term and underpin the destruction of civilisation in the centuries ahead. What the empire did not do was to prepare people for the time when it was no longer there – but was there ever an empire that did?

Chapter 5

A Nation is Born

(AD 410 – C. 1000)

The Old Road was still there, still quite well-trodden, though seldom repaired. Around it, however, the wilderness was starting to press in from those few unfarmed places where it had survived. Brambles extended rooting stems from the tangled hedgerows, thorn thickets spread in the pastures and ranks of blackthorn pressed closer to tracks. The seedlings of oak and ash dashed to become saplings in fields now deserted by cattle or sheep. Travellers straying from the road would encounter countrysides plummeting swiftly from prosperity into abandonment. They might peer around the doorway of a silent farmstead and recoil from the stench of the bodies within. Then they might wonder whether to blame the plague, foraging native war-bands, foreign mercenaries-turned-freebooters, common robbers or some other cause. The crows, buzzards, foxes and kites did not care. Each day brought them the carrion of crises, and theirs were the only numbers that increased.

It was a land where nothing really worked anymore, and had not done so for quite some time. If just one great system was failing, human ingenuity might have been harnessed and focussed to fix it. The problem was that several systems were stressed, collapsing, and helping to bring each other down. Public health was undermined by recurrent plague epidemics; the administrative system, once so pervasive and uncompromising, was fragmented and falling apart, and as it fell, so, too, did the confidence to invest in new enterprises. Meanwhile, the environment, following centuries of severe over-exploitation, experienced crises that interacted and multiplied.

What was worse, a land in turmoil and collapse was burdened with an enormous population inherited from the times of efficient organisation. The massive imperial trading with overseas markets hungry for British produce had created confidence. Income from the trade in lead and farm produce had allowed the natives to raise larger families; the imposition of peace helped to keep them alive. But the continental and garrison markets had gone, as had the imperial trade network that bound them together. In the towns that once had sucked in the rural produce, remnants of urban populations made gardens of the vacant house plots. Peas twined over rubble. Now, the deterioration of the transport infrastructure would have made commerce difficult even if the markets could have been resurrected. In many localities, the drive to fill the granaries of the empire had left soils exhausted and unstable. People stood out in the winter rain and watched their fields slowly slump and slither down slope. At the head of a field, the pale, stony subsoil had been exposed, and at the bottom, the lobes of migrating ploughsoil were choking the stream. Blocked, it backed up and spread out, inundating the plain upstream. The markets gone, most farmers had reverted to self-sufficiency and survival. However, for the moment the massive population of imperial times remained. It could not be supported. There would be a time of dying.

It had not seemed so grim in 409, when the Roman legions had abandoned the island to defend Rome and had left the British to their own devices. The British leaders had daringly quit the empire and people could be heard saying how lucky they now were to have the foreign oppressors off their backs. The truth was that the long experience of Roman rule and Roman culture had left the home-grown aristocracy and governing class equipped only to assist in the operation of the empire. They really knew nothing about governing an independent country. However, the successive generations that had experienced and adopted Roman values had taken people too far from their roots for the world of tribal kings and tribal territories ever to be recreated. They were lapsed as tribesfolk and third-rate as Romans. There could be no resurgent *Brigantia*. If anything would bind the world of Nidderdale and the Craven Dales together in the centuries to come it would be that sometime imperial religion, Christianity.

As so often would be the case, the bright hopes of independence celebrations were followed cruelly and with unseemly haste by escalating disillusionment. The parts of Britain under Roman rule had been united only by the increasingly frayed and tattered bonds of imperial government: remove the bonds and the country would gradually come apart. It would unstitch, mainly along the traditional seams, and its innards would spill out for any scavengers to find. When this did happen, there were no forces trained to intervene. When the whiffs of internal disunity attracted more raiding by barbarian tribes, the death, four centuries earlier, of the British martial traditions was a special cause for regret. Rome had a long history of recruiting and deploying foreign, even barbarian armies. This had nowhere been more obvious than in Britain, where the Roman elite had been vastly outnumbered by soldiers from the Balkans, Central Europe, Iberia and elsewhere. Given their own rusty or non-existent military skills, British leaders, particularly those in the threatened south-east, thought that the way to counter the English (Anglo-Saxon) piracy and coastal raiding was to recruit English mercenaries of their own to fight against them. Doubtless, they thought this with the aloofness of the retired cavalry officer who redeploys the village poacher to guard his pheasants, confident in the belief that his hireling gamekeeper would never dare to wrench him from his charger.

The Romans had already established these pagan savages in various strategic locations. The barbarians camped outside towns and were settled in the most impoverished corners of declining estates, ready to fight when their compatriots attacked. There, they filled their hours by farming, taking British wives and hatching plans to improve their situations. Times of crisis belong to the warlord and to those who have nothing to lose and are desperate to gain. People of more comfortable stations and more compromising dispositions have only indecision and fear in store for them. In thrall to the past and bound to their heirlooms and possessions, they could not cope with the desperate ones. In the USA, the descendants of the Irish famine would one day outstrip the members of the hallowed Protestant establishment in the league of income, just as in Britain where the penniless immigrant Indian shopkeepers and Hungarian refugee businessmen would flourish where others failed. The English took rather longer – two or more centuries – to gain a political mastery, and several generations came and went before their successes in the south were repeated in northern England.

Before this happened the lights of hope would be extinguished, one by one, and all parts of England would endure a night as long and as dark as any in the history of the country.

As the world around them slowly fell apart, the people of the Valley still looked to the old Roman administrative centre at Aldborough. It was a long time since the wagons loaded with lead had ceased to rumble, sagging and creaking along the Valley, to the head of navigation on the Nidd. Ages had past since a Roman grandee was lowered in a lead box within a stone chest to begin a disgusting burial beneath a sealed lid of Greenhow's metal. It was decades since the last patrol coming down from the army bases in the Pennines had crossed the Valley, dusty but relieved, on the road to Aldborough.

At Aldborough now, the hollow corner towers or bastions and the rectangular wall towers that had been added to the towns walls in the latter part of the fourth century still seemed quite new, their Millstone Grit was still more the colour of honey than of mouldy bread. However, the 55 acres (22.3ha) inside these walls had assumed a derelict appearance. It had never recovered the bustle of those days when Valentinian was emperor (AD 364-75) and part of a field army was stationed there. Now, most of the tanners had gone, along with the weavers and black-smiths. Newts wiggled and glided in the water cisterns, autumn gusts sent dry leaves rattling across mosaic floors to gather in the sludge of decorated plaster-work slumping from damp, unroofed walls. A sign of the changing times was the irreverent removal of bones from their privileged owner's stone sarcophagus and its re-use as a crude kiln.

Though debased and decaying, Aldborough remained the hub of a vast estate. 'Hub' however, may not be the best word, for rather than being centrally placed, Aldborough lay near the north-eastern limits of a territory that ran southwards to the Wharfe and the Roman station at Ilkley, that incorporated the whole of our Valley and that had the Ure as its north-eastern boundary. The geographical centre of this huge estate lay close to the point where the Roman road from Ilkley to Aldborough crossed the Nidd. The estate did not fall under the control of pagan English speakers until the early seventh century, at least eight genera-tions after the Roman legions abandoned Britain. When they did take it over, the estate came to be known as 'Borgescire': 'the shire or division of the fort', the fort or borough concerned being Aldborough.

The rediscovery of Burghshire was the achievement of Professor G.R.J. Jones, a geographer of Leeds University. He recognised that this was a geographically diverse estate with a broad spectrum of resources, including fell pasture, woodland and ploughland. This was what we now know as a 'multiple estate', a huge terri-tory subject to a head manor or *caput* and divided into a multitude of smaller land units, each of which was responsible for rendering specialised resources and prod-ucts to the head manor. In Burghshire, different townships would have provided fleece, cheese, wild honey, barley and so on. Over time, the old estate fragmented, with an early stage in the disintegration being the split into two estates, one con-trolled from the ancient capital at Aldborough, the other, from Knaresborough. With the passing centuries, royal land grants, inheritance, marriage and sales of land almost rendered old Burghshire invisible, yet even after the Norman con-quest, traces of the Roman estate were evident in Nidderdale churches that were linked to Aldborough and in pockets of land (berewicks and sokelands) which still were linked to the old centre.

Some threads from the past ran through into the Dark Ages or early medieval centuries. Others snapped and vanished. To understand the differences between the Roman heyday and the times of the semi-mythical Arthur, we must explain how a land that was stretched to its environmental limits to support a massive rural population and various cities was transformed into a place of wildernesses and decayed and desolate towns? Uncertainty and economic decay must have played a part. Warfare can peg back population, though each new generation of upland Brigantes seems to have recovered from the last revolt and to have felt ready to stage a new one. Epidemic is the most potent of the mass-murderers, though even the Pestilence of the fourteenth century eliminated very few villages permanently. The more the pulse of trade with the continent and beyond quickened, the greater the likelihood of importing some strange and frightful disease towards which the British had little resistance. There are very few records for the fifth and sixth centuries and those that exist are terse and often concerned with religion and polemics. There do appear to have been severe epidemics in continental Europe at this time; similar ones probably occurred in Britain and they might have been early visitations by the Black Death, whatever that was, for its nature is now questioned. We are also becoming aware of hyper-plagues, where lethal viruses migrate between different species, and something of that kind involving infection by a virus transferred from animals might have occurred. Depleted by war and disease, threatened, leaderless and with communal confidence now in shreds, people in the Valley and beyond it in all directions could scarcely cope with the revenges of an abused environment.

There are hints, in a Saxon font, a pre-Conquest cross and a commanding church site, that Middlesmoor may have been an early centre of Christian worship. It certainly has all the scenic attributes of a Glastonbury.

Roman Aldborough decayed, its successor was partly abandoned when people drifted to settle in the planned medieval town built by the new bridge at Boroughbridge and the once proud Roman local capital was partly colonised by Aldborough village.

✳✳✳✳✳✳✳✳✳✳✳✳✳✳✳✳

Strangers, now, were mistrusted. These days, anybody benighted on the road had best keep away from any farmsteads and hamlets. Dusk; the priest was approaching the rotting bridge where the Old Road crossed Ripley Beck when the man from the Beck-side farm set the hounds on him. His foot went through the slimy boards and the splinters ripped his shin deeply as, panicking, he pulled free. Then the greyhound nipped and pierced and the bloodhound pulled away a flap of flesh. He struggled across the neck of land between the beck and the river and plunged in. The dogs, enraged, swam more strongly than he could, savaging as they went. And so he gave up the struggle and let the force of the river bear him away, trailing a streamer of gore.

When consciousness returned, he found himself gazing at the moon through the undercut roots of a riverside oak. His legs were numb, but he hauled himself through a nettle bed to the crest of the bank. He looked at his punctured and tattered flesh and realised that without help, he would probably die quite soon. He prayed. When he opened his eyes, as if in answer, he saw a small house with post and daub walls and a thatched roof standing just 30 paces away. He cried for help. He called again and again, till his throat was dry. Then he saw the cloud of flies in the open doorway and the rats scuttling in an out. He did not bother to shout again. The pain from his wounds was intense, but after some time he realised that the worse it became, the more he felt able to detach his mind from his ruined body.

He had been lying, scorched by the sun, in the thistles on the edge of the run-down meadow for most of the day, gazing at a little lagoon in the riverside. He saw a grass snake slide from the bank and weave across the flat water. The silver-olive hue of its sides and the yellow patches on its head seemed to be colours far more intense than any that he had ever seen before. Rainbows radiated from the faint ripples born from its wending body and the up-welling mirrors on the water seemed to pulse in time with his heart. The flies drawn to his blackening wounds were like blued-metal bees and starlight flickered from their wings. The picture was so profoundly beautiful that he longed for his brethren or for just anyone to share it with. For a while, this urge to communicate exceeded the agony of his suffering and impending death.

There still was river water in his lungs, but he was parched: consciousness slipped into his fevered mind and then, blissfully, floated away. He thought of all the things that he had wanted to be. He had planned to be a scholar, a reader of books and a recorder of events, and these he had done. One day, God willing, he would carry Christianity back from this sacred island and take the scriptures to the Godless ones on the continent, those who bowed to beasts and trees. History had gifted the leaders a Christian island, a tamed landscape packed with grain and fine cattle, energy and endeavour. But those frauds had let these hopes and promises trickle, like gold dust, through their fingers. Instead of just government there were tyrants, intrigues and wars. Instead of missions and converts there were retreats and betrayals – and, meanwhile, the pagan lords snatched more and more from this outpost of Christendom. Soon, not a single dream would remain in the graveyard of hope, this forsaken, embattled and leaderless land. He prepared to die.

He thought he had jerked back into consciousness, for things seemed much clearer now. The air was suddenly so very, very clear and one might see forever. Was that a cavalcade with trumpets, drums and banners riding out on the Old Road? Was that a blessed bishop and were there priests in white and gold with retinues chanting the gospels? There were so many hands raised up in prayer. Surely triumphant processions such as this belonged to the lost times? A rider had detached and was cantering across the pasture, though soon the hoof-beats were muffled by the woodland. Now he was much closer: a chomping and jangling of harness, a brushing of branches and a veil of chain mail glinting among the trees. Then they burst out, horse and rider, like the sun exploding through a cleft in thunderclouds.

The horse was white with feathered hocks and hoofs as big as trenchers. The rider's armour was burnished bronze, with the symbol of Christianity glowing in raised relief on the breastplate. Similarly, the pennant on his lance was embroidered with the *Chi-rho* (the first Greek letters of the Saviour's name superimposed), with the *alpha* and *omega* letters in the angles of the chi, signifying that Christ is the beginning and the end. His helmet was in the Roman style, with a crest of red horsehair radiating around it like the rays of a sunrise. All the glory and piety of the lost days were condensed in this knight, whose strange, silvery aura shimmered on the edges of focus.

'Who are you?' gasped the dying man. 'I am the one they call "The Bear". I am Arthur'. The horse plunged and steadied. The rider lowered his lance and the man hauled himself up on it and slumped into the saddle in front of the horseman.

Turning, he whispered, 'Why are you here?' The knight's face was radiant but it would not seem to focus. He replied, 'You made me. You created me to save your faith.' The horse checked, reared and galloped away through the clouds and into the firmament.

Far below, a pack of feral dogs had discovered the fast-cooling body. This was a good time for feral dogs, though not for humans.

❋❋❋❋❋❋❋❋❋❋❋❋❋❋❋

In Roman times, the Valley, like the remainder of Britain, was a Celtic-speaking area. There were quite pronounced dialects within the Celtic-speaking province, and that spoken by the Valley people was closer to those spoken by the Cornish and the Welsh than by the Gaels of Ireland or their descendants, who would later colonise western Scotland. Meanwhile, the Picts of northern Scotland may have spoken either Celtic or a pre-Celtic language. The fact that the Celtic tongue was replaced by (Old) English has been taken as proof of an overwhelming surge by Anglo-Saxons – a cultural tsunami that annihilated the Romanised Britons or drove them into the mountain fastnesses. This seems unlikely.

Recent history shows that within a few decades around the close of the nineteenth century, English became a *lingua franca* throughout much of Africa and the

Indian sub-continent, even though the English colonists were never more than minute elements in their populations. This ascendancy was accomplished not by numbers, but more by psychology than by battlefield victories. The English (Anglo-Saxon) conquest was not sudden and absolute and Celtic communities lived alongside those of the English-speakers in many places in the Dales and elsewhere. Some of them can be recognised by place-names like 'Walden' (off Wensleydale) that includes the English *walas* denoting Celtic-speakers. The English may never have outnumbered the indigenous populations of the Dales, but their culture and their leaders did gain an ascendancy that was not challenged until the arrival of Danes and Norsemen.

This was reflected in the renaming of virtually every spot in our Valley, and it is impossible to discover what the old Celtic names of places where. The 'brilliant' river itself preserved its Celtic name (originally something like the *Niamde* of Irish Gaellic), though this would be combined with the Danish genitive of 'valley' to produce 'Nidderdale'. 'Dacre' might also refer to the river and derive from a Celtic word for a running teardrop, though it could, quite differently, denote a Dane, or something else entirely. The Germanic domination of language in the Valley provided the basis for a wonderful dialect but it has robbed us of almost all the Celtic names: names for places that were usually apt, perceptive and evocative. Of course, the Celtic influences (experts are not quite sure what 'Celtic' is, beyond language and artwork) deprived us of all the place-names of earlier prehistoric times. The tongue spoken by those who worshipped at Thornborough is entirely mysterious.

The manner in which the English cultural domination arose was complex. The confrontation between the Roman revivalism of the British and the aggressive expansionism of the hungry English had several facets. It arose at the moments when the English ceased to act as mercenaries hired to protect the civilised realm against their fellow barbarians or when they were no longer content to be planted in the desolate corners of estates that nobody else wanted.

It was a confrontation of haves and have-nots; an opposition of differing cultures, traditions and languages; a struggle between Christianity as part of an international Christian realm and aimless (though environmentally more responsible) paganism, and it was a battle between institutions and disorder. Had the British been able to preserve their institutions then the disorder that allowed the English to expand could not have taken place. The fact that the pagan, barbarian have-nots – or rather, their patriarchs and culture – emerged triumphant need not necessarily signal the irresistible nature of their challenge. It could, instead, signal the utter demoralisation of a hybrid Romano-British culture that lacked the flexibility to respond to any serious sort of challenge.

In north-eastern England, and doubtless in the Valley, Christianity had a prominent place in the issues. At various times within the empire, the religion had been suppressed and the faithful persecuted and at others, it was favoured and promoted by the establishment. Now, however, those who continued to worship would know nothing of the splendour of mass in a great city church. For many, there were no churches and the encounters with priests were increasingly uncertain. Still, for all the multiplying difficulties and dangers, the light of Christianity continued to smoulder in the north.

In the Craven region of the Dales and in Elmet, the area around modern Leeds, history provides glimpses of Christianity and of beleaguered Christian kingdoms lingering into the gathering gloom of the Dark Ages. Located almost between these kingdoms and close to both, probably within one of them, the Valley, too, must have shared in this perpetuation of the Roman faith. Priests will have plodded the riverside paths, holding masses in halls, beside crosses and in open places, moving up the Valley, towards the darkness.

The pagan advance was gradual, sporadic and yet remorseless. English kingdoms covered the country south of the Trent and in the second half of the sixth century, their realms in the north-east joined arms across the Tees to create the powerful kingdom of Northumbria. At the start of the next century, the Christian British territories that survived in Yorkshire were alone and embattled. To the east of Leeds and to the west of Tadcaster, forces of conscripts and volunteers dug and shifted great masses of earth to build networks of banks and ditches to protect the exposed eastern flanks of their exclave of Christendom against barbarian attack. With their leaders and armies having been depleted in the Saxon victory at Catterick at the start of the century, the ends of Christian Elmet and Craven came in 617. Edwin of Northumbria overran the British territory and Ceretic, son of Guallac, the last Celtic-speaking king, was expelled. If priests now moved in the Valley, for a while they must have done so furtively, though perhaps not as dangerously as did Catholic priests holding masses there 1,000 years later.

After their victory, some English warrior-peasants will have followed the Old Road and spilled into the Valley. For perhaps the first time, conversations in the Old English tongue wafted across the river. It is unlikely that a massacre of Valley people followed. Surviving nobles may have been roughly ejected from the better lands, but this was still a country in the grip of environmental and economic crisis. There were plenty of empty corners waiting to be filled. Language was perhaps the greatest casualty. The linguistic ballet dancer gave way to the foot-slogger. Across many hearths there were British wives who were now learning to swap the silent consonants of their own tongue for the long English vowels and to exchange the Celtic lilt for the bumping plod of the

Northumbrian drawl. The political and cultural agendas were now being set by the new ascendancy, though doubtless they found pleasure in the lightness and colour of the British imagination.

Attention was swung away from the fast-receding world of Rome and its emperors. It turned, instead, to the North Sea and the barbarian maritime nations clustered around its border. Pagan the new perspective might have been, but there was a verve and vibrancy about the salty world stitched together by ships, trade and plunder. As for religion, it is unlikely that much was done to suppress Christianity. The pagan deities (deities that were not so very different from those that competed with Christianity in the earlier days of empire) were probably not promoted with much missionary zeal. Perhaps they were as much sources of amusement and pegs for story-making as objects of belief. After all, it took a fair stretch of the imagination to believe that, on dark and stormy nights Woden might be found riding across the sky in his Wild Hunt, with lost souls for companions. In quiet places and amongst friends, Christianity probably lingered on in and around the Valley. When it returned to favour, there will have been those ready and waiting to greet it.

It did not have to linger for long. Soon after the English conquest, the North found itself caught in the vellum jaws of a closing theological vice. Yet again, the Valley people would find themselves standing on the threshold of historical events of profound importance. While the English had been exporting their mastery northwards and westwards, the Christian Church, which had gone native and survived in Ireland, had eventually discovered a mission to convert pagans in mainland Britain.

After colonising Iona in 563, it took the Celtic monks about seventy years to establish an eastern base on Lindisfarne. The conversion of Northumbria came from a different direction and, in part, from less elevated motives. The southern kingdoms had already been converted and so when Edwin sought a dynastic marriage with the sister of King Eadbald, the Kentish monarch insisted that the northern king should convert to Christianity. This he did, and in 627 this opportunistic conversion took Northumbria into the Christian fold. While Celtic Christianity had been making its introspective advance in the North, in the South events were more focussed, for in 597 Rome had intervened directly and a mission under Augustine had landed in Kent. About a decade after the English victors had entered the Valley, a new archbishop, Paulinus, was enthroned in York, the first to be recorded since 314, when an archbishop of York attended a church council at Arles.

At an instant in history, the ambitions of two versions of the same religion (the one quirky, remote and steeped in Atlantic fringe regionalism and the other inflexible, internationalist and proudly rooted in tradition) came face-to-face as rivals. The zone of this confrontation ran right across our Valley.

Soon, an incursion by pagan Mercians ousted Paulinus. At this time, an opportunity for Celtic influences to dominate was provided by Oswald. He led the Northumbrian recovery, and his father, Aethelfrith, was a covert of Iona. Oswald invited Aidan to establish Celtic monks at Lindisfarne. For those who had endured the hardship of unadorned life on spray-lashed islands or who, unarmed, had faced the pagans in their lairs, religion and its proper observance were issues of supreme importance. Centuries of effective separation had opened a rift between the now-competing faiths, with the austere Celtic tradition inclining to introspection and being rooted in monasticism, and the Roman church being based upon diocese and organised by bishops. The Valley people watched history unfolding before their eyes. Doubtless the recently and, perhaps, superficially converted English had to refer to their longer-established neighbours and relatives for explanations of what was going on. Woden and company had posed far fewer problems; nobody was much bothered about his testimony or how it should be observed. The business of the wives of Wayland and his brothers turning back into swan maidens one day and flying away was child's play compared to some of the difficulties these Christians got into.

A single figure, whose presence must have been familiar to many Valley people, then shaped the course of history. Wilfrid (634-709) had a sad childhood and was packed off to serve in the court of the Bernician king, Oswiu (of Bernicia r.642-70 and Northumbria, r.664-70), at the age of 14. Queen Eanfleda must have been impressed by his clerical potential and supported his transfer to Lindisfarne, and then to Rome. There, Wilfrid was immersed in the dogma and liturgy of the Roman church, then, staying for three years in Lyons, he showed no great compulsion to return to England. When he did return, Alchfrid (King of Deira, r.656-664), Oswy's heir, granted him the monastery at Ripon.

In the middle of the century, Abbot Eata of Melrose had established a Celtic monastery at Ripon, between the fords on the Skell and the Ure. It was inevitable that the Celtic community would soon be offended by the theology and practices that Wilfrid had acquired on the continent. Before long, they abandoned Ripon and returned to Melrose, and Wilfrid's reputation for failure as a conciliator was established. For the next few years, Wilfrid busied himself imposing and enforcing a Roman code while, strangely, serving as Abbot at Ripon for five years *before* becoming a member of the priesthood.

The hold of Christianity in Northumberland was too young and fragile to survive a rivalry between two competing perspectives, so in 664, about a year after Wilfrid became a priest, King Oswiu convened a synod at Whitby in which Colman of Lindisfarne and Wilfrid of Ripon would debate their respective cases. The calculation of the date of Easter provided a focus, though, essentially, the debate determined which brand of faith would live, and which would die.

Wilfrid and his cause emerged victorious. Perhaps his arguments were more convincing, though for a politically astute monarch, the choice of whether to join a small, schismatic church of the Atlantic outposts or to combine with one that embraced, and to some extent marshalled by far the greater part of Christendom, might not have seemed a difficult one to make. (However, the really astute king would have seen an advantage in exerting clear authority over a Celtic monastic system rather than skirmishing indefinitely with the supremacy of the Roman church.)

Colman's monks left Northumbria for Iona, while Wilfrid was appointed Bishop of York. Scarcely the magnanimous victor, he refused to be consecrated by northern bishops, men he still considered schismatics, so he crossed the Channel and was consecrated in Compiègne. His tarrying, once again, on the continent must have exhausted Oswui's patience and he installed Chad in York in Wilfrid's place. Wilfrid returned to Ripon but was then restored to the bishopric in 669. He spent the following years in a characteristically confrontational manner, purging the diocese of Celtic influences, establishing a Benedictine monastery at Ripon, falling out with Ecgfrid (r.670-685), the new king, exacerbating marital differences in the royal household and defying the authority of the archbishop of Canterbury. The quarrels about his standing at York culminated in Wilfrid's departure to Rome, where he won papal support but returned to face imprisonment and then exile in Sussex. A reconciliation brought his restoration as Bishop of Hexham, and then of York. Yet again his quarrelsome intransigence had him heading for Rome bearing complaints about his archbishop, and once more he returned victorious after another prolonged absence on the continent. There was another reconciliation and Wilfrid died in the Midlands, in charge of Hexham and Ripon, though not of York.

Wilfrid began rebuilding the dilapidated church at Ripon in stone in 672, giving the Minster some kind of claim to be England's oldest stone cathedral after York. The contrast with the humble, thatched Celtic churches was deliberate and it was here that Eddius taught the Gregorian chants to his fellow clergy. Wilfrid was said to love ornately adorned churches, liturgy, splendid vestments and the spectacle of ritual pageantry. The imposing and highly adorned churches that he created flaunted his disdain for the Celtic monks and the simple austerity of their buildings. His grandest churches embodied the work of specially imported continental craftsmen and would have been glazed in the progressive manner, as opulently decorated as the times allowed, and endowed with finely illuminated volumes and with relics housed in magnificent reliquaries. The relics in the bowels of a church were crucial: the sanctity of the church depended upon their holy radiance.

We can but wonder what his congregants in the Valley thought of this otherwise ascetic man who yet had obtained extensive landed estates and variously supported an armed retinue. How could they fathom this contentious patriarch

Ripon retains its Saxon crypt, though the Minster above has experienced various disasters and rebuildings.

who read the gospels of forgiveness and brotherly love and yet hounded those who sincerely espoused different nuances of worship with all the implacable tenacity of a bull terrier? What could you make of a man who promoted the cause of a church that was so fiercely wedded to authority and hierarchy, yet who defied and affronted his own superiors at every turn?

How they must have marvelled in the Valley when they heard how he brought the anger of King Ecgfrith down on his own head by persuading the Queen to retreat to Coldingham as a nun! Who else would do such a thing? How the tongues will have wagged when his infatuations with Rome and France prolonged his continental absences beyond all acceptable limits. 'Is he back yet?' some would ask, just to relish the gasps of indignation when it was revealed that he was still abroad.

Across the hearths they recalled stories of his remarkable durability: of how, in 691, he made a bid to be Bishop of all Northumbria, provoking King Aeldfrith (r.685-704/5) to seize Ripon Abbey estates and banish the over-reaching abbot. Yet no sooner had the pest been driven off to Mercia than he resurfaced as the Bishop of Leicester! Perhaps the people took him to their hearts, as people in Britain sometimes still do with old curmudgeons. Perhaps they recognised his integrity, the various churches and abbeys that he had founded and the many conversions he had made in Mercia, the Frisian Islands, Sussex and the Isle of Wight?

Before the era of the English-speaking kings had passed, Wilfrid had acquired his own special cult at Ripon. Almost 150 generations after pilgrims had left the Valley to worship at Thornborough and the Devil's Arrows, Valley people were now treading exactly the same tracks, veering from the river after crossing the Ripley Beck and heading due north on their reborn Pilgrims' Way. Now, their journey was a little shorter: one could be back home by supper and there was no need to ford the Ure. At Ripon the pilgrim tracks converged and the church, with its walls so unusually of stone, its Romanesque arches and the slanting sun rays flashing from its glass, was seen rearing over the River Skell like a great buff eagle with a silver serpent writhing in its talons.

You could enter the church, gape at the painted plasterwork, see towering piers in the nave arcade surging like forest trees, and you could wait in line to peer down a vertical shaft. When you did, you could see the relics that Wilfrid had brought back from Rome – or at least the reliquaries, banded in gold, plated with amber and studded with garnets, that contained them. They gave the church its sanctity. Down there in the crypt the assembled relics pulsed out their energy like the rods in a reactor, but in infinitely more benign a fashion.

The crypt has survived since 672 and is the oldest complete example in Britain. St Wilfrid's shrine attracted visitors until the Reformation forced an end to such pleasures, many of the pilgrims staying at the precursors of the Unicorn on the market square. When Wilfrid died at Oundle in Northamptonshire in his seventy-fifth year, his body was carried back to his favourite church and buried to the south of the high altar. It soon became a magnet for pilgrims. While the crypt has endured, the remainder of Wilfrid's church was destroyed in 950. The rebuilt Minster was wrecked by the Normans during their harrying of the North. A Norman Minster replaced it in 1080, and a century later it was rebuilt in the less monolithic Transitional style. A west front was gained in 1220 and the central tower collapsed in 1485 – and again in 1660. All things considered, the survival of Wilfrid's crypt beneath the present cathedral is rather remarkable. Meanwhile, a town grew around the great church, and in the thirteenth century the archbishops of York reorganised the settlement. A rectangular area of about 5 acres

At York, the focus of Wilfrid's ambition, the Minster stands directly upon the headquarters of the legionary fortress of Roman York.

(around 2ha), about twice as large as the present market square, lying to the west of the church, was designated as a market place for what was effectively a new town. House plots for traders with frontages of about 15 or 30ft (about 4.6 to 9.2m) were marked out surrounding the square and the street pattern was rear-ranged. Medieval Valley people who were familiar with Ripon, as most must have been, would have no difficulty in navigating around there today.

The role of the Valley people as onlookers to the great events of history did not end with Ripon and the synod of Whitby, for another great synod would be held in the Valley itself. According to the almost contemporary history of the English church and people written by Bede, the Jarrow monk, a synod was held near the river Nidd in 706. It apparently concerned Wilfrid's squabbles with King Aeldfrith, the succession to his throne and the restoration of Wilfrid to the bishopric of York. At the synod, Aelfflaed, the fifty-two-year-old princess and abbess, revealed that the dying king had forgiven Wilfrid and wished for his return.

Just where this great council was held is a mystery. The village of Nidd is a favoured choice, perhaps only because it shares its name with that of the river. Any gathering would need to be at a place that was accessible from various directions. Nidd did lie by the Old Road, though it is unlikely that a village existed here at this time. Other things equal, probably the most likely setting would be where the routeways that are likely to have been used by the participants crossed or came close to the river. In the medieval period, the Nidd was navigable to commercial shipping as far as Nun Monkton, just downstream from Knaresborough. However, with a few portages, a light river craft would have no difficulty in reaching the Ripley area. Here, the river formed a great loop (the one that had nudged the Roman road northwards) until it was straightened in 1665. These works, by the then Ingilby lord, severed the old meander, leaving just the Ripley Beck running in the channel where once the Nidd had flowed.

By the ancient church site here, an embayment in the river bluff produces an amphitheatre-like landform that faces the sun and that would have provided an excellent setting for open-air debate. It was here, close to where the road from Ripon, the Old Road and the largely Roman road from York intersect and approach the river, that a rescue excavation produced an ornate fragment of metalwork. Expert opinion considers that it might well have come from the binding of a Saxon bible.

With a Christian monarchy and people of Wilfrid's steadfast kind around, there would be no back-sliding. Even so, people perched on the watershed between faiths sensed certain unease. Christianity was preoccupied with the dominion of mankind over the birds, beasts and inanimate components of nature, while paganism was concerned with the closeness of all creation. Ironically, while the saints had really been human, in a strange way Woden, Wayland, Helith and their chums, for all their improbable antics, seemed to have more down-to-earth humanity. One could quite easily imagine meeting wise, old, one-eyed Woden on some shady lane at dusk. If the old rogue was in the mood, perhaps he would lower his hood and swap a few words. Even the Christian British people felt a need for a more intimate contact with nature, for she had to be coaxed away from causing famines and plagues. You had to get her on your side. So when a church was founded beside the site of the synod, it was placed on a cramped shelf between two holy springs. The Christians were quite opportunistic. The springs had been dedicated to pagan gods since time immemorial, but why abandon such socially significant places? Let them now be Christian holy springs. Then they could clasp the church in their holy embrace

The Celtic tongue was fast retreating. Within a few generations, only the shepherds on the high ground at the head of the Dale would use it. Then it receded to the Pennine fastnesses, lingering for a few medieval centuries in Lakeland, before vanishing from northern England. While the old language was declining in Nidderdale there were some relatively settled times, times disturbed only by the inevitable dynastic wars between rival family members and jealous kingdoms. As Britishness seeped out of the Valley, like wine from a leaking cask, the time of wounds became a time of healing.

The countryside was poised on the brink of revolution. Down south, the scattered farmsteads with their little fields spread around them were starting to give way to villages with churches and churches with villages, and they were surrounded by immense strip fields where the ploughland was being ridged up and furrowed like ripples on a brown lake. When brows were furrowed like the ploughland, it often reflected the anger and distress caused by the Danes. They had begun to materialise like wraiths from the North Sea mists and to fall upon churches and abbeys, pillage their treasure, slaughter a few innocents and then vanish.

In 865, this hit-and-run piracy entered a more threatening phase when a Viking army wintered in East Anglia. Two years later, Ivar the Boneless took York and a Danish army landed in the Humber. Wars, or at least skirmishing, were a part and parcel of life in the Dark Ages. For those who were not killed in the clashes and raiding, the really serious wars were those in which one dominating culture was forcibly replaced by another. Just as Englishness was being established, it happened again. Though some of the Danes came from places like the Frisian Islands, abandoned by migrating Saxons a few centuries before and the target of a mission by Wilfrid, the Danes and Yorkshirefolk were rather different.

Now, in a great example of historic irony, the English had the role of the learned, bookish standard-bearers of Christian civilisation. They had become the ones with vested interests in maintaining peace in an increasingly prosperous country. Now they were the ones who faced desperate Germanic pirates and invaders. Mindless ravaging and soulless genocide had become the vocation of the peasant farmers, small-time traders and fishermen of the hungry, worn-out fringes of Norway and Denmark.

The Vikings destabilised the English realms in the ninth and tenth century, though, strangely, the village/church/open-field revolution continued to progress right through the tumults. In Yorkshire, the invaders virtually destroyed the traditions of worship that Colman and Wilfrid had launched; the region was left studded with ruined Benedictine houses. On the other hand, eighty years of rule by Danes and Norsemen propelled York back into its long-lost role as a leading North Sea and river port and commercial capital. Also, the virtual conquest by the Danes demonstrated the unviable nature of the little English kingdoms and the need for a united monarchy.

✽✽✽✽✽✽✽✽✽✽✽✽✽✽✽✽

They stared at each other across the plank and rope bridge at Summerbridge. On the one side were the brothers, two with spears and a swordsman with a moulding leather helmet. The rings on their hide tunics were rusting and they smelled of the ditch in which they had slept. On the other side of the bridge was a hastily assembled force of local people with bills, scythes and pitchforks. For a long time, the parties glowered across the bridge. Then the swordsman made a hilt-forward gesture with his sword, and the leading elder shrugged and beckoned the brothers over the river.

Once, they might have been flayed alive and their skins nailed to the Minster door. Now, everyone was just tired of it all. The brothers' people still had some influence in York and, well ... there was rather a surplus of daughters in the Valley, to say nothing of widows from some fairly recent clashes. With the tension gone, the climate became quite ridiculously jolly, and simplified Germanic banter in Old English and Old Danish skipped back and forth. 'We've got a couple of your lot here already', said the elder, inventing a pidgin form of Old English as he towed the older brother along by his arm. As yet the Germanic languages of Atlantic Europe were insufficiently differentiated to prevent an English-speaker from communicating in some meaningful sort of manner with a Scandinavian. He hailed a lanky, pale-skinned man over from the line of hoers. 'There you are!', he said proudly. The brothers exchanged a few words with the man, turned to their host and explained with upturned palms and with fingers to their lips that this was not one of 'their lot', but a Norseman. He had come from the frozen fjord country. They were Danes. But to the locals gathered all around, all Vikings were 'Danes'. Danes were devils (though the evidence of recent decades was less conclusive). And yet, if Danes could be cured of their Danishness and devilry by absorbing them into their communities and exposing them to the gospels, then that could only be good. It had all gone on too long.

And so they were absorbed into the Valley community. One brother died repelling a raid by his countryfolk – he recognised his killer, who came from the same village near Esbjerg that he had left years before. The other two became local patriarchs. Their slightly throaty accents became stronger when they sat around the hearth and entertained the local children with their sea songs. Children who had never been within miles of a boat hauled on imaginary ropes in time with the dirge. They told of their Swedish cousins who had travelled through Russia, the broad rivers that ran, like sword thrusts, into the heart of France, and the great rock guarding the mouth of the Mediterranean. But when it came to looting English churches and torching village thatch, they fell quite silent.

❋❋❋❋❋❋❋❋❋❋❋❋❋❋❋❋❋❋

Around the farmsteads, hamlets and new villages, a landscape that would last for more than half a millennium was taking shape. Below the ancient commons were the shared strip fields and then the common meadows. Church towers began to add a vertical emphasis to the scene as old churches were rebuilt in stone and new estate churches joined the Minsters, though these were always far fewer than in the southern lowlands.

Among the work-bands, the women who pounded washing on the riverside stones and the children scurrying around the farms, a new language was being formed. Most of the British words had been lost; *darach* became *ac* or oak and the wood or *coed* became a *wudu* or wood. A few old words would survive, like the *topyn* which became a toppin or head of hair in the Nidderdale vernacular. With the coming of the Scandinavians, the English names were in turn displaced from some places, as the *wudu* and *fyrhth* sometimes became the *vithr* ('with') or *lundr* ('lund'). As words were swapped, dropped and assimilated, a northern dialect that blended the cultural influences came into being. The Norse settlers provided the Valley with a wealth of words, most of them fathomable in their original form by English speakers today: *akr*, a plough field (or 'acora' in the quite recent language of the Dales); *tré*, a tree or wood; *sustir*, sister; *sumar*, summer; *steinn*, a stone. A glorious integration of different linguistic traditions, our Northern dialect thus became a living vindication of cultural integration.

In the couple of centuries before the Norman Conquest, Upper Nidderdale became a cultural melting pot as Celtic-, English-, Danish- and Norse-speakers developed a dialect and created a galaxy of place-names in their various languages.

Into the lifetime of many people reading this book, a Dales dialect circulated in the Valley and was understood by most of us there. Now, you can spend a day there and never hear a word of it. When we look at what we used to say, we find that it was not some sort of parochial gibberish, but was rooted in words that very largely arrived in the area before the Norman Conquest. A 'force' or waterfall was the Old Norse *fors*; a 'keld' or spring was the Old Norse *kelda* and one might cross it at an Old Norse *wath*, or ford; while a 'royd' or woodland clearing was *rjódhr*. The Norse Vikings also gave us *tík*, 'a bitch' which became our 'tyke' or rascal. Their Danish cousins gave us numerous words, like gimmer, 'a ewe lamb', from their word for 'lamb', *gimmer*. Very often, the different Germanic speakers had words that were very similar to each other and that became embedded in the Dales dialect. 'Lake', our word for play, resembles the Norse *leika* and the English *laecan*; 'fettle', the word that we used for mending things comes from the Old Norse *fetill* or the Old English *fetel*, both signifying a strap or belt (such as might be used for binding something up). 'Beck', which we in the Valley preferred to 'stream' or 'brook' is *bekkr* in Norse and *beck* in English, while 'bank', the once very common word for a steep slope or valley side, and 'banky', meaning 'hilly', came from the Old English, *banc*.

As I sit back and look at my computer screen, I see a multitude of red dashes. They are underlining the words of Dales dialect that Microsoft decides have no place in the modern English language. Microsoft will soon be entirely right. On the shelf to my left is a thick dictionary of Lowland Scots. It is quite remarkable how many words from the dying Dales tongue survive in the still-living Scottish dialects: 'loaning', a lane; 'ganning' which means 'going'; 'lither', meaning 'lazy'; 'gay', pronounced 'gae' and meaning 'very'; and a multitude more. It is to the north that our cousins live; perhaps we should get to know them better? If any from a different direction should imagine that the language of the Dales amounted to no more than a quaint accent with a few funny words tossed in, they might look at the abbreviated dictionary that the Victorian Joseph Lucas added to his book of Nidderdale studies. Between 1868 and 1872, when the language was still very much alive, he collected enough words to fill 66 pages of very small print.

✳✳✳✳✳✳✳✳✳✳✳✳✳✳✳✳✳✳

Celtic-speaking returned to the Valley in a very small way. Clothra came with her husband, her brother-in-law, his wife, their farm servant and her parents-in-law. For her, the journey had been a fairly short one: just two days spent crossing the fells from their impoverished holding in Cumbria. Her husband had travelled much further. He had left the farmstead that his father had founded on Skye to go a-Viking. He had stayed with cousins on the Isle of Man, harassed the Irish and then gone to recover from his wounds on an uncle's estate in Cumbria. That was where he had met his wife. His father had travelled even further, sailing west from a fjord near Stavanger on one clear May morning long ago and making landfall amongst former neighbours who had settled on Orkney. There he stayed, until a feud with another little dynasty of Norse settlers saw him setting sail in a hurry for the Minches.

Now, they came stumbling eastwards across the fell, materialising out of the mist one-by-one. She, already homesick for Cumbrian places and people, was singing her sad Celtic ballads which seemed to have 1,000 verses. The old ones were grumbling to each other in Norse, while the little flock of frizzy-haired sheep trotted ahead, forever trying to stop and pick at the heather shoots. At one moment, the Pennine plateau had seemed to stretch endlessly ahead, misty, with winter lingering into April. The next moment, the land was falling away in front of them. There was the Valley forming a wide trough, with the bouncy, youthful river just a wandering dark line in its bottom. It was still fairly empty in its upper reaches. The grass had started to grow and there were not enough sheep to graze away the rank invaders and young thorns. The old man sat down amongst the coarse grasses. He was tired. He had gone halfway round the world. This was where he would die, though not just yet. He would walk as far as the first river bend and that was all. So they might as well start looking for stones and earth to make a house. He had seen some useful bake-stones just a while back, and plenty of peat to heat them up.

After a while, the 'intruders' or 'squatters' became 'neighbours'. They might have pinched some poor common grazings and there had been some threats and harsh words exchanged across the new wall line. But they had killed a couple of wolves, they bought some salted butter, one of the lads was pretty good at smithing and nobody could keep the children quiet like that little foreign lass with her fairytales. They did have some funny ways; they kept making you laugh. They were talking of getting a young horse (which would be very good to borrow), and he called it a *fóli*, the lass called it a *foilid* and everyone knows that a young horse is a *fóla*!

✳✳✳✳✳✳✳✳✳✳✳✳✳✳✳

The old names linger with places. The picture in the Valley has two distinctive aspects. Firstly, it seems that the majority of Scandinavian settlers there were Norse rather than Danes. By the time that they arrived, more from the north-west and over the fells than from the east, their interest in fighting and raiding may have evaporated. Their backgrounds were in the Norwegian fjord and mountain country, in the Scottish hills and the Lakeland fells. Therefore, they will probably have found more to please them in the rough and chilly banks and fellsides of the upper Valley than would have suited flat-landers, like the Danes.

The second point of note is that so many of the names of places tell of a merging of different cultures. 'Spittle Ings' could be the (Old English) hospital by the (Old Norse) meadow. 'Wath' is a Norse word for a ford, but originally Wath in the upper Valley was Acchewath, probably named after a Dane called 'Aki'. Similarly, Woodale takes its name from an English word for a wolf and the Scandinavian words for a valley. The legacy of so many of these bilingual or tri-lingual words is evidence of a bubbling process of cultural integration. If people were borrowing words they were probably also borrowing other things: sharing equipment or draught animals for example. And if people were doing that they were also probably helping to put up each other's houses and co-operating with the harvest work. It is also interesting that in a few places, personal names of the Middle English period are combined with Scandinavian words, showing that the Norse/Danish influences remained strong in the Middle Ages, thus we have the Ermina who owned Armathwaite or Hoodstorth, where Hude had his young wood.

What these diverse people and the melting pot of the Dales achieved given just a few centuries of relative peace is simply amazing. They reorganised a failing landscape, put the countryside back to work and, while doing all this, they gave birth to a nation of Dalesfolk.

CHAPTER 6

THE RED RIVER

(c. 1000 − *c.* 1100*)*

For the thousands throughout history, life was framed in martial terms. For the millions through history, life was about recovering from the devastations wrought by the armed minority. It was about bringing land back under the plough, building new homes in the ashes of the old, restoring some shape to existence and waiting for the next onslaught of the martial men.

So it was in the Valley. It was not the sword or the spear that kept communities alive there while the English, Danes and Norsemen charged and hacked or as rival dynasties fought like terriers for the English crown. As the battles and skirmishes rolled to and fro, the ordinary people of the Valley did not campaign against each other. Rather, they fought the harvest downpour, the potholed lanes and their own arthritic fingers, and in 100 such ways they maintained life whilst lives were being shed all around them. Their doggedness was miraculous and yet it was unexceptional: throughout the length of the kingdom other ordinary people were doing much the same.

They must have regarded those historical events that would find their ways into the history books with a certain resignation: let the aristocracy worry about the code of loyalty obliging one to die with one's lord. Let the thanes and militia men of the *fyrd* do the fighting. Hopefully, it would all pass over; if it did not, one would just have to drive the cows deeply into the woods and slip away for a while. Whatever the name or character of the lord, the impositions of the system were more or less the same. However, even ordinary people had their senses of identity. Knowing who they were and where they were from gave them some of the strength needed to survive amidst chaos. The Valley had been very heavily affected by Scandinavian settlers; up to half the names of places were derived from the Old Norse and Old Danish rather than the Old English. Also, there was already an awareness of a Northern or Northumbrian cultural identity, while in all but a political sense the Valley people had more in common with those of southern Scotland than with the of southern English. Somehow, over the centuries, the centres of power had drifted southwards, and this was cause for considerable suspicion. Even ordinary Northumbrians sensed it.

Harold was king and he was rumoured to be a just and capable leader. However, his father, Godwin, an Englishman who had been granted his Earldom of Wessex by the Danish conqueror Cnut, had been a fearsome political manipulator and was widely distrusted. Perhaps worse, as holder of the Wessex Earldom, he was very much a Southerner. On the other hand, the Godwinsons were at least as much Danish as English, a factor that should have won Harold some support in the northern lands. (On a visit to Denmark with Cnut in 1019, Godwin married Cnut's sister, Gytha, who became mother of Harold, Swegen, Edith, Tostig and Gyrth.) But yet again, Harold's half brother, Tostig, had been a deeply unpopular ruler in the north following his appointment as Earl of Northumbria in 1055. At first, he mounted a successful and welcome campaign against anarchy and robbery, but his reign became increasingly tyrannical, even murderous. Ten years after he took over the northern earldom, more than 200 noblemen met in York and chose a Midlander, Morcar, brother of Edwin, Earl of Mercia, in his place. Predictably, a battle between the supporters of Tostig and Morcar ensued. When Harold intervened, he supported Morcar, who was his brother-in-law, rather than his brother – an exercise in statesmanship that must have won him more friends than enemies in the North.

In the middle years of the 1060s, the levels of political activity were high, but that was not too unusual. The extent to which the heightened climate of intrigue and foreboding influenced life in the Valley is uncertain. An unpopular Earl had gone and, hopefully, the other troubles might just wash over the ordinary people. One thing that will have caused great disquiet was the appearance, in the April of 1066, of Halley's Comet. There it hung and there it seemed to grow, in skies that were then truly as black as night. People who knew said that comets were harbingers of bad news – very bad news. But then skirmishes, epidemics, famines and the like were familiar parts of life, and things could scarcely be much worse than them ... could they?

For the people of the Valley and the regions for miles around they would be very much worse indeed. Half a year after the sighting of the comet there was a flurry of movement as armed foot soldiers from the militia and some thanes on horseback were seen hurrying south-eastwards along roads and trackways, sometimes even cutting right across the grain fields. Word spread that the hated Tostig had returned in a partnership with Harald Hardrada, the giant Norwegian king, whose atrocities were considered frightful even by the standards of his time.

After the flight to the east, there were a few days of calm before soldiers, far fewer than had left, came trudging and limping back, some stained with sweat or blood and some dying and being towed back to their halls on litters made from homestead doors. Edwin and Morcar and the forces of Northumbria, it emerged, had been defeated at Fulford, near York. However, five days later, at Stamford Bridge, the Norsemen were taken by surprise by the fyrdmen and huscarls of an army under the King Harold. It had made a forced march northwards, covering almost 200 miles in just five days. It was also said that Harold had since turned south to face a Norman invasion force under Duke William of Normandy. For the people of the Valley, that was largely that. Tostig and the Vikings were gone; Harold had headed south, and now there should be some peaceful time to get the harvest away. After that, the campaigning season would almost be over, and hopefully, all the bad luck borne by the comet was now done with.

Within a week of the events at Hastings, the Valley people learned of the death of Harold, his huscarls and a large portion of the English nobility. At the time, it was not considered a major disaster; Harold had only been king for a year and feelings about him in the North were still ambivalent. Soon, the estates of the English dead and some of the evicted gentry were taken over by Normans, mostly the descendants of coarse Viking raiders who acquired a veneer of French civilisation and converted to Christianity after settling in Normandy. However, neither people in England who could remember the pure dialects of Old Danish nor those versed in Old Norse could understand a word they said. Wherever they took charge, any bonds of kinship between master and retainers disappeared. But taking charge in the North of England was not easy and the roles of Edwin and Morcar were crucial. In the event, they supported the legitimate English claimant, Edgar Etheling, and led the armed opposition to the Norman occupation, though their resistance crumbled when the Conqueror sent his cavalry north, took York, burned its suburbs and harried the surrounding countryside.

This brought alarm to all those who aspired to nothing more than a return to the drudgery of peaceful times, a community that included most of the freemen, tenants, bondsmen and slaves in the Valley. Soon, it was plain that the price of acquiescence was to see the land pinned down by castles and controlled by foreigners who stood apart from the old English traditions. In the world of the townships and manors, tradition ruled supreme and was more jealously defended than values such as justice. Would the foreigners honour the ancient customs of the manors, which had given a measure of order and dignity to otherwise downtrodden existences?

Edwin and Morcar rose again, driving out Earl Copsi, the Norman puppet ruler in Northumbria. Then, Edgar and the thane Gospatric led a Northumbrian and Scottish army to free York. By this time the people of the Valley, the more prominent of them with fathers, husbands or brothers summoned into the insurgent army, knew that those peaceful times that they had been dreaming of could be a long time away.

Again, in 1068, the Conqueror marched northwards and took York. Peace did not follow and soon a conflict between Gospatric and Robert de Cumin, rival English and Norman claimants to the earldom, was tearing Northumbria apart. A confederation of Northumbrians, Scots and Danes took to the field in 1069. In torching some houses in the suburbs, the Norman garrison accidentally burned down the Minster and its library, and were then slaughtered when the English and Danes stormed the city. Enraged by the massacre of his 3,000-strong garrison, William raised a mercenary army on the continent and laid siege to York, its defenders finally succumbing to famine after six months of resistance. This was the beginning rather than the end of affairs.

The Valley people were hoping that, after four years of bloodshed and intrigue, they might at last have some respite from the ambitions of nobles and the clashes of dynasties. The hopes were soon dashed as rumours of skirmishing cavalry in the vale to the east were heard. Travellers reported seeing plumes of smoke in several directions with, seemingly, a curtain of fire following the distant road from York to Thirsk and Northallerton. Shortly afterwards, a mercenary cavalry force came clattering in from the Old North Road. Leaving William de Percy's estates at Spofforth and Plumpton alone, they harried the Valley lands around Knaresborough and then began the devastation of every house and holding on the estates at Bilton and Rossett. Wild, blood-soaked bands of skirmishers and larger forces led by Norman aristocrats began to arrive. The royal lands around South Stainley, Killinghall, Whipley, Felliscliffe and Timble were not spared, and with the lower Valley silent and wreathed in smoke, the war bands merged and systematically exterminated every human and source of food they could find from Tang Beck to the head of the Valley. Nor did the neighbouring dales fare much better: fire-stained skies were seen to the west above Wharfedale and the Washburn valley and over Wensleydale to the north.

The people had little warning, while flight beyond the Valley homelands ran counter to all tradition. A farmer, whether free, a bondsman, tenant or a slave, was bound to his oat land and pastures. Detached, landless and without a lord he was nothing, scarcely different from an outlaw, and if there was nobody to milk cattle and sheep and swing the scythe, his family would starve. Now it was winter, too: there were no crops out in the fields, no hedgerow fruits to pick and no nuts left in the woods. Some Valley people did flee. Cowering in the woods in daytime and striking across the fells at night, fractured families might meet, shivering and starving in the lands beyond the Tyne.

The scale and ferocity of this, the harrying of the North, set it apart from the dynastic feuds and Scottish incursions. A swathe of countryside some 80 miles in width and stretching from the Tyne to the Humber was ravaged. The guilty ones were foreigners without links of kinship with their victims or ties of place with their setting – they could not even understand the pleas for mercy from their victims.

Orderic Vitalis, a careful chronicler born just six years after the Norman recapture of York, described what had followed when William ... :

> ... made no effort to restrain his fury and punished the innocent with the guilty. In his anger he ordered that all crops and herds, chattels and food of every kind should be brought together and burned to ashes ... so that the whole region north of the Humber might be stripped of all means of sustenance ... so terrible a famine fell upon the humble and defenceless population that more than 100,000 Christian folk of both sexes, young and old alike, died of hunger.

Another chronicler, Simeon of Durham, described the more gruesome aspects of the slaughter, with corpses lying unburied as there were no relatives left alive to bury them.

So it was in the Valley. The first to die were the insurgents from the fighting around York, speared from behind and run down in the lanes by the horsemen as they fled for the wildernesses of the high fells. Then the families of the farmsteads and hamlets were hacked down, often before they realised what the fracas erupting in their midst was about. Next, there was the flight of the survivors, the solitary dwellers and the escaping relatives of those cut down. Along with some who were forewarned, they scrambled through the Valley-side woods with the hammering hoofs pounding ever closer, gasping as they struggled to reach slopes too steep for the pursuing horses. Then, with corpses spread around, the mercenaries began burning the granaries, firing the hay lofts and torching the thatch. With piglets, geese and hens slung across their saddles they galloped on to choose the venue for their next massacre.

When the fires had died down and they were sure that the soldiers had gone, the dregs who had survived events two months earlier slipped back from the distant refuges. The return to the Valley was stalked by forebodings. Approaching the old homesteads they saw the ragged corpses of their family and friends still lying where they fell. They were partly decomposed and dismembered: drawn from the high fells and far woods by the stench of blood, the wolves had taken their fill. So, too, had the boars, kites, crows and the farm dogs. A few tattered bodies found eventual rest in a far-off churchyard; most were buried near where they lay, though sometimes the returning ones, few and weak, could do no more than consign remains of their dead to ditches. The survivors now faced the challenges of building shelters where the homes had stood, of raising crops with the granaries burned and the seed corn gone, and of sustaining livestock without the fodder needed to see them through the last and hungriest part of winter. All this they did while thinking that at any time the cavalry might return. In some parts of the Valley, people returned to hunting for a while, with the escaped cattle, sheep and pigs and hens as their prey.

The pattern of destruction was uneven, with the zones of devastation charting the routes of the invaders. There were places, like Scriven, Ripley, Nidd and the manor of Knaresborough, where their work was incomplete. Here, there may have been enough barley left to keep a family alive and to sow a few acres of ground, and sufficient plough beasts remaining to haul the plough. All along the Valley, the struggle for survival began. It seems a strange trait of humans that men may freely gamble their lives on the battlefield as though life was but a bauble of little value and yet people will struggle to survive in the face of horrors and adversities so severe as to put, or so one might expect, survival beyond the reach and will of human endurance. In the upper Valley, the patterns of human occupation were erased, but lower, where the current slowed and the river wound, enough remained to be built upon. The acre sown yielded the seed to sow three more; the shelter of branches became a shack, the shack a hut, and the hut a home. Flood meadows were mown for the first time in years. Thorn and oak seedlings were dug from the pasture. Babies were born and the milk cow moved back under the thatch.

Then they returned, but with their swords held flat. This time there was little burning or screaming, just a rounding up and a marching off of families. The harrying had been too thorough, so now there were profitable manors in the Vale and its margins that produced far less than before because of the labour shortage. To the lords and their officials, it seemed foolish to have families of bondsmen struggling to re-colonise the wet, stony, peaty and wooded lands of the upper valleys while the richer lowlands were neglected. From Dacre, Bewerley and hamlets and farmsteads further up, survivors were set on the road leading downstream and out of the Valley. Perhaps these upland people had the broadest of Anglo-Scandinavian accents and maybe they were mocked on their new manors, like the Gaellic-speaking 'teuchters' from the Highlands were scorned in the Lowlands of Scotland. Without being offered a choice, Nidderdale's uplanders became lowlanders and the upper reaches of the Valley once again became silent. Foxes looked in vain for chickens but found fleet moor fowl instead.

After the Norman Harrying, areas of countryside in Upper Nidderdale, like this view towards Gouthwaite, will have been almost entirely stripped of their populations.

So now there was the peaceful time that all the Valley people had craved. Sadly, most of them were no longer there to enjoy it.

Travelling across its landscape, we would see many changes in the countryside mosaic. The best land, slightly corrugated by old plough ridges, had now largely fallen out of cultivation, so that where barley, rye, oats and wheat had grown, there were now docks, dandelions, brambles and the seedlings of trees. The wood pasture that covered so many slopes displayed fewer changes, though the neglect of pollarding was beginning to result in trees of a top-heavy stature. The same was true of hedgerow trees, while the hedge shrubs were more than ready for laying and deer had opened some gaps in the networks. Rank, un-mown grass plastered the flood meadows and the seedlings of alder were gaining a hold there. In the woods, the neglect was less evident and coppice woods were far fewer than they would become by the close of the Middle Ages. Those that existed displayed thickets of branches that had grown too thick for wattle or faggots.

Further up the Valley the pastures seemed much as before from a distance, but when approached, it was clear that the deer and feral sheep were not maintaining the pressure of grazing needed to halt the spread of thorn scrub. Clumps of nettles, their roots sunk into the rich layer of domestic detritus, marked the spots where some houses had stood. Often, there were decayed hurdles with frayed wattle tracing the old stock pens and paddocks. Now they were slanting or else lay toppled on the ground. Grass, brambles and a myriad of colonists from the roadsides had camouflaged the old trackways. The upper Valley was now patterned in tones of green and to see the brown of ploughsoil or the gold of ripe grain one needed to go downstream, around Ripley, Nidd and Killinghall.

The commissioners charged with compiling an inventory of the kingdom's taxable assets were not long in Nidderdale – there was little there now to detain them. Ordinary people, who were in awe of the way that estates and their contents were, it seemed, being recorded for all time, called it 'Domesday Book'. Tersely and with innumerable frustrating gaps and ambiguities, it catalogued manorial resources and dues owed to the king. It is plain that in the Valley, the fifteen years of healing time were far from sufficient and the wounds from the Harrying still gaped. Nidderdale was still essentially a wasteland, even allowing for the fact that there was not a clear discrimination in Domesday terminology between commons and land that was ravaged and torched. There were pockets of productive activity, as around Whipley, a hamlet doomed for much later extinction, and there were places around the mouth of the valley, like Plumpton, that still prospered. It was only as one approached the north-eastern flanks, where the Valley broadened and the topographical pendulum shifted from upland to lowland, that the return to normality became marked, with ploughed fields covering sizable areas around Ripley and Nidd. Mainly, though, the Valley of Domesday Book was a place unnaturally empty of people, their noise and bustle; it was a place were wildlife multiplied and the wolves became ever bolder.

As we have seen, the less accessible parts of the Valley had reverted to an Eden-like aspect. Woods expanded, trees grew up to maturity and then beyond. Throughout it all there was a great rustling, flapping, darting and swooping of wildlife. The abundance of herons, ducks and doves might have confused the falconer, while red deer on the fells, roe deer in the woods, the foxes and the otters tugged the hunting packs in all directions.

This Eden was built on human carnage, but this was of little concern to the hunting parties that hawked and galloped across a semi-wilderness unsullied by the cloying clag of ploughland or foolish flocks that fragmented, so diverting the hounds. The shortage of dead hedges, hurdles, dwellings and ditches meant that there were fewer obstacles underfoot, less to break the purity of the canter or the gallop. For the struggling tenants of the huntsmen, however, there was hard work with the mattock to hack the seedlings from the pasture, much slashing with the billhook for wattle to make new hurdles that might keep the boar away from the lambing ewes as well as more furtive work to scare the lord's deer into some other garden. The masters of the Valley were not slow to recognise the improved hunting opportunities that the slaughter had created. Above the areas of rehabilitation, the Valley became a Chase, a formal hunting territory, and any other activities took second place.

The great landowners found their domains and obligations set out in the great book. King Edward the Confessor had owned several estates in the Valley: Cayton, Killinghall, Whipley and Scotton and neighbouring estates at South Stainley, Timble and Brearton, and these passed to the Norman king. Gospatric, a noble English survivor with a large estate centred on Kirkby Malzeard, held lands at Bewerley and a swathe of territory in the valley from Dacre through Birstwith to Ripley. He had led a perilous life. Despite having been heavily implicated in one rebellion, Gospatric was appointed by William to the Earldom of Northumbria, though the Conqueror soon had second thoughts and tried to replace him with a trustworthy Norman, Robert de Cumin. This provoked the renewed Northumbrian insurgency led by Gospatric, the noble Waltheof and the English claimant Edgar Etheling. After the siege of York, William showed uncharacteristic clemency and restored Gospatric to his earldom.

Nobody in Norman England was so lucky to be alive. As he rode from Dacre to Birstwith through the partly desolate lands, he may have mused on this. Perhaps he also wondered how many of his kinsmen and dependants might have kept their lives had he simply acquiesced to Norman rule. When he did think thus, he surely realised that without revolts and acts of courage, tyranny would have intensified its hold on life until all its meaning was lost. The other important landowner was the Archbishop of York, whose lordship was centred on Ripon. He controlled estates in the rolling country to the north of the Valley, where the name of Bishop Thornton still preserves the link. Perhaps the thorns around the 'tun' or farmstead only grew after the Harrying, though the Bishop's holdings in the Valley recovered more quickly than most.

By 1132, those who had been born around the time of the Harrying were old people by the norms of their day. New generations had grown to adulthood. People left forever numbed and diminished by the memories of what they had seen were almost all dead now. Very slowly, a sort of order descended: the Valley was healing. As the communities stumbled towards recovery, rumours began to spread of wild monks who were living in a most un-monkish squalor in Skelldale, just to the north. It was said that they had broken away from the great abbey of

St Mary's in York. This gave rise to competing accounts. Locals of a more generous or gullible persuasion said they had heard that these monks were looking to lead lives of real sacrifice and devotion – that was why they had turned their backs on the comforts of St Mary's. Cynical voices argued that monks were always bragging about the dangers and privations they had endured. This made a good impression on the minds of the more credulous benefactors. Those who believed them thought that the Almighty must have intervened to save His chosen ones in their hours of need. 'You wait', they proclaimed, 'Soon you will be hearing tales of survival on crags and mountain slopes, with violent robbers all around'. (And so they would.) 'Give *us* a few acres in Skellsdale and we won't complain', they added. The outcasts, it was said later, had been adopted into the Cistercian order, whatever that might be. However, its focus on the abbey at Cîteaux in Burgundy linked them with the all-pervasive and Frenchified Norman influences in the minds of many Valley folk. Simple minds: simple, sensible answers.

Soon, the Cistercians became more than mere curiosities. As their abbey of Mary *ad fontes* or 'at the springs' (Fountains) began to rise beside the Skell, woods were plundered for tall straight oaks, quarries were opened and bondsmen were diverted from their farm work to help with operations. Hardly any in the Valley were of sufficient breeding, learning or piety to enter the community as monks,

Violent disagreements among the community of St Mary's York caused a splitting of some monks away from the Benedictine Abbey and the establishment of Fountains.

though there were many places available for lay brethren – the half-educated workers who did the physical work of the abbey.

Though now highly active *in* the Valley, the white monks were never *of* the Valley. People remarked that while the old Benedictines had been rather aloof – as one might expect people who were well-born and literate to be – at least once you got them going you could have a good chat. Corrupt and even debauched at times, they still knew all manner of interesting things, and they knew how to enjoy themselves too! These Cistercians would have nothing to do with you. Whether you were a fellow Christian or a pagan well-worshipper made no difference to them. They made you feel as though you were a fly in the buttermilk or a pig at the spring head. Didn't the Bible say that Christ preached to the masses? These people would have turned their backs on them. Apparently, the Cistercian God was to be found in desolate wildernesses, well away from all those folk that He had created in His own image. But if desolation was the goal, post-Harrying Yorkshire was the place; there were wildernesses enough to set it on Heaven's doorstep (as though its location was ever in doubt).

Born out of adversity (though nowhere near such severe adversity as their promoters claimed), the Cistercians had risen very swiftly to a position of immense power. The white monks had a distinctive image to purvey. It was based on austerity and on a withdrawal from the evils of the world to places '... remote from the comings and goings of the people' (the category of 'people' helpfully included bishops arriving on visitations). Many folk of influence became quite excited by this. Never had a quest for poverty produced such wealth! Their success had fed on the consciences of great landowners, whose undoubted religious convictions were affronted by the manners in which they had actually lived their own lives. By renouncing the avarice and materialism of the Benedictines, the Cistercians found themselves awash with gifts of desolate land. Endowments bought masses; each acre bequeathed improved the donor's prospects on Judgement Day. So long as there were land-rich people with uneasy consciences who believe this, the abbey's prospects could never falter.

As it grew and as its estates expanded, the abbey became a great force in the Valley. Even so, it did not participate in local affairs; rather, the abbots would marshal their influence to grab whatever assets they desired and then the monkish community would retreat back into isolation. There was a darker side, too. The people of Herleshow, living in the shelter of that great knoll and landmark that signals the approach to the abbey from the Valley, were among the first communities to suffer. They lived almost on the doorstep of the abbey; some of the villagers had helped the pioneers. Then, they were got rid off: evicted in a countryside where empty places in which to live were fast decreasing. Their crime was to be

Fountains Abbey, beside the River Skell.

ordinary. As such, the Cistercians saw them as a source of contamination, as people whose presence nearby would pollute the purity of devotion at the abbey. Was the Almighty repelled by the villagers of Herleshow? How strange that the Christian message could become so distorted that now the meek, no longer 'blessed', inherited not the earth, but the roads to trudge and their ditches to sleep in.

The Valley was trapped in the pincers of monastic success. Byland Abbey, another Cistercian house, gained a commanding presence in Upper Nidderdale, its patrons, the Mowbrays, being landowners there, having taken over Gospatric's lands in about 1110. These lands became the hunting territory of these lords of Kirkby Malzeard. Whether for want of cash, salvation or both, Roger de Mowbray sacrificed rights in his chase to both the Cistercian abbeys, and thereby rerouted the course of history for many of his tenants. Fountains had already secured an estate in Dacre and in the 1170s, Byland gained the rights to farm in Stonebeck Down from Roger de Mowbray, who then sold rights in what would be known as Fountains Earth to the other abbey for the cost of a journey to the Holy Land. He then attempted to retract, and a series of disputes, claims, adjustments and counter claims followed. When the dust began to settle on the map of property, de Mowbray had kept his hunting rights for a while but Fountains had gained Brimham, which would be shared by a monastic grange and a deer park. The abbey also controlled Dacre, Bewerley and the eastern side of Upper Nidderdale while Byland dominated its western side. The jaws of the pincers had closed on the head of the Valley, while much of the middle Valley was also controlled by the monasteries.

Generations of countryfolk had experienced countless changes of master. Usually it simply meant that someone new was collecting your rent and exploiting your labour. This was different. Soon the people of Cayton, a village lying on the slopes just across the beck from Ripley's high common, were experiencing the same fate as those of Herleshow and so eviction had come to the Valley itself. Nobody, now, could know whether an abbey would take over their township, and if one did, whether eviction would follow. Cayton departed village England and became a grange, worked by lay brethren for Fountains, nearby. According the Cistercian code, a grange should be at least a day's ride from the abbey, yet Cayton was scarcely a stroll; already the pious rules were bending. This fate may have threatened Hartwith and Winsley, lying right beside Brimham, but with good fortune the lay communities survived while the whole of the upper Valley was being divided into granges. In other places, the accumulation of monastic landholdings within a township was a constant source of concern, Ripley's lay people being fortunate that the balance never quite tipped against them. The abbots, who combined spiritual, political and financial power, exerted immense leverage in the Valley of which they owned so much. One wonders whether the two Ripley landlords were really pleased to surrender the ribbons of territory needed to run a monastic right of way from the abbey and its new grange at Cayton to Hampsthwaite bridge. Soon the Valley was criss-crossed by rights of way, some of them old trackways and some imposed. They were needed to tie the abbeys to their granges and the flocks to their pastures, and while some were gained by coercion, in time they became useful to lay people as they pursued their day-to-day affairs.

※※※※※※※※※※※※※※※

1145. Old Oda awoke and saw the faint blush of dawn through the tiny gaps in the tattered thatch above. Gradually, sensation returned. He sensed a louse twitching in the seam of the garment of unbleached wool that warmed him day and night. There went Wulfric's cockerel! As reliable a time-keeper as ever one might wish. Not to be out-done, three other

This long-forgotten monastic right of way linked Fountains' grange at Cayton to the river crossing at Hampsthwaite.

cockerels then joined in from different corners of the township. But where were the other sounds of daybreak?

Then he remembered: he was the only one left. Ten years earlier, the monks, the white ones, had got their hands on 200 acres (about 81ha) of land here. The monks had been gifted the land, but the villagers of Cayton were gifted the road, its ditches and hedge bottoms. A week ago the abbot's agent had ridden across to tell them all to get out. Some had moved down to live with relatives elsewhere in the Valley, others had gone to seek new lives in the estates of the Vale, while a few had been transferred to pad out the labour forces of the abbey's lay-tenanted estates.

Oda just stayed. He could not comprehend a world that did not stop at the skylines that he could see beyond the neighbouring Ripley common to the west and the farmlands of Newton and Nidd, to the east. Something in his bones told him that there was a great deal wrong – disconcerting, evil – about places that he had not seen. The places that he *had* seen were very few indeed. Some of his former neighbours had been to Knaresborough; most had been to Ripon, while a few claimed to have been to York. To Oda, York was a faint smudge on the horizon, nothing more. That was what it was, and that was what it should stay. If people left the village for other places, might they not stir up the soldiers, raiders and demons who also lived in those other places? Then they might come here. He was not going to shift.

He sat and watched the sunlight warming up the cleft that contained the Newton Beck. He looked down towards the ford used by travellers when they reached the threshold of the great abbey. Those white monks wanted to dam the beck up and have a fishpond there. If God had wanted it dammed He would have dammed it Himself. He had tried to argue about it with one of the lay brothers. All he got was, 'Who knows more about God's will, you or the abbot?' Even Oda knew better than to answer 'Me', though that is what he thought.

He felt the light tap of a staff on his shoulder: 'Come on uncle Oda, time to be going'. He looked round and saw Brihtric, that red-faced lad from Thornton, now in the garb of a lay brother, with two others at his side. He replied with the Anglo-Danish equivalent of, 'I kenned thi faither', surely the most damning phrase of all time. Brihtric took one elbow and his comrade the other and they lifted the old man up from his perch on the valley crest. When he twisted his head around, he saw that his home was now a pile of sticks and straw on the ground.

They put him on a donkey and led him away to the boundary of Clint township, pointed to the track that continued westwards and left him. This country was as utterly foreign as ever Devon or Norfolk could have been, so he turned around and walked back. Two hours later, he was sitting beside the wreckage of the house. The eviction was repeated several times, with similar results. One day Brihtric came back and found the village site empty. He thought that the old man had come to his senses when he saw a grubby, blood-stained garment under a thorn bush. The wolves must be bold this year. He wondered whether the cold had got the old man before the wolf. Then a silly thought came into his head, but he realised that any request for a mass for old Oda would meet with derision.

❄❄❄❄❄❄❄❄❄❄❄❄❄❄❄

While abbey lands were being transformed, elsewhere the healing continued. It was most apparent in the lower Valley lands, where the Harrying had been less severe. Villages were starting to gel again. Hampsthwaite was taking shape as a straggle of homesteads aligned along a stretch of the old Roman road where it led down to the ancient ford on the Nidd. Across the river, Owlcotes, later doomed, lay at an intersection of monastic roads on the pagan pilgrimage track that curved eastwards from the little bridge at Scarah. Killinghall, a string of farmsteads and a manor stitched along the edge of a common, overlooked the Nidd from its plateau. Cayton was gone, while hamlets that might have aspired to be villages, like Whipley and Rowden, would ultimately perish. No places of village proportions existed upstream of Hampsthwaite at this time.

The twelfth century proved to be a time of filling in, a time of making good the damage of 1169-70. Gradually, more and more details were added to the map as farmsteads proliferated; villages took shape; and the advancing tide of the woodland and scrubland was turned while routeways criss-crossed the map to join up all the new starting points and destinations. The century was more than just a time of recovery, for the division of ownership was expressed in completely different ways of occupying and exploiting the land: the farmstead and the grange; the hunting lodge and the homestead; the lay household and the grange's farm-force of lay brethren; semi-sufficiency and commercial monastic farming, the local and the estate-wide perspectives. All these represented different visions. The marks of these quite different ways of working land are still apparent, as are the contrasts between the utter devastation inflicted on the upper Valley and the partial destruction caused by the Harrying in many of its lower parts. Meanwhile, the time of destruction and desolation was yielding to one of the most explosive times of expansion and landscape creation that the Valley would ever know.

CHAPTER 7

THE SWELLING BUD

(*c*. 1100 − *c*. 1300)

There are great tides coursing through history. Ride these swells and mere events, like the wretched baronial wars during the nineteen years after 1135, become like reefs or wrecks: the waves of hope may break on them but the tides of destiny surge on. As the terror of the Harrying passed out of living memory, the Valley people felt the tightening grip of the feudal gauntlet as they saw their homelands divided and consumed by the different lordships. All spaces for laxity or levity were squeezed out, like the air in a cheese press, and lives in bondage became marshalled and constricted almost to the point of suffocation. And yet ... there was a tide of optimism and exuberance running that surged too strongly to be stifled by any lord, steward or reeve. This tide had its sources in land that basked under a friendly sun, in fertile silt that trickled through the fingers like gold dust, leaving scarcely a smear, in sheep that ambled free of foot rot and in woods that beckoned to those who might live in the spaces on the edge. This was a time for the Valley people to shape their rural mould and then swell to fill it until not a nook or cleft was left unused.

Long ago, Aldborough had been the command centre of the Valley world, some ancient ties still touched churches and manors, but now Knaresborough was assuming that role. It lay close to the zone where the Valley ended and the Vale began, though the Valley did not gently grade away. Instead, the 'banky' uplands had their final flourish in a gorge bounded by cliff-like bluffs that announced the imminence of the lowlands. For anyone with an interest in defence and domination, the attraction of the gorge was obvious, for it would defend one aspect of a castle and allow defenceworks to be concentrated on the other sides. This castle could also dominate such traffic as there might be on a portage-ridden and unruly river. Despite its grandeur, the gorge, cut by meltwater seeking an escape to the Vale, is really a merging of upland and lowland geological characters. It was engraved so deeply into the Magnesian Limestone belt that forms an eastern hemline to the Dales that the meltwater torrents of the reborn river cut down into the Millstone Grit, symbolic of the upland valleys, which lay deeply buried below. The castle was the stopper in the narrow neck of the Valley bottle and it regulated every life and deed.

Scarcely more than half a century after the Harrying, the new stronghold established a royal presence on the northern side of the gorge, and in 1173 the Honour of Knaresborough came to be held by the de Stutevilles. A new borough or townlet had recently been established on the castle's doorstep and the locality was set to flourish. William de Stuteville was a rising man, far more than a mere custodian or constable of the castle. His tenure of the Honour obliged him, when required, to supply three fully armed knights for service with the king. Thereafter, the line between royal and baronial control became somewhat blurred. In 1205, John (one of a pack of cubs who seem to have inherited only the very worst characteristics of their remarkable parents, Henry II and Eleanor of Aquitaine) appears to have dispossessed Nicholas de Stuteville. He used the ploy of demanding an impossibly high figure for the 'relief' required to allow Nicholas to assume his inheritance. Ten years later, the council leading the baronial resistance to the king demanded that John's constable return the castle to the ownership of the de Stutevilles. Brian de l'Isle refused, garrisoned the castle, and Knaresborough remained, precariously, in royal ownership through the Baron's War.

Thereafter, if not before, the kings realised the great strategic significance of their castle. So far as foreign wars were concerned, it was largely irrelevant and any northern invaders could pass by it at will. Its importance lay in its assertion of a royal presence in a territory of troublemakers who were often ill-disposed to the Plantagenet monarchy. In so doing it became one of the most important royal castles in the kingdom. In the years preceding the war, large sums were spent on a great rock-cut ditch to protect the exposed, landward side of the citadel. It was probably the garrison's demand for weaponry that gave birth to a local armaments industry producing arrowheads, quarrels and spurs. Iron was scrabbled from the ground; hilltop furnaces sucked air from the winds and forge hammers pounded in leafy backwaters. Work on the castle continued with only the briefest respites for the next century as it assumed the form of a monumental stone keep with walls 10ft thick overlooking the curtain walls and turrets of inner and outer wards. Then, as now, the wheels of war and the wheels of commerce were engaged together. The industries of fortification and administration energised and vitalised the borough that spread in the citadel's glare. And then there was the hunting …

In the Norman era, Knaresborough emerged as a royal castle town and hunting base for the adjacent Forest and deer parks.

❉❉❉❉❉❉❉❉❉❉❉❉❉❉❉❉

The girl from the high end of Hampsthwaite was out in the field, milking. The side of her head was pressed into the warm flanks of the little red cow and she did not hear the approach of the hunt until the clattering hooves were almost upon her. Before she sensed that horsemen had burst out of the hollins behind, the coarse, raw-boned greyhounds had passed. Wild and demented, a straggler snatched at the calf. Twisting free from the jaws, it dashed, bawling blindly, into the path of the horses and was run down. In this instant the girl saw her family's year end in catastrophe, but she stayed cringing behind the cow until the riders and their entourage were well on course for Swincliffe. One of the hunt servants stole the body of the calf. As the huntsmen went by, she noticed that the local nobles were reining back, allowing a stout rider with a narrow circlet of dark hair like a tonsured monk to hold the lead. Even the fleeting glimpse revealed his bulbous lips and posturing manner. She had met her king. John had not met her, and that was just as well.

❉❉❉❉❉❉❉❉❉❉❉❉❉❉❉❉

Once, the kings had never even heard of the Valley, now they were becoming familiar with the bends in the river, the fords and the overlooking woods. John was particularly keen on visiting his castle and what, like wine or salted herrings, it could not supply he would have carted in. Wherever he went, he seemed like the bait for snaking, lurching convoys of wains and wagons, all engaged in an unending quest to keep pace with his appetites. He kept a large pack of dogs and a couple of handlers at Knaresborough castle to await his visits. He needed to show that his rule ran as firmly up here as it did down south – and where in the south could one find such a profusion of game and such invigorating hunting terrain?

The great emptying of the countryside had rent holes in the pattern of human occupation and the deer, boar, birds and small game had multiplied and filled them. It was inevitable that these resources would not go unnoticed, allowing the Valley people to recover steadily, in peace. The Harrying would determine the outlines of the countryside for centuries to come and in its aftermath, a new kind of blood-stench hung in the hollows as hunting, no longer a mere pastime, became a main determinant of the character of the Dales. The long-standing aristocratic hunting tradition, the pockets of semi-wilderness and the presence of the royal castle made the creation of the Forest inevitable.

Kings, on the whole, soon became tired of kingly works and longed to rush out to play. And being kings, this is usually what they did. Around the middle of the twelfth century the Forest of Knaresborough came into being, not as a continuous expanse of woodland as most today imagine, but as a mosaic of moorland, common, woods, pastures, meadows and peasant tillage, with a complement of youthful villages and hamlets. All these facets of the countryside were united under the imposition of new controls – the Forest Law – which conserved deer, though at the expense of ordinary people and their working dogs. The Forest stretched from Knaresborough up the southern side of the Valley for around a dozen miles and it spilled over into the Washburn valley. Curiously, it looped across the river to include the township of Clint – maybe Clint's proximity to the royal manor at Hampsthwaite and to Birstwith, where the Crown controlled Gospatric's old estate, were the reasons?

Nidderdale was now firmly a hunting territory in legal status as well as in function, and while the Forest spanned much of the lower Valley, the Mowbrays, hunting out from Kirkby Malzeard, ranged across their Chase covering most of the upper dale. When the king and the Mowbrays were out hunting on the same day they could have heard each other's horns. Before the Middle Ages had ended, the horns of the Abbot of Fountain hunting at Brimham or in his home park, of the Ingilbys coursing deer at Ripley, the Vasavours in Dob Park and the king's huntsmen in the parks of Bilton, Haverah and Haya, would all join the gory chorus as deer were trumpeted to their doom. On hunting days, the Valley must have seemed like one great killing ground. After the eras of the Harrying the Forest, the Chase and the parks, one might expect that each barrow load of its soil would be stained red.

Hunting across the thickets, alder swamp and plough ridges of the Forest offered the thrills of rough riding. Riding down the crops and livestock of ordinary people provided that frisson of cruelty born of superiority that has thrilled the privileged classes right through to the present day. But there were days when time and energy were in shorter supply or days when one wanted to display one's martial skills to less energetic admirers. Thus, alongside the Forest and chases there were much smaller and more tightly confined deer parks, carefully contrived places where walls and pales trapped the deer inside. In these, the creatures had no chance. It was like shooting fish in a bucket.

In the making of deer parks, the Valley people were scarcely more able to resist than the captive deer. In his creation of Haverah park before the eviction of his dynasty from the castle, William de Stuteville took over a common that was an essential component in the subsistence economy of the Killinghall households. About three-quarters of a century later, the additional Forest deer parks of Bilton and Haya were created. Henry III gave his brother, the Earl of Cornwall, who was also Lord of Knaresborough, gifts of deer from his estates in Pontefract and the Forest of Galtres to stock his parks. Presumably, they had to be de-stocked of people first. And since they lay in good farming country close to the new borough, a good few people must have been uprooted.

Quite recently, I made an in-depth study of deer parks in the Yorkshire Dales. As my maps filled with a dense stipple of plots it became clear that the relative emptiness of the region – due partly to the wild and rugged character of terrain in the west and the effects of the Harrying in the east – must have made this the most important hunting territory in the entire kingdom. There were some more surprising aspects, for the parks were not filling voids or wilderness areas that had been passed-over by the cultivators. Instead, for reasons of convenience, they were set close to the castles and manor houses of their owners. Sometimes, the coursing was watched by groups on the battlements or in lofty apartments. The power-centres stood on the better rather than the poorer ground and a marked preference for limestone country emerged. Perhaps the well-drained ground, sweeter soils and more open aspects were attractions. Being founded on grits, sandstones, shales and glacial deposits rather than on limestone, our Valley could not offer the fast gallops across short, springy turf that would much later appeal so strongly to racehorse trainers of Wensleydale. It could, however, provide immensely varied hunting terrain as roe deer or foxes were hounded through the woods and hollins of the Valley flanks, while there were red deer to course when the hunt erupted into the upland commons. There were otters skulking under roots and banks in the river, and abundant targets waited for the falcon, goshawk, kestrel or merlin, from the heron to the dove or quail.

Although the deer parks must have been established with hunting mostly in mind, following the eviction of local populations a range of other opportunities emerged. Many parks had resources of pannage, with swine being admitted to eat up the acorn harvest after the fawns had grown nimble enough to escape their jaws. More profitable was agistment or the renting out of parkland grazings to cattle or horses at a specified rent. The parks clustered around Knaresborough castle were particularly productive of such rents. Specialised cattle farms or 'vaccaries' were established in many parks during the thirteenth century, while Haverah came to be noted for the breeding of horses. The parks were also useful as places where the animals of visiting entourages could be pastured close to the castle or manor house.

Seen from within, these parks must have had some Eden-like qualities. Most contained wood pastures and the old pollards were regularly lopped to produce leafy browse for the deer and cattle. Recently pollarded examples will have looked like the trees in the painting books of children, with thick trunks sprouting pole-like branches topped, lollipop fashion, by billows of fresh foliage. Some trees would be 'shredded' or stripped of their side branches for browse, until they stood bare like slender quill pens with just a plume of leaves at their tops. The surviving deer in these parks must have been terrorised by their experiences of being coursed across the lawns by hounds and will have stepped gingerly among the shadows. The horses and cattle, in contrast, may have been emboldened by the reduction in human contact. The renters of parkland grazings may sometimes have been alarmed to be kicked or charged when checking on their beasts. Cattle seem happier in the dappled shade of thickets than in open fields; when Haya was disparked in the seventeenth century cattle were furnished with bells so that they could be found in the thickets, so dense was the woodland cover.

For the Valley people, however, the Forest added a new stratum of feudal impositions above those that ordinary folk everywhere had to bear. Forest Law was not as draconian as the popular Robin Hood myths relate. To the extent that any poachers had been executed or mutilated in previous times, a charter of restitution issued in 1257, mollified the law and prescribed a heavy fine for poachers who could pay, and imprisonment for a year and a day for those who could not – this to be followed by exile for parties who could not find sureties. Poachers were by no means just the starving peasants of the popular stereotypes: gay young blades, important office-bearers, trusted servants and privileged people indulging desires for devilment were just as often to blame. Also, the servants of the hunt were often its worst offenders.

The medieval countryside in the Valley was made up of jigsaws of peasant farmland, hunting territories and monastic farming. In many places, as in this panorama near Darley, something of the diverse character survives.

For the people of the Valley, Forest status carried a variety of inconveniences and impositions. They were prevented from disturbing game, even if the deer or boar were damaging their crops, though, doubtless, this restriction would only have taken effect when people thought that someone of influence might be looking. They were also supposed to have their dogs 'lawed' or partly crippled by the removal of a toe to prevent them from coursing deer. In a district where shepherding was well established, this would have been a distinct impediment. Also, of course, they were forbidden to hunt, although such strictures applied everywhere (though not always with such intimidating powers of enforcement).

Then there were the Foresters who, having been given positions of considerable authority over their neighbours, often proceeded to abuse it by bullying. Sometimes this was done with the aim of extorting money that the Foresters then invested in drinking sessions. They formed cohorts of louts at venues like fairs and markets, where they provoked trouble with people dwelling outside the Forest. Finally, some communities were burdened with special feudal duties associated with the hunt, being obliged to board hounds, provide beaters, erect temporary buildings or maintain fences. At the same time, the hunting industry created employment for a significant force of Foresters, parkers, dog-handlers and the like, and life on a royal manor inside the Forest had less uncertainty than did the lives of feudal tenants on nearby abbey estates, where eviction might be just a step away.

✱✱✱✱✱✱✱✱✱✱✱✱✱✱✱✱✱

Robert huddled furtively among the stems of a hazel at the edge of the wood. The cold gnawed at a back tortured by thirty years of outdoor work. It had all begun with the loss of the calf. A poor second hay crop had followed, so that the village men had shinned, prickled and bleeding, up every holly tree in their hollins to cut as much as they could of the thorn-free foliage from the tops. When the last of the dried holly fodder was carried out of the little barn or 'helm', the cull of livestock would have to begin. But maybe the folk across the river would trade some hay or holly for a couple of haunches of venison, and might that save the little red milk cow? If the cow was saved, its milk could make all the difference and the children might also survive. If the children survived there might be someone to care for him when his back finally locked solid.

That is why Robert was there, waiting for the deer to slip, ghostlike, from the wood to graze in the fringing pastures. A rustle, a low, moving shape. Not a little squirrel; not a polecat; and not a wildcat – what was it? It did not walk but hopped, its ears were ridiculously long and its tail was no more than a teazel-shaped whisp of white fluff. Robert slowly released his bow and took a grip on his cudgel … one more lolloping step. A fox sidled up, took the rabbit by the neck and vanished into the wood. The rabbit had not even moved. The Normans had set up warrens for these imported lumps of luxury fare on their new estates, but centuries would pass before rabbits were sufficiently well adjusted to survive in the wild in the Valley. Their journey from titbit to vermin spanned a good six centuries.

Robert returned to his agonising vigil. There was some movement in the wood, but something much heavier than the leaf-brushing hoof-point patter of deer. Shadows, scarcely lowered voices, unrestrained chuckling. Could it be the Foresters? If so their dogs would surely smell him out and he was as good as in the Forest court. Then he recognised the voices: his own priest, one Forester, the two youngest sons of that fancy lord from Follifoot way and someone with an in-between accent who sounded like a squire. The Forester was leading a nag, and a roe deer was slung across its back with blood from its open stomach cavity streaking the horse's side. The smell of the blood saved Robert from the padding bloodhound, now gorged on entrails and quite sated. With this stench lingering under the trees, the deer would not emerge. Robert quietly retired.

They ate the cow. The protein boost kept the children alive through the winter, but the great time of dying was in the early spring when winter-weakened bodies faced the latest epidemic. That was when they died. Robert's spine locked shortly after, during the spring ploughing. Then his wife took the plough shafts, but wrestled the lurching oxen with little success and the couple lasted just two more years.

❄❄❄❄❄❄❄❄❄❄❄❄❄❄❄❄❄

One Valley; three worlds. Sometimes the worlds nudged and jostled, but mainly they stayed apart. One world was that of the grange, the worlds of Brimham, Dacre or Warsill where lay-brethren dug ditches, clipped the soiled wool from the back ends of sheep and walled-off lands stolen from the commons. All this was done in the watchful presence of monks whose status elevated them above hand toil, as practised by labourers or artisans, like their Saviour's earthly father. The second world was that of the nobles, also debarred from toil by status and inclination. To them, the Valley people were incidental appendages to the pursuit of recreation and the competition for status. The third world was that of people rooted to the soil by ancestry, station, occupation and law. It was the law that bound them to their manors even had they wished to leave.

During most months and at many times, these different worlds bumped and glanced off each other without the one exerting very much influence on the others. Living in a world of greens, greys, blues and browns, the Valley people would only have seen red at a pig killing or when a sickle slipped, but on hunting days sweat-stained minions leaning on their scythes could look up and see a cavalcade of crimson, scarlet magenta and purple jogging by.

The less energetic the hunting, the fewer the leather jerkins and the brighter the colours. Then, there were the ladies who washed their hair, wore daring necklines and had kestrels balancing on their wrists, hooded birds that stumbled with spreading wings at every little plunge of the palfrey. There were men on mad-eyed stallions, richly dressed, fleshy faced men who side-scanned one another with envy and barged flank-on-flank for places beside the leader. Each longed to be the one to save him from a goring by a cornered stag or to jerk him from the path of an assassin's bolt. At the same time, they tried to gauge his courage, wits and resolve and to judge how successful any attempts at poisoning, rebellion and regicide might be. The king, meanwhile, had learned as a youth how to act the jovial, bountiful huntsman while assessing the intelligence and nerve of his barons. Their trustworthiness was never assumed. Now, in the absence of a rebellion, the hunt became a venue for lobbying and favour-seeking, so that the king had to find the right level of largesse to dispense: to one side lay affront and to the other, weakness. The degrees to which one or the other could be served to each member of the party had to be gauged as though the throne itself was at stake. Sometimes, it was.

While the nobles intrigued and the hunting horns brayed across the Valley, the ordinary people did as they always did when nobody was waging war across their homeland: they increased. Amongst these people there was a consensus that extended far beyond the Valley. The moist, floodable land fringing the river and becks was designated as meadow. This was the ground that produced the hay which, one hoped, would keep the beasts alive through winter. With luck, a second, albeit sparser, hay crop might be taken at summer's end, a few weeks after the main hay-making at the end of June, though, really, there was seldom sufficient hay to go round. Livestock grazed the meadows after they were cut and sometimes they were folded there so that their dung could maintain the fertility. Dung: that was something else permanently in short supply.

The meadows were divided up between the households in each township, so that each feudal tenancy had several strips, 'dales' or 'doles' scattered around the meadow, rather like the plough strips in the arable field. In the absence of hedges or fence posts, largish mere stones marked the boundaries of each dole. It was sometimes said that half the disputes in the community concerned the alleged moving of stones this way or that. The open expanses of meadow attached to Hampsthwaite, and Clint, Ripley and Killinghall made a splendid sight in the early summer as the grasses out-grew the dandelion carpet. The flatlands flanking the river would go shimmering and swirling as the breeze made the tall grasses twitch and lean. The course of a swirling gust could be traced for up to a mile across the un-partitioned meadow grasses. The beaver were gone from the riverside now; hunting had made the otters yet more secretive, but the booming of the corncrakes nesting beneath the stems in the meadow was still a wonder to hear.

The great rural consensus also maintained that the best ground, with a gentle climate and well-drained soil, should be reserved for grain and legumes. They produced more energy per acre than any other use. Oats were good for fodder and gruel; barley yielded malt for making ale in places where water supplies were often undrinkable; and both could be used in starchy mush for nourishing soups and stews. Rye was good for bread and could be mixed with wheat to form maslin, while wheat, which was rather more choosy in its settings, made the best quality bread. The peas and beans were good for people and they were also good tonic for ground whose fertility was ever under stress. The further up the Valley one went, the more the balance tipped away from cultivation towards stock-rearing, but most townships had some stock land. All communities needed oxen to pull the plough, eight of them to a team on the heaviest ground. The oxen were preferred to horses, for while you could not put a collar on an ox without it soon choking, at the end of its day at least you could eat it. You did not eat horses because people did not eat horses – and what better reason could there be than that? You did eat ewes, but not before they had ceased to yield much milk for cheese. Countless centuries of experience in cheese-making in the Valley never amounted to much more than basic production, even though, for centuries, tenants of the monastery paid part of their rents in prodigious amounts of cheese. Whatever it was that Wensleydale and Swaledale had remained their secrets.

Lower down the Valley, where there was more good land, the village households tenanted strips that were scattered near and far across the great fields. How bleak and black they must have seemed in winter, with only the faint glimmer of light reflecting from the soil swells in the corduroy landscape of ridge and furrow to dispel the gloom! In these fields, the strips were packaged together in 'cultures' or 'flatts', and perhaps each flat had its own rotation. This would have created a summer landscape of blocks of different hue and texture: the wheat, then of kinds growing as tall as the reapers, the whiskery barley and rye and the droplet-grained oats giving contrasting notes of cream and gold, and the peas staying green for longer than the yellowing corn. In among all these there were, in that herbicide-free age, sparkling galaxies of wild flowers or weeds of cultivation – poppies, corn cockle, marigolds, cornflowers, feverfew – all nodding brightly among the grain. Later, when the crops were reaped, the beasts of the township were set loose to graze the weeds and grass seedlings of the 'aftermath' and so, to fertilise the ground. Only the villages had open field systems of anything like the textbook type. Hamlets and places up the dale might have small strip fields, shared between a handful of neighbours on their best land.

Permanent pastures gave the Valley its brightest and most enduring greenness. Mostly, they formed a broad zone on the sloping flanks between the ploughland and the higher commons. At first, there were few hedged enclosures and their expansion marked an advance of the private countryside against the common one. Freemen in farmsteads with a few hedged fields grouped around them were embedded in a landscape of common pastures, ploughland and hay meadows; who might guess that one day their compartmentalised countryside would be the norm?

The emerald of the sloping pastures was fragmented by darker tracts of wooded countryside. Here, oak, ash, elm and just a little lime and hornbeam tinted the bobbled canopy. An intermediate stage between the woods and the pasture was provided by extensive though already contracting areas of wood pasture, where cattle grazed contentedly in the dappled shade and rubbed their bites and sores against the rough bark of the oak pollards. On these wooded commons, the deer felt more secure, the pouncing owls found perches and the frequent drumming of woodpeckers added staccato notes among the birdsong. Wood pasture was a very special place, but its time was running out.

The bells of churches (single bells tolling and not fancy changes) provided a counterpoint to the blaring of the hunting horns. In the lower country, where the ox teams hauled and panted under their yokes, there was now the wherewithal to sustain churches. A little wealth was being squeezed from the countryside and the church was not slow to seize a share. Further up the Valley, Godlessness remained more easily justified. A remarkable feature of the early churches in the Valley – Hampsthwaite, Ripley and Nidd – is that, rather than reflecting the new orientation towards Knaresborough, with its flourishing church, town and castle, they were strung like beads along the old Roman road that crossed the Valley. They fossilised the links and orientations of earlier times. The Old Road was still a significant corridor; the ancient links to Aldborough were not yet dead for Hampsthwaite began as a chapel of the mother church at 'Burgh'. The Minster at the ancient capital, operating in its vast parish, must have provided the first Christian worship in Hampsthwaite and the Valley. Now the old territory had fragmented and soon the Roman connection with Alborough would be forgotten.

With an unusual dedication to the archbishop martyred by the knights of Henry II, the Church of St Thomas a Beckett in Hampsthwaite was under the patronage of the Stutevilles, but later became a possession of Richard, Earl of Cornwall. About 1257, he gave the right to appoint a priest to the Trinitarian Friars of Knaresborough, along with pasturage for twenty cows and their calves in Hampsthwaite for three years. The friary was an odd institution. The Trinitarians, founded in 1197 to collect funds to ransom hostages from the Saracens, took income from land and tithes (though other friars had renounced property), did not own their friaries and depended on begging. The Trinitarians seem to have been attracted to the locality occupied by the hermit, St Robert of Knaresborough, who died in 1218. His renown was fast expanding as he became associated with rumours of miracles. His tomb, from which medicinal oils were said to issue, had begun to attract pilgrims The strength and depth of religious convictions in Hampsthwaite at this time are uncertain, and the care that the Aldborough priests could have provided in earlier times must have been minimal. Yet there is no doubting the fact that, while the friars could provide a much better level of spiritual care, a cell of land and people now had to produce more in order to sup-

The medieval church at Hampsthwaite, which underwent a rather heavy restoration in the 1820s.

port a priest, and more again to satisfy the claims of his church. For people living at subsistence level, these were heavy impositions.

The brethren in Knaresborough supplied Hampsthwaite with a priest and they received the church's robes, the endowment of land provided to support the priest, the priest house and the tithes. In 1292, a value of £5 was placed on this vicarage, while at the close of the Middle Ages it was valued at £13 6*s* 8*d*. The most lucrative item in the 1536 valuation (when the friary was still providing a vicar) was the tithe on lambs and their wool. Then there were the payments given at Lent and oblations due on the day of the patron saint: at Christmas, on Easter Day, and at weddings and funerals. Also, there were the tithes on calves, fowls and eggs, and finally, the tithe on hay.

These extractions of cash and kind from a largely impoverished congregation continued across the successive centuries and the dues demanded were itemised in ever more detail. So, in 1743 we read:

> Item.– For every lamb under the number six, there is due to the vicar one penny; at six, half a lamb; at seven, a whole lamb, without deduction. The same in tith-ing wool- only for every fleece under the number six there is due to the owner

one halfpenny for every odd one. For a tithe calf there is due to the vicar three
shillings and four pence; for every foal, two pence. Twopence for every foal com-
municant at the age of sixteen ...

And so it continued, not overlooking the charge of twopence on every plough and a
penny for a swarm of bees. From anyone dying under the burden of tithes, and from
everything else, the vicar took a 'mortuary' of their second best chattel, often a cow.

✳✳✳✳✳✳✳✳✳✳✳✳✳✳✳✳✳

Still, it is unlikely that Master John had the injustices of the tithes on
his mind as he set out from the friary in Knaresborough to become the
priest at Hampsthwaite in 1280. He would miss the companionship of the
brethren; worship in the priory church built in the very cave where St
Robert was entombed; and the thrill of living somewhere rather special
when the king and his relatives were installed, nearby. Still, Hampsthwaite
was a benefice of real value and they had sent one of their best men.
However, he was not a rector like the priest at Ripley, who received all
the tithes and perks, but a vicar, who would stand watching as the best
part of the benefice went off to his friary.

He travelled on the north side of the river, past Knaresborough's
Bondgate, the quarters of the bondsmen, through Scotton, and then he
joined the Roman route at Ripley. Heads turned as country people saw
his striking white habit with its cross formed of a vertical blue bar cut
across by a horizontal one of red. As the Old Road started to dip down
into the Valley, he caught his first glimpse of his church, a stone building
in the Gothic style standing by the riverside and the ancient ford. On the
old floodplain to its east lay the meadows that would be so productive of
hay tithes, while the fields around promised corn tithes, mortuaries and
so much more. The village straggling beyond the church could be relied
upon to furnish a stream of weddings and funerals and, with the priest
now established in the heart of the community, it would be hard to evade
the church's dues. With the chilling waters surging around his shins John
did not care for the ford, but everything else he liked.

✳✳✳✳✳✳✳✳✳✳✳✳✳✳✳✳✳

As he made his way to Hampsthwaite on the Roman road, Master John had
come quite close to the church at Ripley, close enough to suffer the sickly smell

emanating from its churchyard and, so, to make the sign of the cross. The customary stench and the triangular burial ground with its mounds of earth were the only indications of the place of worship. The church was out of sight below, on a narrow river bluff terrace overlooking a sweeping meander of the Nidd. Other than the riverbed itself, this was practically the most uninviting site for a large building in the entire parish. The reasons for it being there, we have seen already: the flanking springs, presumed holy but soon contaminated in their passage through the graveyard, which issued from the sands and silts of the bluff. I have mentioned that this place is a very strong candidate for the site of the synod of Nidd, though quite how long a church stood here we do not know. One Bernard, who was the priest here, is recorded in the years around 1200, but Ripley Church was probably long established by then. The discovery of a metal fragment thought to have come from the binding of a bible of the eighth century might take the span of Christian worship back much closer to pagan times.

(At the close of the twentieth century I mapped the alignment of stones that is all that remains of the last surviving wall of the church. I have been inside various remote prehistoric tombs, alone, without sensing any discomfort. This is the only place where I have ever felt ill-at-ease and watched by invisible eyes. I found

At first, priests approaching their new parish from the friary in Knaresborough will have forded the river just where the Romans had done, though successive flimsy timber bridges were built before the stone bridge appeared after the end of the Middle Ages.

the stump of what seemed to have been a ramp of earth and stones that once led upwards to link the church to its churchyard on the plain, high above. Now the bones of medieval people slowly erode out of their graves there. I think the bluff was stabilised long ago by an artificial revetment of river cobbles, but now this has collapsed and larches stand poised with their roots exposed, ready to topple.)

The first church that Master John had glimpsed after leaving Knaresborough was at Nidd, where the modest and unadorned church was a notable landmark at the side of the Roman road. However, it does not seem to have enjoyed powerful connections and its tithes will have made it a tempting target for the flourishing churches in Ripon and Knaresboropugh. In 1242, it was indeed appropriated by the collegiate church of Ripon. An essentially medieval building survived here into the nineteenth century, though a renovation, described in chapter 12, deprived us of what must have been a significant and evocative building.

Things had changed considerably. Once, the scriptures were served up by foot-sore monks from distant Minsters who might have negotiated flooded becks and mud-swamped roads in order to reach the established preaching places. Often, they stood at a 'mote' or meeting place in the driving rain, talking patiently to groups whose comprehension levels on scriptural matters were minimal. Yet now, the church was acquiring a massive stake in the countryside and its human resources. If it was to extract foodstuffs and income from mainly destitute com-munities it had to offer much and exert a powerful psychological presence. In the period after the Harrying, doctrines of Heaven and Hell were carefully refined. Congregants were left in no doubt that their present conduct, not least their religious conduct, would determine their fates in Eternity. The God they encoun-tered was vengeful and unbending; his reign was one of terror rather than love, and life was a path that led, remorselessly, to death and the Day of Judgement. The common masses seem to have been regarded by their (largely better-bred) priests and mentors as being so dangerous and corrupt that they had, permanently, to be terrorised by the threat of divine retribution.

Heaven awaited the very good and Hell, the bad. But there was also Purgatory, a sort of halfway house, where the soul would experience burning and less easily imagined torments until the tarnished spirit was sufficiently cleansed to win access to Heaven. There was, too, some support for the notion that the souls of the good passed some time lodged in the bosom of Abraham, a sort of spiritual com-fort stop on the road to Heaven. To be good, life had to be conducted according to the procedures and processes of the church, and these involved penance, prayer and masses. It helped considerably to be both pious and wealthy, for then masses and prayers for the soul could be bought and the tedium of Purgatory might be short-circuited. Less pious? That could cost more. Wealth, too, could buy a better resting place, and it was best to be buried inside a church rather than outside in the yard – the closer to its holiest parts and any relics, the better. Death did not release one from the injustices of the class system, for it existed in some form in Heaven. Adam and Eve, the first sinners and presumably Hell's first occupants, were emblems for common people in the iconography of the Middle Ages.

To make sure the message went home, the church walls became colourful hoardings that displayed the awesomeness of the Last Judgement, while cavorting cadavers writhed to the horrors of Purgatory. A certain weighing of good and evil in the life of the departed was often thought to occur, St Michael often being the one who had charge of the scales. Within the parishes, the intellectual levels of spiritual discourse must have been low. The reasons for thinking this are fairly obvious. Firstly, worship in church was conducted in Latin (of which country people had no understanding) and consisted of impressive ceremonial, liturgy and masses rather than sermons. Its impact was sensual rather than cerebral. Secondly, the rectors and vicars came very largely from the privileged classes; many were the younger sons of lords and quite a few were, themselves, knights, and so they were not accustomed, or often inclined, to any engagement in dialogue and debate with ordinary folk. Next, the dialect of the Dalesfolk and other country people of the High Middle Ages was rich in terms connected with agriculture and nature, but not in the vocabulary for abstract thought. People tended to look for allegories with the familiar, natural world in forming their ideas. Images in sculpture and wall-painting conveyed simple warnings. Finally, the persistence of pagan beliefs is often exaggerated but superstition was a very important part of daily life and thinking. Given the ever-presence of death and disaster, this is hardly surprising. In general, the church seems to have co-existed with the leftovers of paganism with surprising ease. Witch-burning belonged to a later age.

In the minds of the people who stumbled, often reluctantly, to mass, there were probably some notions that devils would gather around the deathbed, hoping to seize the soul when it emerged. This soul had a human form, perhaps that of an adult, maybe a child. For the people who moved, respectfully, to the verge as Master John approached his benefice, death was not an instant. Death was something that had to be approached properly, with repentance and new assertions of belief. The soul had to be nurtured through the process with prayers and tears. Then, it was necessary to ensure that the person really was dead and their soul departed, and here old local lore and potions might be employed. There was a horror of consigning the living to the world of the dead. From folk songs that may root back into the Middle Ages there are suggestions that even death did not break the bond between a wife and her widowed husband, though too much weeping at the graveside disturbed the corpse and prevented the spirit from resting.

❋❋❋❋❋❋❋❋❋❋❋❋❋❋❋❋❋

Master John's first task on arriving in Hampsthwaite involved administering the last rites to a woman crushed against a wall by a startled ox. Laying on a straw-filled sack, she gasped out a confession and was granted absolution and each portion of her body was forgiven and blessed for any wickedness it may have done (the scope in medieval Hampsthwaite was not great), and then she took a sip of holy water. A significant spiritual landmark had now been crossed for, in the minds of the more devout villagers, if she should now contrive to recover she would have to lead a blameless and abstemious life or the rites would somehow be debased. A cluster of neighbours had gathered to witness the scene and Master John waved them away from the open door and window: the soul must be free to escape.

Thus far things were going well: Blanche had survived the accident for long enough to make her confession and she was dying in the company of others, including a priest. It was a shame, some thought, that she had not enjoyed a few years of rest from farmwork and housework. A widow, she had just negotiated an agreement with her son which ensured that she would be supported when she relinquished her tenancy to him. On the other hand, she would not reach old age. People were rather uncertain about truly old people: they did not know too many of them but considered that most of those they had met had begun to look and act rather oddly, so perhaps they might be, well ... closer to the Devil? Living too long was not always considered a good thing.

When Blanche died, all the right things had been done and people agreed it was a good death. Someone brought in a chicken feather to tickle her nose, which was now cold, as it should be. There was some discussion about whether the women should dress her body for burial or use her few coins to buy a shroud. Blanche had gasped a request for a wake, and so a vigil was kept over the shrouded body. The next day, a grave was dug in the churchyard. In the absence of headstones or well-surveyed plans, this was a somewhat hit and miss affair, and as the generations in the churchyard increased, hits became more likely than misses. The digger hit an arm and laid the bones carefully in the newly dug grave. Blanche's shrouded but un-coffined body was put to rest and the funeral went well apart from an unseemly wrangle at the end between Master John and relatives, for his charges were higher than those of the previous incumbent. She would have been pleased that the family looked for value and she would have been immensely relieved to know that she was resting securely with the Blood of the Village. In the minds of its people the village and the lineage of villagers were a greater force than its priesthood.

Soon afterwards, John performed a less common funeral. His gaze had lighted upon Roger, who lived beyond the village. John being rather a stickler for procedures and Roger being a leper, some special church work was required. Lepers were regarded as living in Purgatory. This was not to say that they were sinners who must be cast out, but rather they were suffering for the souls of humanity. However, if lepers were in Purgatory, they could not be of the same world as the living and it was up to the church to perform the arrangements needed to establish this fact properly.

John, chanting psalms of penitence, brought Roger into the church. A space had been outlined by burning candles and Roger knelt within it as a black cloth draped across frames was spread over him. He heard mass, confessed and took communion. Then he followed the priest out into the churchyard, where the keen air wafted away the stale smell of tallow and graves. A shovel full of earth was thrown over his feet. Now everyone would know that he was from the world of the dead and not of the living. The churchyard was no longer for him, and when he was buried it would have to be in the grounds of a hospital for lepers.

✳✳✳✳✳✳✳✳✳✳✳✳✳✳✳✳✳

Any member of the Hampsthwaite congregation would have been absolutely baffled by the notion that an archaeologist, burrowing amongst the bones in the churchyard, would be able to form a picture of village life and health as they were in the years around 1300. The fact is that this community probably had many resemblances to the most impoverished developing communities of today. It is hard to know about babies as their remains did not always reach the church-yard. Childhood was a time of terrible danger for little people yet to acquire immunity to a frightening array of diseases, while greatly weakened by famine and endemic malnutrition. Were the reader to be born into a family in one of the Nidderdale villages of this time, it is fair to guess that there would only be about a two in three chance of surviving beyond childhood. Those who escaped the voracious churchyard in childhood might have an inkling that the average life expectancy for men was a mere thirty-five years, while that for women was a miserly thirty years or so. The discrepancy resulted form the terribly high levels of mortality during childbirth; few impending mothers can have approached the event with anything but terror. Many young mothers would end in the church-yards, their newborn babe in a bundle beside them. However, and contrary to popular mythology, those people who did survive to adulthood grew to heights similar to those of the older of the Dalesfolk living today (recent advances in nutrition and growth in mobility-induced hybrid vigour have made the very latest generation or two much taller than their ancestors). Middle age for us was old age for our medieval villagers: little more than one person in ten lived beyond the age of fifty.

The bones of the medieval Valley people would tell us about their lives. If we could do a careful excavation and analysis, we might find that in-breeding among the Blood of the Village had given rise to certain village attributes, in the way that their broad-faced contemporaries in York tended to have pointed chins and their left cheekbones slightly higher than their right ones. Within a village community, such peculiarities could become still more concentrated and pronounced. Severe pain was commonplace. Whether the grain was ground at the lord's mill, or ille-gally at home in stone hand querns, flakes of grit would become mixed with the flour. Quite often, the chewing of heavy rye bread would be broken by a grating sensation as one of these fragments gouged a furrow in the enamel of a chewer's tooth. Over the years, the hard layer would be scratched away and, as a result, some people would suffer excruciating pain, or even death from dental abscesses. Almost one person in ten suffered severe problems with their teeth. Quite a few suffered from gallstones; internal parasites, like tapeworms, were indivisible from medieval life; but it was arthritis that eventually barred many villagers from the fields. Hard work in the rain and snow drew osteo-arthritis to its victims. Any visitor to a Valley community will have encountered people with stiff, aching hands and backs that were rigid tubes of fused vertebrae.

With lives so short and threatened by pain, and with death waiting in every polluted well and open sewer, it might seem that living then was just too wretched to bear. Had this been so, the evidence for mental illness and suicide (admittedly taboo subjects that might be concealed in the records) must surely have been greater? Ordinary people were illiterate and could not record their thoughts, though one does suspect an underlying fatalism. One of the very few places where the doings of ordinary people are recorded is in the rolls of manor and higher courts. Here we meet village people who are 'at the mercy of the court' for little crimes like fighting with cudgels, answering the manorial officials back, failing to perform their 'boonworks' or trying to diddle their neighbours out of bits of land. The impression is of a rumbustious populace – people that would be out creating lots of trouble were it not for the controls exerted by the local courts. What, one wonders, might such lusty people have got up to if raised on decent diets? Still, if we can best them in terms of longevity and health, they lived close to the earth in a beautiful world still not distorted by greed. Their hours were shorter, but their colours, more intense. Their communities were strong and supportive, their folk culture was rich and when they spoke to some-one they will have looked them in the eye. They had no mobile phones, media celebrities, masters of political spin or institutionalised materialism to cheapen their existences. It was tranquil in ways that we, wretchedly, can no longer enjoy, but it was also violent.

❋❋❋❋❋❋❋❋❋❋❋❋❋❋❋

We are in Clint, it is 1324 and the bud of growth has ceased to swell. The inn is a rather shabby place where armourers, spur-makers, Foresters and cloth merchants may pass the odd hour to break their journeys to and from Knaresborough. William, son of Adam, a local Clint man, and another William, called 'del Ridding' (or 'of the clearing') are arguing. They have drunk too much and their voices are raised. Del Sayles (maybe 'of the willows'), who is the landlord and yet another William, is worried. The local boy lurches to his feet; he has seen something frightening in the eyes of del Ridding and he dashes through the door. Del Ridding is well-armed; he strings his bow, grabs his quiver, checks his dagger and follows. De Clint looks around in panic; he has known Agnes Serveys since childhood and he runs into her house. She is flustered, but he pushes her back down the passage. He bars the door and his enemy tries to batter it down; his fear turns to ice as he realises that if del Ridding is prepared to break into a stranger's house he is probably prepared to kill as well.

Perhaps his knowledge of the local topography may save him. He bursts out of the back door, heads towards the manor house and leaps across a succession of the hedges that define the parallel house plots. Arrows fly past his shoulders and even the proximity to the manor house, the moated headquarters of local authority, does not deter del Ridding. De Clint runs past it for another 2 miles, until he can run no further. Cornered and facing his killer, he dies with an arrow in his breast. The murderer makes no attempt to conceal himself, but is arraigned at Knaresborough the following year. The court records recall the events.

❋❋❋❋❋❋❋❋❋❋❋❋❋❋❋

It was as though an invisible line had been drawn across the Valley. On the one side lay Village England, the world of dwellings, churches and ploughland. On the other, there were neither villages nor churches and most land was in pasture, wood pasture, woodland or moor. The large parishes containing the churches extended up the Valley, reaching out for congregants, but the further one got from the churches then, of course, the more difficult it was to reach them and the more easily and readily the strictures of the priests were cast aside. The truly devout might go padding down potholed lanes, up woodland tracks and over becks for 6 miles to get to a church. In terms of time alone, a round journey of a dozen miles plus an hour or two spent standing in church left little time in the day for seeing to the livestock or warding off any wolves that might stray over from the high marchlands of Wensleydale. It is, in short, hard to imagine that very much serious worship took place in the more remote parts of the Valley during the Middle Ages, except in the abbey granges and lodges. A grange chapel survived at Ramsgill in the upper Valley into the nineteenth century. Only the east gable remains, clasped by the churchyard wall, after the demolition of the rest of the chapel in 1842.

In the absence of a far-reaching system of chapels of ease, it is hard to know how some communities disposed of their dead. The medieval period was well advanced before an agreement in 1484 between the Prebendary of Masham, the Vicar of Kirkby Malzeard and leading people of the locality allowed a chapel and chapel yard to be established at Middlesmoor. The reasons cited were the distance from the mother church of Kirkby Malzeard (outside the Valley) and the '… difficulty of the road to convey their children to be baptised and their copses to be buried'. An older, unlicensed chapel seems to have existed there. In the Dales in general, corpses were placed in wicker coffins and carried across miles of rough country by bearers on foot – sometimes through blizzards and across rivers in spate. It is perhaps discomforting to wonder whether this was always done and what would happen when communities were completely snow-bound. An edict from the Archbishop of York in 1351 noted that people in the Pateley Bridge-Bewerley-Dacre area were '… living in a certain beastly manner to the peril of their souls … far distant from any parish church, to the which for the swellings of waters and other tempests greatly in winter season some men cannot pass without great difficulty and corporal danger'. Pateley Bridge had gained a chapel in 1321, but there were problems over tithes: the (minority?) who did go to church in the new chapel had claimed exemption because they lived in locations still attached to Kirkby Malzeard. Do we see an early demonstration of Dales character here?

The middle section of the Valley was linked to the celebrated Minster church at Ripon, around 10 miles away as the crow flies, but people were not crows, the river might intervene and the ground was far from flat. The territory of Ripon

Middlesmoor Church resulted from an agreement of 1484 to provide a chapel and graveyard owing to the distance from the parent church at Kirkby Malzeard.

was divided between seven canons and the Valley was in the care of the vicar of the canon of Studley, which was scarcely any closer. It is unlikely that many serious attempts to challenge the geographical realities were made and the middle Valley people were probably touched but lightly by organised Christianity until the chapel of St Mary was built at Pateley Bridge, far beyond the hearing of the Hampsthwaite bells. Sited on a slope that tested the calf muscles, this church may have been located in an existing hamlet or have attracted one to grow around it. Ultimately, the chapel fell into ruins and the settlement appears to have slipped downhill, perhaps lured away by the commercial potential posed by traders using the bridge, below. Later in the Middle Ages, in 1402, a chapel was built to serve people at Thornthwaite, just beyond the long outreach of Hampsthwaite parish. In this or the next century, the Beckwiths had a chapel made in their own hall at Clint (somewhat self-indulgently since their parish church at Ripley was scarcely more than a stroll away).

In the Valley, conversion was not a brief and brilliant event. It took more than 1,000 years for each cell of community to gain a church or a chapel of one persuasion or another. Now, for lack of interest, they are losing them and car-owners find it harder to get to church than did the footsore beck-forders.

The monks were rather like the lepers in their divorce from the world of the living. Fountains had its grange and fishpond at Cayton on the threshold of the abbey, its

Pateley Bridge gained a chapel in 1321, though the settlement seems to have slipped down to the river bridge since then. The abandoned church has fallen into ruin.

grange and park at Brimham, a clutch of granges and lodges in Dacre and Bewerley in the middle Valley and a string of them on the eastern flanks of the upland section. Byland, whose people must have resented their dependence on the other Cistercian house for rights of access to their estate, held a similar string of granges and lodges on the western side of the upper Valley. Monastic control was an uncomfortable burden for the Valley people. It could mean eviction, while if not, it meant exactions and impositions by the stewards from the abbey. For those who were not bondsmen, the claims of the monasteries conflicted with the hallowed privileges of free families. Sometimes, all pretences were set aside and the gangs of laymen and lay brethren set to fighting with cudgels or to rustling stock. From time to time, the monastic bands would fight each other, with the lay brethren of Fountains having various sets-to with the Augustinians of Bolton Priory in Wharfedale or their servants. Great personages in the monastic centres of power tended to take a utilitarian view of their tenants and estates. Both existed to generate the wealth needed to finance the latest magnificent building phase at the abbey. Those who impeded work that glorified God might well be considered to be in the pay of the Devil.

Accidents of history had brought the Cistercians into the North Country and the accidents of success changed and distorted their lifestyle from the one based on self-sufficiency and austerity that was at first intended. They had attracted too much luck, too much land and too much manpower to remain in poverty. As their estates expanded, they needed roads to reach the territorial extremities, and so they learned how to coerce their neighbours and win rights of way. As they established sheep, horse and cattle farming on their new territories, they discovered which extra tracts of land they needed to complete a grazing, where a vital beck could be stolen to provide a watering place or where to secure a useful ford or bridge.

The abbey estate was composed of cells, often old townships that had existed for centuries before the monks arrived. These estate and township cells frequently became fairly self-contained monastic farms or granges. Granges were usually subdivided into lodges that were rather like farmsteads, and on the granges and lodges the shepherding, farm work, building and walling were done by lay brethren. Each grange had a hall with a small oratory and the supervision of its affairs was undertaken by a monk, sometimes just one, or sometimes two or three of them. They oversaw the work of the grange, provided religious services for the workers, maintained discipline, imposed the rule of the abbey and dealt with any abbey tenants that there might be in the vicinity. Every few weeks, there would be a great ordering of farm work and tidying of accounts in anticipation of a visitation by the cellarer, who had ridden out from the abbey. Very rarely, he would be accompanied by the Abbot, whose majestic presence and gorgeous raiment would draw a small crowd of countryfolk away from fell and fold to line the roadside. It was even better than the show when a merchant from Florence rode in, well-mounted and swathed in furs, to count the sheep, judge the pasture and formulate a bid for the wool crop of some future year.

❋❋❋❋❋❋❋❋❋❋❋❋❋❋❋

Henry seemed to be sidling aimlessly among the sheep on the slopes near Lofthouse. He did not look directly at the limping one and seemed to have passed it by when his crook shot out like a lizard's tongue and took it by the neck. A couple of seconds later, it was on its back between his knees and Henry was trimming back the overgrown points on its hoof and scooping out the foot-rot, avocado-fashion. He sat down to clean his blade. He looked across the Valley of an excitable young river that had not too long since emerged from the ground. The grey-green banks below the heather line were not compartmentalised into a field of patchwork and almost the only walls that could be seen were those of sheepfolds.

Was that moving grey fleck by the skyline a wolf? He narrowed his eyes but could not be certain. There were less of them than before, that was for sure. Bounty hunting was putting paid to their games. He wondered if the wilderness and deserts in the scriptures looked like this, with circling pewits and no more than a distant birch or rowan to detail the scene?

Sometimes he felt unfortunate, or dare he say ... cheated? He had a reflective side and would love to have been a monk, but his breeding, his demeanour and one or two things in his past closed that door. He hoped that by becoming a lay brother he might be halfway to his goal. So, too, did many others; there was no shortage of recruits. What he had discovered was an abundance of hard work but little to fulfil a mind that was relaxed and receptive after the day of physical toil. At Fountains, life had been anything but contemplative or reclusive. Beneath their accommodation had been the seemingly unending cellarium, where all the commodities from the far-flung estates were gathered. There was the endless groaning and creaking of wains and waggons – louder when they arrived laden than when they departed. Sometimes, he wanted to dash down the stone steps and grease the axles himself. There was the endless mutter of checking, recording and tallying by the cellarer's assistants and an eternal sound of unloading, piling, shifting and stacking. Cheese, fleece, butter, salted meat, eggs – all coming in or going out.

Still, if life in that crowded lay brothers' accommodation, overlooking the River Skell at Fountains, had been far from solitary, there was solitude aplenty to be enjoyed after the transfer to the head of the Valley. He relished work, but he had expected an education to go with it. Now, he discovered that the monks deliberately kept their *conversi* or lay brethren illiterate. One, who had arrived literate, was severely punished when he tried to teach the names of the letters to his friends in the dormitory at night. Henry worshipped at dawn and dusk but received communion only seven times a year; he longed to be able to open one of those great Bibles and read a page from it. But the dazzling illustrations were all that he could understand.

Shepherding offered the pleasures of solitude and inexhaustible opportunities for contemplation. Out on the banks and fell-sides, the clutter of civilisation did not get in the way. But there were some practical disadvantages. Some of those lads that the brethren had bruised with clubs and staffs in a boundary battle might catch you the next day, alone on the fell, undefended and beyond assistance. This was a threat, but Henry was still more bothered that he might be a serious sinner. Grown grey and lean on the prescribed diet of grain, pease and fish, he found himself glancing

Nidderdale was as much dairying as sheep-raising country, and scenes such as this will have been common. The monks had many 'vaccaries' or cattle farms, while abbey tenants often paid the bulk of their rents in vast amounts of cheese.

hungrily at the remains of an old ewe that the wolves had torn apart. He looked at lambs in the same way, seeing the meat beneath the wool, and also at the milk that squirted into the pails when the women came in to milk the sheep. That was something else: he was not allowed to speak to a woman without supervision and no females were allowed inside the hall.

The company of the brethren was all very well, but now he was having fundamental doubts about the whole Cistercian code – or at least, how it was lived. Most of the Cistercian lands were not devoid of people, as required – or not until they monks and *conversi* made them so. The prescription against taking rents from tenants was openly being broken in scores of places and was not he, himself, just an instrument whereby the monks could increase the wealth they should not have? But it was not just the monks: the lay brothers, who were uncompromised by religious vows, had started to buy wool from lay outlets and to resell it along with the monastic produce at a better price. The monks did not interfere because they had become deeply involved in speculation and forward buying and so the '*collecta*' from the lay brethren helped to bridge any gaps between the hoped-for and the actual production of wool. It would be for later generations to find a name for that economic system which contaminates every aspect of human relations through the quest for wealth.

These doubts penetrated the core of all those beliefs that he had tried to build his life around. However modest his vocation, he had never wanted to bully harmless country people out of their scraps of common or bludgeon them into using the abbey's mill. Still, the system was far bigger than he was and had done nothing but expand for the last two centuries. Perhaps he was wrong and perhaps those who could read had discovered answers that he could not comprehend. He looked for a brighter side. So long as the priest in charge of the grange was not too aloof or too much of a martinet then the little all-male community could be very affable and the banter and ragging were enjoyable, in moderation. And for all the rules about abstinence, neither a monk nor even a lay brother had ever died of famine, so far as he could recall. Life was more secure than back in the village, so why did he miss it so much?

✻✻✻✻✻✻✻✻✻✻✻✻✻✻✻✻✻

Now, the cogwheels of time, which seem to have run in reverse during the Dark Ages, were running faster. Change was visible. It was accelerating. A couple of centuries on and Henry's world is transformed. Now we can encounter real people with real names. In 1496, the monks were gone from the grange and Miles Rayner, a layman and former grange-keeper, was now renting a whole lodge on the old grange of Lofthouse from the abbey. His rent was considerable: 13s 4d per year. In addition, he was required to keep forty of the abbey's cows and render their yield to the monks. He was to deliver 26st. 8lb (around 169kg) of butter at 1s per stone (6.4kg.) and 53st. 4lb (around 338kg) of cheese at 8d per stone, as well as twenty yearling cattle. His total rent came to £7 15s 6¼d. Miles seems to have found all this very burdensome, because his relatives, Roger and Christopher, subsequently seem to have taken over portions of the old lodge tenancy. Countless agreements like this show that the Cistercians had abandoned all pretence of toiling in a wilderness and were running their estates, now often tenanted, as sheer revenue-raising operations.

The pattern of churches mirrored the spread of villages, for churches usually needed a village to feed on. Those in the Valley were not like the ones in the vale to the east, where most villages were reconstructed from the ruins of settlements devastated by the Harrying. The villages over in the vale were set out and planned in precise and repetitive designs under the supervision of the agents of their lords. Stewards went out with measuring rods and marked out the ground. In the Valley, village growth was more leisurely and less restricted.

Hampsthwaite had its form determined by the course of the Old Road. It began at the ford by the church, straggled across the old floodplain and then up the lower slope of the valley side. This basic layout of a routeway lined by dwellings gained a little variation when the king, as lord of the manor, granted himself a market at Hampsthwaite in 1304. Also included in the package was a summer fair at the feast of St Thomas the Martyr, from 5 to 8 July. The rise in status required some adjustments. The old village had a rather 'y'-shaped form, with a short spur being formed by the lane which headed up the Valley. Standing on a terrace above the floodplain and just to the river's side of the junction of stem and spur lay the manor house, with its associated outbuildings. The market required a venue, and there was nowhere better than at the junction of routeways almost in front of the manor. Here, a triangular green was inserted into the village layout, probably at the expense of a few roadside houses. This green endures to this day, partly as green and partly as shop-front parking spaces, though road widening has consumed plenty of the market-place, too.

Nidd had its church by the Roman road, though the village itself developed southwards from it, along Town Lane, which formed a winding link between Knaresborough's road to Ripley and beyond and the way to Ripon. Endowed with a church but not a market, Nidd survived until its owners terminated its life in the nineteenth century. Owlcotes was another village that straggled along a road, in its case the ancient pilgrimage road on the northern side of the Valley, where it ascended from Godwin's bridge or Scara Bridge before bifurcating into branches heading for Ripon and for Knaresborough. Owlcotes was soon to die, and Ripley would then take shape.

There was another village, lacking both church and market, at Killinghall. Here there was a manor house, but the village did not have the compact form of those of the Midlands; rather, it was largely composed of a loose line of farmsteads strung out along the margins of a great common. Clint seems to have been more coherent; it was an upland settlement, and Pateley Bridge apart, the last outpost of Village England to the north of the river. It, too, was an elongated settlement and straggled along the roadside, and the eastern part of it lined the flanks of an oblong green. It ran from the manor house in the west, where seventeenth-century ruins now stand, to the bifurcation of its lane in the east. Again, the convergence on lanes was an important element in its plan. The curious intrusion of the Forest boundary meant that Clint was lassoed as a Forest village, like Hampsthwaite, though unlike its neighbour across the Valley, it never gained a church and was probably without a market, too.

The villages that were taking shape in the Valley tended to be straggly places that would always lack the population sizes and complex forms of most lowland villages. To focus just on them would be to overlook the wealth of smaller settlements, for detached farmsteads and hamlets were always more important. Even in the lower part of the Valley where the villages gelled, hamlets were present in force. They are less evident today because they proved even less durable than the villages. Some of them are known by name, like Whipley, which sat by its little green between Clint and Ripley. Others can be recognised as archaeological traces of short lines of dwellings on one or two sides of a road. Hamlets like this came and went during the Middle Ages and the centuries that followed; usually we know nothing about them, not even their names.

Now there was a sound more pervasive and more insistent than the 'dong-ing' of bells or the blaring of horns. At close quarters the axes went 'chunk!' and 'thwack!' but from a distance they sounded a higher, ringing tone. The sound came from every quarter, as though the people and the woods were at war. The ringing told of wooded pastures, spinneys, groves and hursts – places that had served people well with their browse, fuel and timber for centuries – that were being sacrificed by communities with a insatiable gluttony for growth. One could not support more people on traditional resources; more calories were needed, and that meant more grain. And this meant fewer of everything else: you paid for your rye, oats and barley with timber, hay, grass and fuel.

Travel eastward along the road to Clint Bank after frost or a light snow. Look across the river at the north-facing slopes, and there you will see the traces of slight corrugations frosted in white. Look at countless other places in the Valley and, under the right conditions, you will see the same: plough ridges. This is not the rumble-tumble, helter-skelter pattern of ridge and furrow that you might see in the Midlands, with ridges rising knee- or thigh-high above a boot placed in the furrow. Such great corrugations took centuries of continuous cultivation to form. No, these are faint plough ridges born of starvation and a desperate urge to grow some extra grain. Cold, sour, sun-skirted and hungry land might be broken in and ridged-up for a few years of cultivation until it had nothing left to give. It was desperation that carved these faint wrinkles on the brow of the Valley and harsh reality that brought their abandonment.

The green at Hampsthwaite must have resulted from the decision to establish a market on the royal manor.

❊❊❊❊❊❊❊❊❊❊❊❊❊❊❊❊

Adam sat on a log outside his door at Owlcotes. Beyond his house plot there was a ribbon of meadow and then the river. For once, that direction did not interest him. Nor was he staring, as he often did, to the left, to see if anybody of interest might cross the beck on Godwin's little bridge by the mill. His brother, Henry, had become a lay brother and he often hoped he might see him again, striding out along one of Fountain's rights of way. Occasionally, he hoped that he would not. Many monks and lay brethren came out of the Valley but none remained *of* it. Henry had always had a zealous sort of piety and after a few years with the monks, he could well despise his brother as a sinful bondsman. That would be hard to bear. This day, however, it was the high ground to the north that had captured Adam's attention. Trees were being felled around the edge of the common and bonfires of twigs and damp leaves were smouldering. It was dank and misty; only reluctantly did the brash kindle and release a dark, tangy smoke. Then Adam did glance behind, 'Hemmed-in and hedged-about', he muttered. There, in the meadow and on the slope across the river, were his strips of land, tightly bracketed by those of his neighbours. Wherever he looked they lay side-by-side, earthy cheek to loamy jowl; there was no leeway, no space for expansion.

It was as though the whole world of the village was bound around by a tight belt of iron.

He had not expected that so many of his children would survive infancy, and that was a fact. That was the problem, too. Instead of one son to take over the holding and look after him when he got old, there were now four very lively lads. At least two of them could be expected to live, maybe more – plus a daughter to marry-off. The good weather could be blamed for this. It made you healthier, and that meant more children. Nobody wanted a famine, but honestly, two children would be more manageable. Anyway, Adam reminded himself, it did not do to get attached to your children before they had left the cradle and

The feverish assarting of the thirteenth century came at a terrible price of lost timber, fuel and browse. Even the tough hornbeam yielded firewood and hard timber for cog wheels.

infancy well behind. If you did, then it was more likely than not they would go and die on you, just when you had got used to having them around. But now he was starting to get fond of them – all of them; too many of them.

This was what his interest in Birthwaite was all about (*Birken thwaite*: birchwood clearing). Up where the lane broadened to form a funnel at the entrance to the common, a team of the Owlcotes lads had started to clear away trees. A small village of roadside dwellings was taking shape. It was almost in shouting distance of a couple of manor houses, with Fountains' bells donging out their commands just over the brow, and yet there was that strange frontier feeling of release – of freedom up there. There was still a zone of woodland to clear, as well as the pollards in the common pasture. Adam strode up from Owlcotes. He prodded the leaf-strewn embers with his staff and peered at places where the felling had laid soil bare, 'Yes', he muttered, 'Yes, we *will*'.

He collected his mattock and headed back up the track, the track along which he had led his cattle so very many times before. 'Room for one more?' he asked when he got up with the men, and they showed him a plot at the end of the house string. Within a few weeks, the family had moved into their cottage beside the old track. Its tannin-scented beams rested on good rubble footings, blades of oak-formed gables, and it was so unusually solid that it might not need much rebuilding for the rest of Adam's lifespan. For a while, it seemed strange to leave the old common and not need to make the trek down to the old village. Not quite a home in the sky, though perhaps halfway, but winters were a shade keener up there. Now Adam and the boys had some new land to add to their shares in the old ploughland and meadow. Of course, the lord fined them for 'squatting' on their new holding, though this amounted to nothing more than accepting what had happened and taking a rent for it. Throughout his lordship and those of all his neighbours, people were felling and grubbing out old roots, hacking, burning, clearing and, all the while, spreading like mould over an apple. Cottages sprang up in mushroom-fashion and the authority of the manor was overwhelmed. Feudalism had encountered a greater power: the cradle.

Seven springs later, Adam sat his bare haunches down on the clammy plough soil. He explained to his sons that this was a way to test if the soil was warm enough for planting. The low-level view was rather disturbing: he could swear that when he first came here, the soil was browner than this. Now it seemed yellowish, and when he rubbed a pinch of earth between his finger and thumb it felt more gritty. Already, a bank of the finer silts seemed to be building up against the hedge, below. It was the same problem that they had known back in the village: not sufficient stock to fold on the ploughland to keep it in good heart. But if you wanted more animals you had less space to grow beans and oats, to say nothing of hungry barley – and then you couldn't support one village, let alone Owlcotes *and* Birthwaite. Adam remained convinced that little people, like himself, could not answer big questions. To try to could be usurping the work of God and his clergy and tantamount to sinning. Adam had to do his own work: to feed his household and to pay his dues to his earthly lord (including the ridiculous ones about giving chickens and eggs at Christmas) and then to support the church. No matter how desperate the situation might be on his own holding, he also had to perform his feudal services on the lord's demesne. These 'boonworks' he was presumed to do out of love for his lord, but it was the fear of the manor court that dragged him away from his own over-ripened harvest and into his lord's demesne. He thought of all this and of his family and their ever growing appetites. He looked at his sons; their drawn faces and weak-jointed bodies told of scarcely survived famines and vitamin deficiencies. 'Lord, forgive me', he thought, 'I cannot afford to fall ill'.

CHAPTER 8

WHERE DISASTERS COLLIDE

(1348 – 1380)

It was not the slate skies or the nagging patter of the drips falling from the thatch. What really turned his nerves into bowstrings were the recollections from his grandfather. There he sat, with a sack around his bony shoulders and his grimy feet on the warm bakestone, and not an hour would pass without him nattering about days that had been so hot and sunny that the lads would down their sickles, quit the demesne and charge fully clothed into the river. Of else it would be about how his posh uncle would rest by the dusty track and fry eggs on his scorching breastplate as the old king led his armies across the frontiers to bash this lot or that lot. 'When I was a boy we'd be picking wild gooseberries by this time of the year', came the voice.

✳✳✳✳✳✳✳✳✳✳✳✳✳✳✳✳✳

When one thing went wrong, people would tackle it. Practicality was etched on their genes. This was different: *everything* was going wrong and you had not fettled one thing before another needed fixing. There were some things that you simply could not fix, and since the start of the century the climate had simply fallen to bits. Places on the edge where once one could just wrest a living were being washed out and wasted. So then their people came back to the heartlands of the Valley hoping to resettle, but they found crops moulding in the fields, sheep hobbling across the sodden turf with rotting feet, cows coughing and oxen dropping in their yokes. Just across the watershed in Wharfedale, the canons at

Bolton could not cope with the soaking of their moorland pastures and disease was devastating their flocks. In the space of just a year, the priory flock was reduced from 3,000 to 1,000, while murrain assailed their cattle. In 1314, the summer was dull and grey; the next year, rods of rain drove down the harvest. In 1316, conditions had deteriorated so badly that Britain experienced a famine of a severity that was unknown to living memory, after which disease ravaged the enfeebled communities.

Longshanks, the old king – a psychopath or political genius depending on your point of view – had died in 1307. Already, unresolved differences over Scottish status and the legacies of misdeeds committed there by English armies were undermining confidence and stability in northern England. The reign of Edward II was just a few years old when the terror of Scottish raiding advanced southwards from the Borders into the north of England. Soon, the little communities of Dales hamlets and the families of secluded, bank-side farmsteads were drawn into Bruce's campaign for recognition as the independent King of Scotland. Longshank's son had inherited neither his appetite for campaigning nor his gift for it, and duly led the army to the biggest defeat that anyone could recall. As a result, the Scots warriors might appear on the homely old roads of the Valley at any time, as, quite often, they did. If the thirteenth century had seemed quite hopeful, the fourteenth century seemed to be a place where disasters collided.

✳✳✳✳✳✳✳✳✳✳✳✳✳✳✳✳✳

Walter did not belong to the nobility, nor did his family have mercenary traditions. Nevertheless, he craved to see something of the world, to make his fortune and to share in adventures. During his formative years, tales of the old king and his latest victories had enlivened many a gathering. Now, Walter wanted to immerse himself in the colours and splendours of chivalry, a code that increased its romance and allure with each passing day. An opportunity was provided by the fact that he came from a family of free tenants living on the Plumpton estates of the warlord Percy dynasty: here might be an entry into the martial world. The next king, Edward II, seemed a much less inspiring leader, but when Henry, the 1st Lord Percy of Alnwick, rose against him, the usurper's cause had little glamour and fewer prospects. Henry was forfeit but soon restored. The next march of events seemed to offer all the glory and the plunder that Walter could wish. Scottish resentment against English interference was bubbling over, and by 1312 it was a serious threat to the North. Soon, Wharfedale was too dangerous a place for civilised life and the unfortunate canons of Bolton fled their priory, some trekking south and others finding refuge in the Clifford castle at Skipton.

Now the tide seemed to be turning. In 1314, along with Neville, the other great northern lord, Percy, was advancing into Scotland to relieve the English garrison of Stirling Castle. Walter had gained a place as a foot soldier in the army. His uncle's old helmet had already rubbed a red weal at the top of his neck when he inhaled the salty air wafting in from across the Firth of Forth and saw the distant mountains ranged in a wall along the Highlands' edge. The damp countryside was still pristine and spring-like in this Scottish June as the 22,000 Englishmen, Welsh bowmen and their camp followers approached Edinburgh.

Walter found himself among a group of foot-soldiers, minor squires and grooms; their conversation was all about plunder, feats of arms and triumph. All were mesmerised by the splendour of the fiery Spanish chargers and the elegant palfreys, as highly bred as their riders. They were entranced by the surcoats emblazoned with the arms that were beginning to identify their owners, by the lustrous sheen of the new plate armour and by the unending procession of the celebrities from the chivalric myths with their sweeping moustaches and commanding gestures. When the hardened old troopers in the sweat-stained leather jerkins failed to respond, the novices thought that they were affecting superior airs. For those new to arms, the main fear was that the Scots would be so devastated and trampled by the charge of the heavy cavalry that there would be nothing left for the pikemen to fight or loot.

They saw Stirling Castle on a great rock that was like an intrusion of the Grampians into countryside that seemed more English than Scottish. It towered over the wooded slopes and the wet meadows and marshes below. A detachment of English cavalry attempted to reach the castle, but then the novices witnessed a most amazing sight. Moray's spearmen formed a 'schiltron', a moving formation that bristled with elongated spears like a porcupine backing into its attacker. The English knights were poked away and then driven back, unable to reach the spearmen through the thicket of shafts. Then Bruce himself emerged from a wood with a regal circlet around his helmet. His light mount side-stepped the lance of Sir Humphry Bohun and then Bruce split the knight's helm with his battleaxe. These preliminaries only made the English ranks more eager to engage. But when the Bannock Burn was crossed and battle was joined, it gradually became clear that the Scottish schiltrons were far better able to cope with the muddy ground than the ponderously armoured English formations. When the Scottish light cavalry under Sir Robert Keith charged the exposed Welsh archers, the once unthinkable English defeat became a possibility. Meanwhile, nimble Scottish archers dashed in and out of the shelter of the schiltrons, whose massed spear points sent the English back and ever closer to the burn.

Looking around, Walter saw the proud pageants of chivalry passing before his eyes. The mail rustled with a silky shimmer, the great swords, laminated in the forge, flashed and swooped. Burnished plates slid over each other with every move of the knights, exactly as the armourers had intended. Heraldic devices in red, gold, black, silver and green identified their bearers and whatever valorous actions they might perform. There were streamers, horses plunging and biting and war cries. Was that the white saltire on a red ground of the Nevilles at this time, and could that be the Percys' silver crescent? But other devices were pressing in on his view, the blue lion rampant of the Bruce and the Glendinnings' black and silver cross. The clashing, the colours, the pressure of armoured bodies forced together, the awesome power of a warhorse pushing on one's shoulder – battle was a remarkable intensification of the senses.

Warhorses backing away from the Scottish spears converged on him. He felt himself trapped between two immensely powerful sets of hind quarters. He was being carried backwards, his feet helplessly pawing the air. Then it all became blurred as he dropped and a hoof pressed his head into the mud. As he lay trapped, he thought that something was wrong: all the amazing craftsmanship of the armourers, the ingenuity of the dyers and embroiderers who had made the banners and surcoats and the patience of the grooms was being dented, torn, muddied wasted. War was not supposed to be like this. Tired bodies were trapped in the mire and trampled as the townspeople of Stirling, along with some Highlanders and the camp followers, charged down on the survivors with their knives and clubs. The English army disintegrated, with the burn and its marshy flanks gradually vanishing from sight under a mass of muddy, armoured and jerkin-clad bodies, some heaving, some now still. The Welsh archers retreated in good order to Carlisle, but large companies of knights were seen galloping across country to the border and some nobles took ships for England from Dunbar. Walter was not with any of them. His realisation, an instant before his death, that war is not a game had come too late.

✳✳✳✳✳✳✳✳✳✳✳✳✳✳✳✳

Now the doors of the North were wide open. The northerners had better fend for themselves; there was not much that their king would do to save them. Humiliated, pressed between the leaking clouds and the sodden earth, the communities of the northern valleys had to face the revenge of the Scots. With the Bannockburn summer still extant, a great army under Edward Bruce ravaged Northumberland, next Durham and then entered Richmondshire, leaving the castle but raiding all the country around. For once, the pillage (cattle, ransom, booty and ransom-worthy prisoners) was flowing northwards. In saner times, it was realised that people on both sides of the border shared interests in fellowship and peaceful trading. But Scottish pride had been crushed and bruised too many times. There would be bands of freebooters scampering swiftly southwards along the high trails and descending under darkness on the byre and paddock. Wayward Borders barons would rampage outside the walls of castles, looting, rounding up the village herds and taunting their lords to come down from the battlements to fight. Occasionally, too, larger armies would advance on broad, destructive fronts, leaving swathes of blackened fields, burning villages and ravaged towns behind.

Four years after Bannockburn, the pillaging began in yet more earnest and it lasted for a further four years and then erupted from time to time in the years to follow. One never knew just where the invaders would strike next. In 1318, the area around Knaresborough was burned and pillaged, as was the town itself. In the year that followed, a Scots victory at Myton, close to Boroughbridge, took raiding to the historic capital of the Valley, to several places in the Valley itself and around the Old North Road. Winter this year did not bring its customary respite, for it was associated with one of the worst eruptions of the cattle murrain. In 1320, the Archbishop of York received a royal charter allowing him to operate a market and fair at Pateley Bridge, this being compensation for the losses caused by those Scottish raids that the king had proved unable to prevent.

In 1322 Edward took another army north, but the curses of dysentery and famine were themselves sufficient to turn it back, and to add to the insults its baggage train was captured near Rievaulx. A desperate establishment was reduced to imploring the Franciscans at Richmond to offer an Indulgence of forty days of relief from Purgatory to local people who would resist the Scots. Many of them must have felt that they were already in Purgatory. The Bruce died in 1329 and then the raiding lost momentum. However, the issues were not resolved and the destruction caused in and around the king's Haverah Park in about 1334 may have been a deliberate attempt to humiliate the English monarch and his ally, the pretender Edward Balliol. Park-breaking was a well established form of insult.

Modern visitors to pretty Knaresborough are seldom aware of the terrible fourteenth-century burning of the town by Scottish invaders.

Villagers in Hampsthwaite, Killinghall, Ripley, Clint and several other places will have seen the red glow illuminating the cloud base and have realised at once that it hung over Knaresborough. The king's castle had done nothing to protect them and at the very time when the garrison should have been preparing to face the aftermath of Bannockburn, in 1318, there had been a ludicrous squabble in which the constable had been obliged to break open and recapture his own castle from a supporter of the Earl of Lancaster. The king's authority was in tatters and he certainly did not appear to be greatly concerned for the fate of his humble subjects in the Dales. No sooner had Roger Damory begun the repairs to the castle inflicted by his own siege engines than the Scots appeared. They did not attempt to take the castle. Instead, they set about burning Knaresborough under the very noses of the garrison that was there, (partly) to defend it.

The town had its own defences, of a sort, comprising a surrounding earth bank and ditch which looped out from the castle moat. They proved worthless. People fled into the nearby woods and parks with their livestock, but the raiders followed and drove the stock away with them. When the flames shrank back into the embers it could be seen that about ⅞ of all the houses in the town had been burned down. Survivors hopped and gasped as they tip-toed among the smouldering charcoal of rafters and beams to pick among the wreckage for possessions. Some camped among the scorched orchards on the town bank; others spent the day walking to York and a few returned to their native villages in the Valley. Nobody came to Knaresborough market that Wednesday, or for some Wednesdays to follow. Religious houses were seldom spared in medieval warfare and St Robert's friary was a victim of the raid. The plight of the friars was recognised in a suspension of their taxes and a grant of the tithes from the ruined church at Pannal, which had also been plundered by the Scots.

Surrounding places, like Ripley, Fewston, Pateley Bridge and Hampsthwaite had been hit, yet in the very year that followed, adversity returned in the quite different guises of disease and cattle sickness. With their oxen falling sick and seldom recovering, villagers were compelled to adopt the novel action of harnessing whatever horses they could find – presumably nags – to the plough. The raiders could arrive in various forms and often without warning. The northern castles, Alnwick, Richmond, Middleham, Newcastle and the rest, might as well have been made of papier mâché for all the good that they did for the people of the Valley. Coming via the high trackways or down the lowland corridors, the raiders by-passed them at will. Whether the men at the threshold were merely rag-tag border reivers, the retainers of the fearsome Black Douglas, who gave the word 'blackmail' to the English language, or members of a royal army made little difference. The feudal English peasant had no martial traditions: he could not fight back.

Even after a hard day in the fields, sleep did not come easily. One lay on the hard pallet and listened: dog fox; screech owl; nightjar; stoat and rabbit, another owl – or was it? Whether to waken the family and scuttle away or try to sink into sleep for a while? Time after time and place after place the Scots would materialise among the familiar landmarks. With a few minutes of warning, the people of the villages and farmsteads would flee to the woods or otherwise they would be evicted from their homes at spear point. In either event, they would cower in the woods nearby, and after a while the acrid scent of burning thatch and wattle would come wafting through the trees. There would be no resistance. After a few hours one emerged, knowing that the home had gone but wondering about the church. The sty and henhouse would be empty, while as for the cattle and sheep, they were part of a bigger herd now, soon to be driven northbound across the windy upland pastures. Along with them might go any captured notable who seemed likely to be worth a ransom, so then the tenants would have another feudal burden to bear. People who were stretched to the limit to endure famine and diseases amongst themselves and their stock must have found these extra blows to be almost beyond endurance. The threat continued, though much diminished, until Flodden in 1513, when an English army, stiffened by Northumberland men and well-stocked with vengeful recruits from the Dales, turned the tide of war. The wars had been totally unnecessary and purely destructive. The price for Longshanks' bullying and lust to dominate, had been born by generations in the North, and here the ordinary people generally suffered far more than the nobles.

✳✳✳✳✳✳✳✳✳✳✳✳✳✳✳✳✳✳✳

Alice was talking over the hearth with old Tom, the badger. This was not the animal that she knew as a 'pate', but an itinerant dealer in farm produce. There was no impropriety, for John, her husband, had been driven in by the interminable rain and was sitting in the corner, splitting hazel rods with a billhook. His eyes had gone and he was as much a danger to himself as to the rods. Tom was saying that he had sold some eggs to a merchant out Nun Monkton way a few days ago, and *he* had said that there had been a great dying down south. Alice leant forward and stirred the black pot of lentils, oats and beans, as well as some chunks of rabbit from you-know-where. (They had become more frisky and rather less feeble.) 'Well', she, said, 'there was always a great dying somewhere'. It might be the bloody flux, or famine, or a murrain among the cattle. 'We're all gay keen to meet us mekker', she said, crooking the youngest in her arm.

Then Tom mentioned that he had dropped by to look at the new houses going up in Knaresborough, had stopped a couple of nights with his nephew in Nidd and then crossed over to have one of his ponies shoed in Hampsthwaite. Oh, but the river was high, still! He often thought he'd be safer staying at home. Alice looked for some platters, took a handful of sand from a pail and reached out into the rain for some long grass. With these she scoured the soiled surfaces (apart from the cracks that had opened after the wood was turned and which were now packed with residues of dozens of meals). She ladled out three helpings. John, who was offended that he had got the tree butt to sit on while Tom had got the three-legged stool, worked his gums in silence. He always ate outdoors on the grass when he could and hated the gloom and fug of the house, which, along with so many others, he regarded more as a refuge from unfriendly weather than as a home.

At least all the rain had encouraged the grass and now, with a little window of sunshine in prospect, the women had joined the line of scythes. Alice swung her scythe with great deliberation, though not with the effortless fluency of the well-practised men. She was not going to risk her ankles or those of her neighbour for a few bundles of grass, so soon she and Maud were left a few paces behind the men. Maud chattered incessantly and it was easier to nod from time to time than to pay much attention. But Alice began to take notice when Maud mentioned rumours of a Pestilence in places a few miles downstream. Then she said that old Tom was dead. They had found him on the roadside, all blackened, spotty and covered with boils and with his ponies gasping for water nearby. He was taken into the farmstead but he was cursing and oozing blood and it was a mercy when he died. What was more, his own nephew in Nidd had just been taken badly. And him that did smithing at Hampsthwaite, he was badly, too. Alice stopped swinging her scythe; she did not need to listen any more. She leant on a hedgerow tree and the pounding of her heart seemed to pass through her and resonate in the trunk. There was a gap in the line ahead and dear old John was leaning forward on the shaft of his scythe and coughing. She thought of her child.

※※※※※※※※※※※※※※※

The Black Death arrived in Dorset in 1348 and spread swiftly northwards. At the time its cause was not known, although divine intervention or else a corruption of the air were popular suspects. In modern times, it was identified as bubonic plague, a disease carried by rat fleas, which would abandon their conventional hosts when they died and their bodies turned cold, and would then transfer to any humans who might be available. Most, recently, however, the nature of the Black Death has again come under scrutiny. It has been seen that the symptoms described by medieval contemporaries do not seem particularly close to those of bubonic plague and the rat-spread disease does not appear to have that terrible virulence associated with the Black Death. Now it is argued that the epidemic, whatever it was, must have spread directly from person to person with immense speed and potency. Rat packs would not want to traverse the country at rates of 2 miles per day, which is what the plague achieved. An early outbreak of ebola might explain the internal haemorrhaging often described, though the illness could have originated in livestock and have crossed the species divide. Various animal epidemics existed at this same time. A viral explanation seems likely, and a virus with a long incubation period would allow the illness to obtain the very high rates of infection that occurred. The real Black Death agent could have become extinct, or yet be surviving in some colony and waiting to return.

Mentions of the impact of the Black Death on the Valley and its surroundings are largely confined to records of the death of priests there. These seem to accord with the national fatality rate of more than a third to almost one half of the population. This was a continent-wide catastrophe and we can fill in details with some confidence from contemporary writers. Giovanni Boccaccio (1313-1375) experienced the disease's assault on Florence in 1348, when he thought that 96,000 citizens were killed. In 1350 he wrote his celebrated *Decameron*, a risqué collection of tales set in a rural mansion where nobles had gathered to escape the plague. He described how the disease began with the appearance of egg-shaped swellings, sometimes as large as apples, which would spread over the body:

> The disease at this point began to take on the qualities of a deadly sickness, and the body would be covered with dark and livid spots, which would appear in great numbers on the arms, the thighs and other parts of the body; some were large and widely spaced while some were small and bunched together ... These were certain indications of coming death.

He reported that the plague seemed to be passed by contact and associations between people:

> Of this my own eyes had one day, among others, experienced in this way: to wit, that the rags of a poor man who had died of the plague, being cast out into the public way, two hogs came upon them and having first, after their wont, rooted among them with their snouts, took them into their mouths and tossed them about their jaws; then, in a little while, after turning round and round, they both, as if they had taken poison, fell down dead ...

If there really was a transmission of infection between species, the death of the hogs would have taken longer than the 'little while' that Boccaccio mentioned, but he does demonstrate awareness that infection by contact was suspected. Many people were aware that isolation was the safest strategy. Indeed, Boccaccio reported that the plague gave rise to feelings of guilt and caused people to flee from one another. Those who thought they might be infected were distraught in the knowledge that they might have conveyed it to their loved ones, while any friend or stranger one encountered might be carrying the lethal infection.

In some places the structure of society was undermined when priests refused to attend the dying and administer the last rites, while lawyers might not draw up or witness wills. In their desperation and terror, people cast about for explanations and scapegoats. Had the epidemic been caused by foul humours or a planetary conjunction? Was it a form of divine retribution, or might the Jews be to blame? Some people prayed to God, while others indulged in gluttony, believing that they should feast as well as they could before the plague carried them away, too. Boccaccio reported that some people sought survival by shutting themselves away and enjoying fine meats and wines. Some fled the death-ridden streets of the towns, and in so doing exported the Pestilence into the countryside. (In normal times it was the country people who went into the towns to die, for the higher mortality rates in medieval towns, like York, meant that they had continually to be replenished by the influx of people from their surroundings.)

❀❀❀❀❀❀❀❀❀❀❀❀❀❀❀

The tavern in Clint was a glum, if not a sober, place. The room was half empty and the customers there were seeking to spread apart rather than to gather in the usual convivial huddles. The innkeeper was gloomy about the loss of almost half his customers, though some survivors were doing all they could to make up the lost takings. The most earnest of them were those who had been present at the deaths of their families and best friends. You could recognise them from their guilt-ridden expressions and the way they drank steadily and determinedly with lowered eyes until eventually they slumped silently across the board. Those who talked did so, half-shouting, from safer but unusual distances.

    The fuller from Killinghall said that he had seen it all coming. People in the Valley had been sinning in more ways that he could mention. They had tempted the Lord and the Lord had said 'No more!' Could there ever be a plainer proof of the wickedness of mankind and the power of the Almighty? There were plenty of warnings in the Bible – he knew that was so because he knew someone that could read it. The gravedigger, who had staggered across from Ripley, caked with earth, exhausted but driven by a monstrous thirst, disagreed. How could it be, he asked, that the Almighty would reap so many priests and other monks and so many very good people if He was exacting His vengeance on the sinners? Why, his very own rector has just been carried off, and a more Godly soul one might never meet. The keeper's servant from Brimham deer park had an answer for this. Lowering his voice theatrically as though his masters might be listening, he announced that everyone knew that the Cistercians, Benedictines and the rest of them were as corrupt as could be. Look how fat some of them were; you did not get like that by abstaining. Where in the Bible did it say that abbots should hunt all day and feast all night? Who pocketed all the Indulgences? How many people might they name who had 'celibate' clerks, including abbots and priors, for fathers? Go on, how many Clarksons, Abbots, Priors and Bishops could they name?

He sat back with a contemptuous gesture that challenged anyone to disagree (and indeed, everybody present could name a Clarkson or two and even an Austin and a Monk). The itinerant turner, driven in by the rain had from the coppice, agreed that the established orders were riddled with corruption, but the friars, he claimed, were quite different. They were not too proud to preach to ordinary folk and they didn't even own the places in which they lived. You could get more hellfire and devil-smiting in an hour from a friar than any rector could utter in a lifetime. 'Do you know Bob Friar?' the cheeky keeper interjected, but nobody was really in a mood for jokes or banter. Of course, the dialogue went nowhere and the descent into drunkenness was the only common denominator. In its final phases the Jews were invoked as culprits and then someone speculated that lepers might be to blame, though nobody could quite work out how. A more relevant topic would have concerned which of the company would contract the plague through visiting the tavern that day.

As they divided at the tavern door, each found his sorrowful way home through the drizzle and across countryside in chaos. In some fields the rows of scythes or sickles could still be seen, but now the rows were shorter, ragged and saw-toothed as survivors shunned the close company of their workmates. Nobody had an ankle slashed that summer. A few farm tools were left where their users had sunk down- valuable equipment that nobody bothered to steal. Occasionally, widows could be seen with small children tugging at their skirts as they tried to keep up a tenancy after the death of a spouse. Perhaps the hard toil helped to divert their thoughts from the possibility that they and the children were already condemned to follow. Other holdings were completely derelict and abandoned to bloated cattle or thirst-craved horses. And all the while, stray dogs from the plague-struck homes were padding the lanes, obscenely sleek and better fed than they had ever been before. A sickly smell hovered over the Valley, such a smell as would not be known again until 1954, when myxomatosis filled the warrens, ditches, fields and briar patches with countless thousands of rabbit corpses. The plague pits near the churches were the main sources of the stench, though some farmsteads, scattered cottages and ditches played their part.

❋❋❋❋❋❋❋❋❋❋❋❋❋❋❋❋❋

The people that one passed, and who stepped aside with suspicious glances, were trying to cope with the horror in different ways. Some, who had seen half their friends and all their close relatives die horribly in blood and filth after three days of intense suffering and degradation, moved around dazed and unable to comprehend the magnitude of the disaster. A few refused to accept what had happened and adopted a reverse set of emotions. They were seen joking, dancing and singing, for which they were sometimes made to pay. Some, confronting what seemed like the inevitability of their own demise, turned to extreme forms of hedonism. Others, who had been devout all their lives renounced a God that could inflict such wanton evil, though others, still, anticipating the flagellants on the continent, became intensely devout and guilt-stricken, and sought for ways to punish themselves to atone for the wickedness of their kind. Very few people emerged from the ordeal with their integrity enhanced. The commonest emotion amongst those who survived was an intense sense of personal culpability. It was compounded partly of feelings that they were unworthy to have survived in the face of such suffering and partly of awe for a deity that could inflict such extremes of suffering upon poor sinners. Those who felt this way might not turn to the church, for its mission seemed discredited by its failure to affect the course of events. Instead, they craved personal encounters with the God that, without explanation, had overlooked the harvest of their own souls.

There were others, just a few, who tried to direct the course of events during the plague years. In 1350, having slaughtered around four people out of every ten, the Pestilence vanished as swiftly as it had come. But it returned again many times that century, taking away children, survivors, townspeople and villagers. It would still erupt in Shakespeare's England, cause terror in Pepys' London, and it was still a lingering presence in the time of Daniel Defoe. Ripley had been just a corner of a backwater, though it was lucky to survive being completely assimilated in the empire of Fountains Abbey after Thomas de Ripley bequeathed estates at Godwinscales to the monks in the 1230s. About eighteen years before the plague arrived, a Thomas of a very different kind appeared on the scene, when an ambitious outsider, Thomas Ingilby, married Edeline Thweng, the local heiress. Two years before the plague, Thomas became an advocate; at the time it arrived in Dorset he was a Member of Parliament for Yorkshire, while his efforts through the years when the Black Death was scything down the population, made him a Judge of Assize in 1351. A decade later, he became a Justice of the King's Bench, and before his death in 1369, he was knighted. His tomb effigy in Ripley Church shows him in this guise: moustached and in plate armour with a hood of mail beneath his helmet and Edeline at his side. He survived the first storm of the plague and its various revisita-

The new church that the Ingilbys built at Ripley using rubble and timber work from the recently renovated church by the pagan springs.

tions, like the awful one of 1361, which came at about the time that Thomas seems to have gained the adjacent manor, at Nidd.

It is quite plain that Thomas did not allow the convergence of catastrophes to deflect him from his driving legal and dynastic ambitions. When the establishment that he served was seeing the institutions of society perish with the onslaught of plague, Thomas seized Ripley and dragged it into the latest and last phase of feudal control. He became sufficiently prominent to court and win the favour of Edward III, thereby furthering his ambitions to join the ranks of the landed aristocracy. Obtaining a right, in 1356, to hunt small game on his scattered demesne lands at Amotherby, Flask, Hutton Wandesley and Ripley helped this purpose, though some other changes were of more of a commercial and modernising nature. From the king, he gained the right in 1357 to hold a market at Ripley on Mondays plus a three-day feast around the day of the Assumption of the Blessed Virgin. Possibly the plague reaper caught up with Thomas in the end, for both he and his rector at Ripley, Joseph Mauleverer, died about 1369, during the third major return of the Black Death.

Sir Thomas passed on the genes of unswerving ambition to his successors. The second Sir Thomas continued the plans to reshape Ripley as an Ingilby Manor;

perhaps much of what was undertaken was done to assert the domination of the de Ingilby dynasty over what had been backwater territory. The old church, bracketed by pagan springs though fairly recently rebuilt, was dismantled and the current church came into being, incorporating the stone, the penitential cross and the rood screen from its predecessor. The fresh bones of the old Sir Thomas and Edeline were removed and reinstalled in the new church, as may those of rector Joseph have been. Perhaps the grandest creation was the village of Ripley itself, set out to a 'Y'-shaped plan in the vicinity of the old manor house and new church. Whether it was created at the time of gaining the market, or around 1390 when the church was shifted and rebuilt, or around 1414 when the third Sir Thomas was reorganising his demesne lands, is uncertain. However, we can be sure that far-reaching changes to the local system of roads and tracks were needed in order to connect the new village to the local system. In turn, the new roads cut across existing fields so that tenancy and farming arrangements had to be re-cast.

There may well have been an even greater change. While researching Ripley in the late-1990s, I discovered the site of the substantial deserted medieval village of

The gatehouse of the fortified manor at Ripley, built by Sir John Ingilby in 1434-57, a time of civil disorder and plague.

Owlcotes on the north-western margins of the deer park. The pottery evidence suggested that Owlcotes declined about the time that Ripley was created. Did Sir Thomas I or Sir Thomas II take advantage of the disruption and disorder caused by the plague to replace a straggling 'traditional' village standing beyond the close view of the manor house with a new, 'modern', chartered settlement placed right under the eyes of its lord? If not, why should Owlcotes, however plague-struck it might have been, not have been rebuilt and repopulated where it stood, as happened so often elsewhere? The early Ingilbys seem to have been determined to impose their modernising, dynasty-building wishes on the landscape and overcome the most daunting of challenges. I suspect that they made the decision to herd people from an old and probably plague-weakened place – and perhaps from some hamlets and farmsteads, too – and to settle them in new Ripley, standing as it did on a 'green field' (actually, largely a ploughland) site.

During the plague years, people in the Valley reacted very differently to the tribulations that they were compelled to witness. Although they did not know it, the mass of survivors stood to benefit. They had paid for society's inability to adjust human numbers to environmental resources with the blood and suffering of those they held dear. As the fourteenth century passed into history, those still alive opened their lifes' windows on a much brighter prospect. It was true that epidemics of plague and other diseases could still roll across the country, but for the first time in generations, numbers of people had reached some kind of equilibrium with their setting. There was space to move, room to turn. In this respect, we should envy them.

CHAPTER 9

FILLING THE SPACES

(1380 – 1536)

Flap, slap; flap, slap; flap, slap; flap … Ralph suddenly became aware of the sound of his sandals on the floor tiles and he paused. He looked around: nobody there. So he spread out his arms in his coarse, whitish habit and did a little jig step: flapetty-slap. Then he realised just how quiet it all was when he stood still. The year was 1380, and Ralph, now intrigued by the silence, mentally reeled-off the names of his fellow monks at Fountains, tapping-out their names on his finger tips to be sure. Thirty-three of them; thirty-four counting himself. Next the *conversi* or lay brethren: his fingers were sufficient – there were just ten of them now. His eyes roamed the vastness of the vaulted cellar. Then he remembered that there were documents in the abbey archives that recorded how, in 1150, Fountains had sent out no less than ninety-one monks from the community to colonise new abbey sites: six of them in England, and even one in Norway. He also remembered learning that, at the start of the thirteenth century, Fountains had supported more than fifty monks and a great work force of more than 200 lay brethren. My, what a great buzzing and bustle there must have been then! What couldn't you have done with 200 or so *conversi* at your bidding!

Now, the frater, dorter and rear dorter of the lay brethren (where they respectively fed, slept and studied, and had their lavatory) were vast, echoing halls, like barracks abandoned by the battalion or wards in a declining hospital. Still, the *cellarium*, more than 100 paces long, was an ordered jumble of produce, though less tightly stacked than before. The wains full of wool, packed by hired shepherds and tenants, still rolled in from the abbey lodges and granges in Nidderdale, Wharfedale and beyond. The foreign buyers were less in evidence, but the hamlets, villages and market towns of the Dales were now almost bursting with fullers, spinners, weavers and tailors – all buyers for the abbey fleeces.

The bells still toned and donged their commands, like barrel-built drill sergeants of bronze. As before, people hurried, unquestioning, to do their bidding. The community still functioned and lived by the letter (rather more than the spirit) of the Cistercian rule. And yet, life had a hollow, echoing quality. It was like being alone at market or wearing clothes that were many sizes too big.

He knelt facing the altar in the nave of the enormous church. Dreamy sun-shafts created buff galaxies as they lit up the dust specks that hung in the morning air, while the sun's full glare brightened the cloister outside, to the right. His mind began to wander, though several times he hauled it back (it did this too often and Ralph was concerned that it was a more serious sin than the confessor maintained). There! It was off again. Or perhaps it was not sinful to think about why the abbey was declining. Maybe not if it spawned ideas to put things right? Had not the saints and founders thrived on adversity? Doubtless they had, but life was not really adverse at Fountains. In truth, for survivors it was rather comfy, and might the problem lie there?

The Scottish raids had not helped. The activities of key granges, like Kilnsey and Malham, had been disrupted and valuable property was destroyed. But an abbey was more than a commercial enterprise and harm done to the balance sheet could not explain the withering of vocations. Certainly, the plague had hit the religious houses as hard as it had struck the villages – numbers of recruits were bound to be down. (His mind slipped back across two decades to the ghastly scenes of dying in the infirmary. They had fresh, running water, a well-stocked herb garden, knowledge of medicine gleaned from throughout the civilised world and not a morsel of rat-infested thatch, but still the brothers had dropped like white, infected leaves.) But then surely such an awesome exposition of divine anger should have brought intending monks and lay brethren thronging to the gates? They were not there.

There was something that you could sense when you left the abbey on some errand or other. A lack of respect. Heads turned away. Scandalous remarks about drinking and wenching and impudent enquiries about which of his parks the Abbot was hunting in today – these were what one overheard. People did not respect the monks and they no longer felt constrained by their masters to hide their feelings. Meanwhile, those masters were no longer enriching the great abbeys with endowments. Instead, if at all, they were investing for the future of their souls in chantry and guild chapels in the parish churches. Then there were the friars, out on the street corners and cutthroat alleys among the drunkards, preaching salvation and damnation to the filthy masses – and themselves paupers like the poorest among them. Ralph shuddered and sought to purify his mind with imaginings of Kilnsey and Malham, both heavy with the silence of fresh-fallen snow. There were no footprints in this snow.

❋❋❋❋❋❋❋❋❋❋❋❋❋❋❋❋

Thomas and Margaret inhaled the real fresh air. At last, it was thought
to be plague-free and they sucked their chests full of the sweet spring
vapours. The birdsong was very loud this year. The pewits were rolling
on bluff, barge-bowed wings, when their calls seemed to spill out like
wine from a tipping vessel. But the axes were quiet. The great assailant
of woodland in the Valley, Henry Arkel (whose name survives in Hark
Hill Nook in Clint), had perished. His time had passed. The clearings
had come to a halt and the living countryside sang and strutted with
relief. Behind them stood their home – yes, with some stone footings,
reused beams and a wealth of reed thatch it was becoming more a home
than a shelter. The floors were strewn with rushes, the door had a simple
clanky sort of lock and they had even thought of putting in a ladder
and sleeping loft. People were beginning to talk: they'd be looking to
chimneys, dormers and glass i' t' windows next! Chatter they might, but it
was not as loud as before. To the left was a hovel that was emptied by the
plague and rotting. To the right, just the widow from a family of seven was
left, hanging on and growing what little she could.

   Thomas had been wondering why their lord put up with her – she paid
next to nothing in rent and worked just a corner of the tenancy. That was
when it hit him. If they kicked her out there would be another empty
house and no rent at all! And so Thomas then worked his way around the
community, letting it slip that if he did not get a better deal he was off to
find his fortune in York. What could the mighty lord do about that? He'd
never raise a force to drag him back. Also, he had heard of bondsmen who
would arrive in some new place and claim to be freemen. Well, who would
ask awkward questions on a manor that had some of its best land lying idle?
Threats and rumours that would once have seen Thomas castigated by the
manor court and probably set upon too, by cudgel-wielding agents of the
lord, now produced a remarkable dividend. His tenancy was increased by 30
acres to a virgate-a-half (around 45 acres/ 18ha) with no increase in rent; his
remaining obligations to work on the demesne were replaced with a largely
notional rent and all the business about rendering gifts of capons, honey
and so on was forgotten. Thomas had discovered the laws of supply and
demand. He thought of employing a drudge, some cottager, to help with
the enlarged holding – but who, now, need be a drudge?

❋❋❋❋❋❋❋❋❋❋❋❋❋❋❋❋

This was a very good age for the survivor. Of course, like life in general, it was most unjust. Nearly half the people had paid for humankind's sins against the environment with their lives. The other half, no more virtuous, revelled in all that remained (or did so if they could purge their minds of those terrible pictures): a countryside freed of its excessive human baggage. Once they had got over the intoxication of survival or the claws of bereavement, people began to discover the exhilaration of having some space around them. It was as though they had lived their earlier lives hunched and trapped. Gradually, it dawned upon them that they were not predestined to pursue narrow, cramped and totally predictable life journeys like their forbears. They had choices. They could choose what to be, burgesses in some town or countryfolk of some standing, while every manor in the land needed tenants, craftsmen and paid workers. If they stayed at home, they wanted better terms from the landlord. Feudalism had had its day. They did not want to be churls, serfs, bondsmen, bordars or villeins. They wanted to be farmers or weavers or dealers or ...

Local families of lesser gentry like the Beckwiths, or larger Forest of Knaresborough tenants like the Pulleyns and the Woods, began speculating in land and the resources of the countryside. In village after village, pushy little entrepreneurs emerged. Heavy with ambition, they began to see the traditional institutions that had helped the community weather oppression and disaster as impediments to their personal designs. Carve-up the common fields, abandon the complex regulations that had helped the old and feeble to have a share in affairs, let the strong lay hold on whatever they could ... yes, modern life has some very Tudor qualities.

Then, in hundreds of places throughout England, richer landlords who had endured enough of grasping and whingeing tenants, showed what real power was all about. They simply evicted the people and replaced them with sheep. The shepherd presiding from his hut over the stumps of a village and tramping with his dogs across pastures corrugated with the waves of old ploughland became common motifs of the English countryside. Our Valley was lucky. Sheep and people were accustomed to co-existing here and so there was not the tumult of eviction that happened to the east, in the Vale and on the Wolds. The period running through to the close of the Middle Ages was a dangerous one. Its echoes could be heard in the Valley. At West Tanfield, close to the centres of prehistoric worship in Wensleydale, eight (remaining?) houses were pulled down and 400 acres of village land were enclosed in the years just before 1517.

Haughtiness still had its outlets. Deer parks continued to be rammed into the countryside, though the Ingilbys do seem to have bought up tenancies rather than evicting the occupants of their Tudor park at Ripley. The old institutions, whether aristocratic or ecclesiastical, were not always revered. In 1529, a dozen poachers burst into a deer park in the Valley. This was not a remote reserve with a feeble and ineffectual owner. The park was Haya, on the edge of Knaresborough, and its owner was the king – as fearsome a monarch as ever lived. They came with bows and greyhounds and they killed two deer, then a four-year-old buck and then one of two years, as well as injuring two or three more bucks, which afterwards died. The leader of this ridiculously audacious foray was not some anonymous lout who might slink away from the scene. It was Sir John Robinson, the Vicar of Knaresborough.

The worlds of community and individualism were in collision. Confrontation, rage and indignation erupted to foul the air that the plague had cleared. Societies that had seemed to be bonded like rocks in concrete became divided. Old Walter's son, Henry, had lived at a time when the concrete had seemed secure against any chisel or pick, but his actions anticipated what was to come. He had cleared or 'assarted' some common land in Killinghall. The local elders and neighbours were apprehensive. He promised them that once his grain had been harvested, he would remove the dead hedges and throw the old common open to grazing by the village herd – just as it had been open since times before memory. In 1344, he broke his word. Now, he was leaning over his ramparts of thorn, purple-faced, and shouting that nobody would stop him from doing his best to support his family. Those on the other side called him a liar and a thief.

As the years rolled on, such confrontations became ever more frequent. In the process of compacting private holdings out of the myriad tenancies of common land, new roads and trackways were frequently created. They provided immense potential for trouble. In 1454, John Shutt and Stephen Parker were jostling to gain access ways in Kettlesing, where the communal fields were being dismantled. Shutt refused to let Parker have the way that he wanted, and Shutt claimed that Parker had run a dyke and fence across the traditional track that linked his farmstead and his fields. Salvation and opportunity were not bringing out the best in the Valley people.

Today, greed produces ugly, vacuous landscape. It was not always so. The privatisation of the common lands was accomplished by planting mile after mile of hedgerows to mark the new boundaries. These hedgerows were studded with thousand upon thousand of closely-spaced trees, which were pollarded to produce regular crops of fuel and browse. Oaks were preferred, with some elms, ashes on the sweeter soils and a few fruit trees, too. As the hedgerows and trees matured, they became defining features of the Nidderdale landscape. When William Grainge was writing in 1871, I estimate that there were many more hedgerows still extant and about seven or eight times as many ancient trees. This is what he saw in the fields by Elton Bank in Birstwith, where the fields:

The old hedge has gone, but these hedgerow trees in Clint still survive.

… present some splendid specimens of oak timber – some of them old, pollarded, knotty, 'gnarled and unwedgeable' patriarchs of the old forest; others, young tall and straight, have grown up in their shelter, and indicate a soil suitable for the sustenation of the monarch of the British woods. One oak felled in the spring of 1867, presented a perfectly straight trunk of fifty-one feet in length … on the left of the road leading to Hampsthwaite, is another remarkable tree of the oak species … Its trunk is gnarled and knotted in a most singular manner. It is evidently of great age- a genuine relic of the old forest day.

The myth that the surviving old tees are relics of the hunting Forest persists. In fact they are hedgerow trees that were planted in Tudor through to Stuart times as the common countryside was sliced up. For centuries they gave the Valley landscape its personality. In townships like Clint, Ripley, Hampsthwaite and Birstwith, they still do. Now, the last are near the ends of their lifespans and they cannot do so for much longer. We extol countryide that has reached the fag-end of its existence. Imagine how it must have looked in their pomp!

An old hedge and hedgerow trees at Birstwith.

While individual ambitions stalked the old commons, the depleted monastic communities were unable to man the many outposts of their empires. Since there had, for some time, been an unspoken consensus that the granges and lodges were really there to produce income for the abbey, it seemed sensible to lease them out and have them worked by lay servants. Times were less favourable to the feudal landlords, though the countryside did fill quite quickly in the two centuries after the Black Death. In reorganising their affairs, the monks were not going to part with a morsel more than they could, and rigorous conditions were imposed to protect trees and other resources. Leases were favoured by both lay and monastic landlords: they made it easier to get rid of leaseholders when their agreements expired.

In 1536, at the very end of the Middle Ages, Abbot Marmaduke Bradley, who would surrender Fountains to the king three years later, leased land from the grange and lodges at Pott to Richard Atkinson. The stringent conditions had been explained and anyway, they were already bywords in the Valley. Richard would pay 16s per annum, part of this at Whitsun and part at Martinmas. He would keep ten of the abbey cows, two heifers and two yearlings throughout the year at his own cost. He would also deliver each year to the abbey cheese house 13st. 4lb (around 84kg) of cheese and 6st. 8lb (around 42kg) of quality butter. If he did not deliver the full quota, he must pay 8*d* for every missing stone of cheese and 12*d* for each missing stone of butter. As well as the stated 'presents' he would deliver five stirks or yearling cattle from the abbey's cows each year, and would be fined 4*s* for each one not delivered. He would keep a flock of three 'long hundreds' (360) of the abbey sheep on the grange pastures and would pay out rent for a cow pasture called 'Cowe Rake'. He would be responsible for maintaining all houses, hedges, walls, ditches drains and other 'defences' and would surrender the tenement to the abbot when the lease expired. Next, the clerk explained to him that he must not fell any significant woodland without sanction. The section as it was read out was in language that we, today, can almost understand. He was allowed the legal:

> fellynge of holling bowes and other bruchwode at seasonable tyme of yere callyd brusyng for pastour of cattell, and also oke bowes, not tymber, for ther fewell and making of fensez ...

> '... felling of holly boughs [probably in designated hollins] and other brushwood at the suitable time of year, known as "browse" for the pasturing of cattle, and also oak boughs, not heavy oak timber, for their use as fuel and making of fences...'

Should Richard enter any agreement to sublet the holding, he would face forfeiture. He could, however, on the day of his death, name his chosen son as his inheritor and the widow and the heir could occupy the holding for twenty years. Richard gulped deeply as he made his mark. He had pledged a great deal of hard work and incurred a crushing set of obligations. His expectations were far less certain.

Often, the abbey also demanded privileged rights of access and game conservation measures. Thus, when Robert Hardcastle and his son William leased a quarter of the grange at Dacre from Abbot Marmaduke Huby in 1516, the same restrictions on timber were imposed and the Fountains community retained the right to pasture their own livestock in the woods, according to 'ancient custom usual there'. In 1524, the same abbot let land at Thorpe Underwood to Francis Man and Peter, his son, and demanded such ...'*peions*' [pigeons?] as were taken at every flight within the manor to be delivered to the abbot and convent or their deputy and demanded that Francis and Peter should keep to the abbot and convent's use and profit, 'wild bores, dere, heronsewies, shovelardes [shoveller ducks], fesandes, partriches as other fowles and beistes of waraunt breeding within the manor and are not to allow them to be destroyed...'

Most of the grand old trees of Nidderdale are survivors of Tudor and Elizabethan hedge-planting.

The strict and thoroughgoing nature of the leases may have been a worry for the leaseholders, but they give us some useful insights about the use of woods in Nidderdale. The ancient wooded commons were fast disappearing and the rising demands for fuel were being met from the expanding 'springs' or coppice woods. These produced a stronger and more reliable flow of production, though they were vulnerable to browsing in the first few years after felling. When William Scaife and his wife, Elizabeth, leased a holding from the abbey at Braisty Woods in 1518, they agreed not to suffer any of their cattle to enter the coppices or springs, '… durynge the years of fence tyme of the same, that shulde in eny wyse be hurtfull to them or eny of theme and all the heigies [hedges] of the seid sprynge[coppice] maide and to be maide …' Nor would they make 'wilfull waste' by felling the woods for their cattle and would only take sufficient timber for fencing and hedging.

Fence time lasted for around seven years, during which tenants were generally responsible for maintaining the stock-proof fences or dead hedges around each coppiced compartment of a wood. A number of the leases reveal the special significance accorded to holly in the Valley, where thornless foliage from the tops of trees was cut and stored as winter fodder. When Richard and Elizabeth Jackson leased an abbey holding in 1526, its hollins was treated as a separate item leased for 12*d* on top of the 16*s* they paid for their tenement. Leaf fodder from woods and hedgerow trees was very important; at Warsill Grange, Peter and Agnes Smyth were required to feed the abbey cattle on hay, oak leaves and holly browse. Virtually all the agreements distinguished between unlicensed felling, which was strictly forbidden, and the taking of holly boughs, brushwood and the soft branches ('greenhews' or 'watter bowes') of oak. A few leaseholders were shouldered with responsibilities for bringing poachers and trespassers caught in the woods to the abbey courts at venues like Brimham.

The *cellarium* where the produce of Fountains' far-flung estates was stored.

The High Street at Pateley Bridge, running down to the river crossing that gave the townlet its importance.

Pateley Bridge, now less of a distant country cousin of the villages lower down the Dale, had grown since gaining its Tuesday market in 1320, about the same time that the parochial chapel was built on the steep hillside. At some point, the village would slip down from its perch around St Mary's church to be near the bridge on the Nidd that was its geographical trump card. The place where the ancient track from Grassington and the Wharfedale hill country came hurtling to its junction with roads leading down the Valley and up to its head was something of a divide. Downstream lay the leased farmsteads in many kinds of ownerships where cattle munched and browsed in the shady pastures, though above, the world of the grange was almost universal. Where once lay brethren had shuddered when yelping wolves closed in on a hind, now quotas and rents were the common causes of concern.

Sheep were more abundant here, though this was not entirely sheep country by any means, and Lofthouse and Bouthwaite both supported large cattle herds in the mid-fifteenth century. Across these pastures, milk was being converted into cheese and butter for delivery to the abbey. There were even some favoured patches of arable land where a little horse fodder, barley for brewing and stews or oats for gruel might be grown. Some pastures were reserved for cattle. Beasts were driven down in autumn from the fells, while upland commons, like the old winter cattle parks, had probably been used in this way since prehistoric times. Valley pastures became the sheltered abodes of wintering flocks, which huddled in their hollows before heading for the more nutritious pastures of the limestone fells in the spring. Byland had withdrawn its monastic herds from the Valley and its granges were being sub-divided between lay tenants, while Fountains' flocks were very much smaller than before the Black Death. Most of the sheep seen on a ramble in Upper Nidderdale towards the close of the Middle Ages were in flocks of tens and twenties and were kept by leaseholders or else were modest perks enjoyed by lay grange-keepers. There were still some larger flocks in the care of shepherds hired by the abbey. The picture had become complicated. In 1529 Richard Thakwray was the keeper of Brimham deer park, though by this time it was only functioning as an estate farm. He lived in the old park lodge and as well as keeping the abbot's cattle he could feed three of his own and could keep another cow at the abbot's discretion for a rent of 3s 4d. He could graze thirty of his own sheep with the abbey flock and also keep a horse in the park, but he was held responsible for overseeing the land and could sell no wood or grazing without permission.

Once, the granges had been worked by lay brethren, who delivered the produce to the parent abbey. Next, the abbeys tended to install laymen as keepers in charge of granges, lodges and other portions of granges. These people were the servants of the owning abbey and were paid in wages of a portion of the production and often allowed to keep their own livestock alongside the abbey stock in their care. Then the keepers of abbey holdings were expected to deliver quotas of produce, like cheese, butter and livestock. Finally, some granges became more simple tenancies not unlike some farms today, with the occupant paying a rent in cash, though the Dissolution intervened before this system made much headway in the Valley. In a sense, the granges did not disappear. Rather, they frequently evolved into lay settlements and visitors to such places in Upper Nidderdale today might never imagine the monastic origins of the settlements.

As history tweaked and nudged the patterns, times came when the great strings of pack horses and the pitching carts delivering fleeces to the cellarer were seldom seen. Badgers would no longer fall asleep against roadside trees as they waited for the lay brethren to drive a seemingly endless flock past. In their places came nags all burdened with butter walking in the cool shade of evening or the early morn and groaning carts that hauled cheese by the stone into the abbey compound. (How welcome it was, we cannot say, though in later times, Nidderdale cheese was not considered gourmet fare.) Meanwhile the exotic merchant, snuggling in furs with his eloquent gestures, silks and coin chest was replaced by the gruff Yorkshire weavers and clothiers, who may have driven rather stiffer bargains. Of more lasting consequence for the landscape was the fact that, where once there had been a grange peopled by a monk and a few lay brethren, later a farm would often grow around the nucleus of the old monastic buildings. It might wither away, remain a farmstead or grow into a hamlet, like Bouthwaite or a small village, like Lofthouse or Ramsgill. Without the small villages, hamlets and farmsteads that are descended from monastic granges and lodges, Upper Nidderdale would be a desert.

It was in the period after the plague that the industrial character of the Valley became more clearly articulated. Earlier industries, like fulling and the forging of spurs and missiles, had existed and the Valley did have some lead and iron, woods for fuel and a supply of water-power that was more reliable than those of the dry, limestone Dales. On the other hand, it was still a backwater that lacked the craft guild machinery of the bigger cities and was poorly connected to the world beyond.

✻✻✻✻✻✻✻✻✻✻✻✻✻✻✻

The laden wagons in the convoy from the Greenhow lead mines had come down the hill into Bewerley with such scarcely restrained impetus that they had threatened to overrun their draught oxen. One driver claimed that the tip of his brake pole was still smouldering when they reached the river. They did not use the newish bridge at Pateley, but continued along the south bank to the smelter perched on the hillock in Guisecliff Wood. There, amongst the coppices and wood kilns that fed its great hunger, it caught the freshening breeze swooping down the Valley from the north-west. The blast of air turned the fuel from red to yellow and white. Lead was needed for church roofing, water tanks, coffins and the like, but there was not much demand for it in the Valley. The molten lead was cast into ingots and the ox wagons came back into play.

Firstly, there was the Nidd to cross, and this was done right away at a ford appropriately called 'Lead Wath' (later preserved on a map of 1611). The oxen did not like to feel the cold water washing around their hocks. They feared the invisible riverbed might delve into potholes, while crocodile warnings were sounding in ancient corners of their brains. Through their yokes and harness they felt the plank-built wheels scraping and sliding on the loose shingle and smooth rocks. Pricked and lashed, they bawled for the mercy that never came – and then the wagons were pitching and rising at the far shore. Then they rolled along ancient tracks and monastic rights of way with the drivers, peering at the world

The church at Ramsgill was only built in 1842, but Ramsgill was the main grange on the Nidderdale estates of Byland Abbey and the ruins of the grange chapel are incorporated in the churchyard wall.

though sweat and flies, longing for showers to slake the dust. When the rain did come, it came in sheets. Wheels slipped into ruts and revolved ineffectually. Mud-plastered waggoners tossed rubble into the wheel-traps and pressed their shoulders to the splintered rims. When they reached the Roman road at Ripley, conditions should have improved. It was market day; the waggoners all got drunk and some of them brawled with local Foresters.

The next day, they followed the Old Road to Boroughbridge, the town on the Ure that had replaced ancient Aldborough, nearby. It had been set out to a disciplined grid-like plan to the south of a new bridge that was built around 1145. Within twenty years, it had rocketed to borough status, while Aldborough, its parent, sank to become a humdrum village spread across the buried grandeur of the Roman town. At Boroughbridge they had access to the river transport network and goods could sail to York or pass right out on the mouth of the Humber on salty, pot-bellied coasters optimistically bound for Europe's sea and river-ports. From Greenhow to Lincoln, London or Rochester, there was scarcely an hour's worth of secure and comfortable travel.

❊❊❊❊❊❊❊❊❊❊❊❊❊❊❊❊

At Ripley, up above on the Thornton Beck and below on the Nidd, the Valley supported several fulling mills. Some were fairly primitive affairs: walk mills, where the fullers thickened the cloth by trampling on it in the dew or in a beck. Such a mill gave its name to Walk Mill Ing, an old meadow lying by the outlet of the landscaped lake and former mill pond at Ripley. Further upstream, one later developed at Bishop Thornton. Once fulled or dyed, the woollen cloth was stretched on the hooks of tenters to dry. These drying frames gave their names to various fields in the Valley, and to Tenter Hill, just to the east of the original church and green at Pateley Bridge. After the times of fulling and dyeing, lots of little fields in the Valley must have looked like schooners with their topgallants set, all ready to sail away with the next gust.

In the decades following the plague (if not before) a cottage industry of scattered weaving households became well established throughout the Valley, complementing the urban concentrations of woollen manufacture at Ripon and Knaresborough. They introduced the practice of multiple occupations that became common in most places where the land was not rich enough to support populations by farming alone. Shuttles, carding gear and looms became almost as familiar in farmsteads as cheese presses and meat hooks. As the medieval period

Just below the farmstead, the track used by the lead trains approached the ford on the Nidd known as 'Lead Wath'.

drew towards its close, 'customer weavers' appeared; they were mainly cottagers who took the wool or the yarns spun in the farming households and turned them into cloth. Around this time, another kind of textile joined the woollen kersey and broadcloth being produced in the Valley: linen. Hemp and flax were grown locally in the sixteenth century and their presence in the Valley was announced by the pervasive stench from the 'retting ponds', where the harvested plants were placed to rot, leaving just the fibres behind.

The end of the Middle Ages is defined by the end of the monasteries. Over the centuries, the Fountains and Byland had lost integrity, but their presence was buried deep in the heart of the communities and countryside. What they lacked in prestige, they gained in patronage. Let us take the example of Sir Ninian Markynfelde's servant, Thomas Kay. In 1520 Thomas took the post of keeper in Fountains' home deer park. His wages were 26s 8d in cash per annum. He could also take meat and drink for himself and his servant in the abbey hall whenever they were in the vicinity and would receive three gallons of the best ale and three of the next best every week. He was also entitled to three loaves of the best convent bread and three of the second best every week, while every day his hounds would have two grey loaves. He could pasture four cattle and their calves, a horse or mare and two pigs in the park and could gather firewood.

Every year, he would have a new jacket and could keep a shoulder of every deer slain in the park. He also got the occupation of a farm lying within 4-5 miles of the monastery yielding 20s 8d per annum. Once a servant, he now had a servant of his own. Thomas may well have skipped with joy on learning these terms, but without the abbeys, such deals could not be found. The popularity of the uprising in the North against the Dissolution that is known as the Pilgrimage of Grace should not surprise us. The monks were well-known and deeply estab-lished. As such, they were much preferred to the colonisation of abbey estates by the avaricious strangers from the South who were widely expected to pillage a defenceless North.

As the Middle Ages came, contentiously, to a close, the Valley had the qual-ities of a well-fitting shoe. It had been shaped and shaped again to meet the needs of its occupiers. Villages were taking root and markets were busy enough. The local gaps created by the plague had mostly been filled, and if there was a deficiency it concerned churches, with a community far removed from their church at Hampsthwaite building a chapel at Thornthwaite in 1402 and Bishop Thornton gaining a chapel later in that century. We have reached a point in our story when any surviving Nidderdale natives of today could be released into the Valley and, though they would see things that were strange and different, they would not get lost. A traveller today who retraced the course of the old lead wagons bound for Boroughbridge would traverse ancient landscapes; the men

Boroughbridge, Aldborough's medieval successor, was set out to a gridiron plan, so that it is a place of rectangular blocks and right-angled intersections.

who drove those wagons were traversing countrysides that were already ancient. Sometimes, a traveller in late-Tudor times would have had his nose offended by the hemp retting ponds and perhaps some farmyard and graveyard smells as well. It is hard to imagine that he would have seen a single passage of ugly country-side anywhere. Away from the commons, the broad vistas were usually hidden by stout, well maintained hedgerows. To travel was to experience a succession of intimate country cameos: the pollards standing above thistle and nettle patches that were all a-flutter with myriad butterflies; salmon shooting rapids in reverse in rivers flanked by meadows that throbbed to the notes of corncrakes; or slopes banded with rye, barley and oats decorated by a brilliant confetti pattern of wild-flowers. Herbicides, pesticides, mechanisation, planning and other great advances have taken care of most of this.

CHAPTER 10

THE SAFETY OF SHADOWS

(1536 – *c*. 1700)

1537. They heard it quite distinctly at the head of the Valley. It was sudden, somewhere between a 'crack' and a 'thud' and it set the crows milling around. Jervaulx Abbey, on the other side of Masham, had been blown up with gunpowder. Abbot Adam Sedbergh, who had, perhaps wrongly, been implicated in the Pilgrimage of Grace the year before, had been betrayed by one of his own monks and sentenced to die at Tyburn. The recriminations slashed across the ranks of monastic leadership, for the Abbot of Fountains, a former Abbot of Rievaulx and the Prior of Bridlington had been amongst the other victims.

Almost two centuries earlier, the Black Death had given communities, great and small, a new chance to live in comfort and harmony. Instead, their leaders had created a new purgatory in which nobody could feel safe. The more powerful and well-educated a person, the greater his or her complicity in this was likely to be. The fears that were born in the hearts and minds of people became the fuel for intolerance, persecution, war, terror and torture. (Again, Tudor times have so many resonances with today.)

The North was, for all the lost trust and disillusionment, monastic territory. Though the Pilgrimage began in Lincolnshire, Yorkshire soon became its powerhouse. The region was still so heavily dependent on its monastic communities, diminished though they were. The Austin canons shared their churches; the nuns of various brands provided education for the well-born girls; the monks orchestrated the conditions of tenancies and appointed laymen to attractive posts; numerous houses provided priests for parish churches; and the surnames of the monks, like Sedbergh's betrayer, Ninian Staveley, frequently revealed their origins in local villages.

People in Yorkshire realised that the Dissolution would create a vacuum in northern society, and the aftermath of Henry's divorce threw their fears into focus. The London lawyers and merchants with capital to speculate were not figments of northern paranoia. Northern folk recognised that the eviction of the monks from their estates would throw open gates for the deeply distrusted southerners and give them ample opportunities to trade in northern lands and lives. So it was that in 1536, on 11 October, pilgrims from Nidderdale joined with their neighbours from the territory around Masham to defend their old church. They marched up the birch-clad gorge of Birk Gill to Coverham Abbey and then 3 miles further, to the old Neville stronghold of Middleham. They carried torches and set beacons blazing which, it was hoped, would ignite the flames of rebellion in upper Wensleydale and Swaledale, too. However, with most of Yorkshire taken by rebel armies under Robert Aske of Aughton, the insurgents foolishly negotiated at Doncaster and were promised a parliament at York. They believed the Duke of Norfolk's pledges and so they tore off their badges of the Five Wounds of Christ and disbanded. Soon, they were betrayed as a purge of monks was instituted and the monastic world was ripped apart. The wretched North was placed under the jurisdiction of a Council of the North, which imposed oppression and alien interests and values upon it for a century.

Yorkshire was left with a fiercely Catholic capital, York, and a largely Catholic and insecure aristocracy. Almost a generation later, the Catholic Mary Queen of Scots, seemed to offer some hope. In 1569, and for the last time, northerners rose up to fight for the North. They may not have known of the distant occasion when their ancestors marched under the banners of the northern earls, Edwin and Morcar. Some will have had forbears at Flodden Moor, though in the Wars of the Roses, the northern lands had been split between the Lancastrian Percys and Cliffords and the Yorkist Nevilles. Now, the Percies and Nevilles were united. Their northern subjects took up their badges, wearing the half moon for the Percys and the dun bull for the Nevilles. Their revolt collapsed and its leaders were exiled. Countless northerners would fight for England or for Britain, but the days of the North, proud and militant, had ended. The revolutionary flame flickered until 1605, and the Guy Fawkes plot. A little later, the Civil War showed Yorkshire to be as divided as most other parts of the kingdom.

This evil war brushed closer to the Valley than it did to most backwaters. There was fighting at Ripon in 1643, and Prince Rupert's army arrived at Knaresborough on 30 July 1644. The prince had terrorised Puritan Lancashire and was marching from Skipton to York with orders to relieve the city and to engage a Scottish and Parliamentary army. He by-passed a force blocking the road at Long Marston by sweeping to the north-east, crossing the Ure at Boroughbridge and then descending on the northern capital. The armies met at Marston Moor, outside York, and within two hours more than 4,000 Royalists were killed, outnumbering the Allied dead by more than 10 to 1. There is a local legend of a skirmish with retreating Royalists who were caught on the Old Road at Ripley. It was said to have left sixty corpses that were buried on Kiln Green at the end of Ripley Wood. 'Dockens' or dock plants growing there until quite recently were claimed to have blood red leaves as a result.

Lest history should seem to be some meaninglessly remote entity, let me quote from John Thorpe, who wrote a history of Ripley in 1866. He mentioned a local man who had died just before 1820, and whose grandfather had held Cromwell's horse during his alarming descent on the village. He wrote:

> As an evidence of the salubrity of the locality, it may be stated that many of its inhabitants have lived to an extreme old age, and one village patriarch, well known to the author when a boy, attained the advanced period of 104 years. This venerable man appeared to have belonged to a family famous for longevity, for the writer has heard him relate a story of his grandfather having seen Cromwell on his visit to Ripley, and holding the General's horse. He died some time previous to 1820.

Cromwell certainly did come to Ripley. Sir William Ingilby (1594-1652) was staunch both as a Catholic and a Royalist, and in the summer of 1644 he raised a troop of horses from the Ripley locality and joined the effort to raise the siege of York. It is said that his sister, Jane, accompanied him as a trooper in full armour. However it was Cromwell rather than the Sir William who arrived in Ripley on the evening of the battle. As a cavalry general under the Earl of Manchester, he will have been pursuing the routed Royalists. Jane is also reputed to have returned, and to have given the general a frosty welcome, only allowing him to sleep in the castle when he permitted her to retain her pistols – or so the story goes. Cromwell is said to have ordered Royalist prisoners to be shot against the walls of the gatehouse and church. A very competent local historian warns me that the pockmarks in the stone that are said to be the legacy of the musket balls used may be produced by natural processes, though if so, these processes do tend to have produced most pits at around chest height. The Ingilby family relationship with Cromwell left much to be desired, for in Knaresborough the general's troops captured the Ingilby family treasure chest, which was en route for safekeeping with the loyal garrison in York.

Until the Reformation, Valley people had simple choices. The old paganism had withered and amounted to no more than a few superstitions. Folk could be devout Catholics, or they could pretend to be such – that was the range of choices on offer. This was a good arrangement insofar as it left little scope for disagreement. Now, a spectrum of incompatible doctrines and organisations vied for congregants. King, Pope, bishops, covenants and consciences were locked in strife. Faith and fear crept hand in hand through the darkness of human intolerance. Even those who calculatingly espoused the establishment credo could never know that this would not be tomorrow's heresy.

The Valley was a microcosm of the wider world of splitting faiths. It had not been a region, like many in the south or Midlands, where the church, manor and congregation were tightly grouped together. It had very few 'typical' villages, like Ripley and Hampsthwaite, but even these had sprawling parishes. Priests, vicars and curates, some from distant foundations, rambled their territories in dread of the times when a bank-bursting, bridge-busting river, a cloudburst or a blizzard would keep them apart from their hearth or warming house. Some had set off from places like Ripley and Hampsthwaite; others had come farther, from Ripon or Kirkby Malzeard, or perhaps from the grange chapels at Brimham or Ramsgill. Even before the Reformation and the factionalism that followed, organised worship in the Valley had a ramshackle character that owed more to ancient ecclesiastical history than to current needs.

Pockmarks in the stone suggest that Royalist prisoners were executed against the walls at the east end of Ripley church.

For some time after the Reformation, the local Valley communities tended, not surprisingly, to take their religious lead from their masters – and the greater families remained loyal to the Roman church. For such people, living in a backwater had its advantages and Protestant zealots tended to be attracted to the bigger fish in the bigger pools. Leading families like the Ingilbys and the Yorkes, and lesser gentry like the Trappes of Nidd and Swaleses of Clint, controlled churches and/or estates and decided whether to renew leases as well as often presiding over manor courts. Also, their networks of marriage gave them influence over the lesser families like the Pulleyns and the Thackwrays, some of which their people had married into.

A new breed of hooded figure could be glimpsed slipping into the hedgerow shadows of a moonlit lane. They were not footpads or poachers, but fugitive priests. At least three of them, either from the Valley or caught in it, were executed, and those who sheltered them could meet similar fates. Protestant fanatics trailed them with all the obsessive tenacity of later bounty-hunters. Fear was forever at their side and they took fear to every house they entered, yet still the doors were opened to them. When all in the village was dark and still, they might rap gently on the diamond panes at the back of the hall, then slip inside without a light escaping or a word of greeting being exchanged. Damp, chilled and probably lousy, the priest might wash and borrow a robe before sharing a meal with his noble hosts. The latter, unconfessed, had waited his arrival with mixed anxieties.

There, the priest might stay for a few days, like an incubating virus, standing back from any windows until the loyal local tenants were exposed to his treasonable and potentially lethal doctrines on the supremacy and infallibility of the Pope, the status of saints and martyrs and the subordination of kings and queens. Those he convinced, he might simultaneously sentence to persecution and destitution – who knew? If disloyal villagers were thought to be active or if the agents of the High Commission were in the area, the Jesuit or local-born priest might be secreted for long periods in a cramped and ill-appointed priest hole (I recall that one of my first assignments as a cub reporter in 1962 was to cover the discovery of a priest hole in Ripley Castle, one which had been forgotten and overlooked since the persecutions).

❋❋❋❋❋❋❋❋❋❋❋❋❋❋❋

It was some time in the 1580s and the middle-aged couple sat on their valuable joiner-made chairs, half facing each other, with their legs slanting towards the fire. The suspended sides of cured meat and the spit, chains, hooks and roasting gear gave the fireplace the air of a torturer's shop. Normally it was a jolly enough place. This was not an open hearth venting peat smoke by circuitous routes to a reeking smoke hole, like those in the old hovels. The end wall of the house was ascended by a new chimney stack that carried the smoke clean away. Straight out. The room was still open to the thatch, but the roof was made of sound reed bundles that might last as much as twenty years – much longer than the mice and sparrows that already infested it. Everything was very quiet until the door rattled. Was that the wind tugging at the latch or was there a priest out there? The man, frightened, found himself wishing that the threshold was bare, and then reproached himself for his sin in wishing away God's conduit; something more for confession, when he got the chance.

They did not need to glance at each other or to speak to know what each was thinking. Tomorrow they would be presented to the High Commission. What would they say? How should they reply when challenged to explain their three months of absence from church? Should they lie and plead illness and stupidity or ask for forgiveness? How hard they had worked to build-up their farm, and for so long! Could it be right to reward all this Christian diligence with forfeiture? What about their duties to their children? How badly they would fail as parents if they allowed the whole family to be turned out on the road. The boy and his young bride were relying on inheriting. Should they be made beggars with a baby to feed?

The penalties were well known. They could be fined £5 for every week that they continued their boycott of the establishment and its established church. Why, you could buy two or three really good milking cows or around twenty-five sheep for that. Fines of that size would quickly bleed a farming household to death. But then if you went against your conscience and told the men on the Commission the things that they wanted to hear … if you denied your own true God what price would you pay? Surely a prolonged term in Purgatory would be the best that such a sinner could hope for? They looked at each other and did not need to speak. There seemed no escape. If it came to be that way then the road would be bad, but Purgatory must be worse. They still feared their Maker even more than they feared the priest-slayer, Proctor.

✸✸✸✸✸✸✸✸✸✸✸✸✸✸✸✸✸✸✸✸✸✸✸✸✸

Our small Valley contained dozens and dozens of people who, if forced, would face any danger in order to uphold their beliefs and ideals. They may have been mistaken, but their integrity still shines like beacons. Yet what of their descendants? Is she one: bleating into her mobile phone from the voids of her mind as she drives past the strings of schoolchildren? Or him: leaning on the bar and proclaiming his hated of Muslims, the French or any other foreigners he has never met and whose civilisations he has not the wit to comprehend. Could she be a descendant? Her skin is grey and greasy from the Yankee junk food she wolfs while watching the TV greed channels about houses in Provence, designer labels, designer face lifts, purple kitchens with stars on their ceilings, snarling sports cars and drunken holidays in distant places, all of them eviscerated by the tourist industry. She thinks she may find happiness in any of these desires, not knowing that the barrenness of her spirit will follow her wherever she goes. If those genes of courage, integrity and community-mindedness are dead, their death was recent. I remember them displayed in the fitters who had tested the guns on Lancasters, the aircrew who had serviced the Halifaxes, the secretaries who had worked for the Air Ministry, under-fed and in threadbare frocks; Bert, whose war wounds would not heal; George, the P47 pilot; the ex-prisoner returning, shattered, from a Japanese POW camp, and so many more. Giants. Perhaps in the unsung carers, the best nurses and the uncomplaining sufferers we may find those genes surviving?

Given the precarious standing and vulnerability of the Valley gentry, it is remarkable that they retained control over their localities through the Tudor and Elizabethan repressions and then through the dangerous times of the Civil War. Much of English life had been transformed, but feudalism still maintained some powers. The manor courts still permeated rural life like the veins in a blue cheese. The Ingilbys, though lords of Ripley and various other places, were particularly vulnerable and yet they enforced a firm system of local justice. Sampson Ingilby (1569-1604) had been steward at Spoffoth Castle to the Percys, earls who were ardent Catholics and steeped in intrigue. A priest had been caught in Ripley Park in 1598 and executed, while Sir William Ingilby's son, Father Francis Ingilby, was captured and executed in York in 1586, after two years of furtive missionary work. Sir William (1546-1618) himself was arrested as a suspect in the Guy Fawkes plot and was lucky to be released. He had accommodated his brother-in-law, Robert Wynter, a leading conspirator, and furnished him with horses. There were many threads in the web that seemed to converge on Ripley. Nevertheless, the records show that the precariously perched family could still impose order on their neighbourhood.

The only possible, but unlikely, hint of defiance was reported in the manor court records of Ripley for April 1624, when the widow Katherine Scarlett was put in the mercy of the court for breaking hedges belonging to William Pulleyn in a bit of the glebe called 'Parsonflatt' ('Parson's Furlong') at Birthwaite.

William was the priest and came from a local family with many Catholic connections. This bond with the Ingilbys, however, did not give him immunity and in 1597, and again in 1615, he was before the court for failing to scour his ditches, including the churchyard ditch.

The activities of the court show us that, against the backdrop of religious uncertainty and persecution, the appetite for privatised land and common resources that had coloured the late Tudor years was still running strong:

October, 1648, John Flesher removed a boundary stone (soon he was at it again)

April, 1649, John Flesher removed a stone called *le bounder stone* between the lands of lord Vavasour and Scarow Moore [Scarah Moor]

Taking illegal enclosures or pillaging common resources were widespread:

October, 1621, William Steele carried *one wayne load of sande from Skarowe Moore*

April, 1636, *A paine laid that Margatett Stubb shall pull downe the fence in the parke land, and hange Yates* [gates] *in the same, that men may passe as they have done heretofore, … upon paine of iij s. iiijd* (c.17p)

April, 1648, William Reynardson did not pull down his encroachments at *le Newton Wath* [the ford on Newton Beck].

A remarkably high proportion of the cases judged by the manor court at Ripley concerned hedge-breaking. It might be that this reflected hostility to the enclosure of common land by those disadvantaged by it. However, some of the cases involved children and the carrying-off of hedge timber, so a fuel crisis cannot be ruled out.

April, 1628, Anthony Veritie caused his children to cut down wood in a close called *litle Chappellflat* [near the original church]

April, 1629, Thomas Kidd allowed his children to cut down and carry off wood, *in English twistinge* [loppings of browse?] *of oake and ashe*, from Ripley Park

April, 1629, Richard Dearlove broke a hedge at *Sorrowsikes* [beside the castle] and carried off a cart load of the same

October, 1648, Robert Mountaine broke an enclosure

April, 1649, Thomas Holdsworth cut down a tree called in English 'a Crabtree' in
    Robert Bransbye's hedge

This last one leaves various questions unanswered:

April, 1627, Robert Hodgson broke the hedge of a certain close called *Chappell
    Flatt* and placed the horse of Thomas Withes therein

Those who were not breaking the hedges of others seem, periodically, to have
been at the mercy of the court for not maintaining properly the ones that they
owned:

April, 1625, *William Reynardson shall make his fence well and sufficiently between Henry
    Douglas and him in the common peece before St Barnaby day next*

April 1627, *A paine laid that John Browne and Francis Launsdell shall cutt a peece of hedge
    alonge the street…*[to] *Ripon that men may passe with corne and hay over against
    Langbrookes before Candlemas next*

Other entries show the but modest successes enjoyed by the court in its attempt
to impose order on an awkward community. If taken alone, these entries would
suggest a feudal world little changed by the Reformation. In fact they show the
old dynasties effecting control in the most difficult of circumstances:

May, 1617, *A paine laid that Thomas Ingilbie, Miles Reynard, James Cuthbart, Reynard
    Wilson and all the reste of the tenantes within this manor shall repaire there partes of
    the common pindfold within the space of tenn dayes* [the pinfold was a pound for
    wandering livestock]

April, 1627, *A paine laid that all men who hath any parte of the watersuers* [drains] *of the
    back sides of Ripley shall scoure them before Whitsonday next or else for every severall
    default shall forfeit iijs iiijd* (c.17p)

May, 1650, *Leonard Campelshon shall scour his ditch between the churchyard and his
    orchards. Thomas Holdsworth shall repair his shop and his houses. Thomas Peareson
    shall repaire his houses and chimneys.*

These old records of misdemeanours bring the old village world to life. We can
picture the rural English as looking quite like the 'peasants' portrayed in early

Dutch paintings: rumbustious, quarrelsome, irresponsible, sometimes petty or even vindictive, but also bursting with vitality and character.

The stubbornness that was part of the Valley character was evident in the hundreds (albeit a minority of the total population), who simply refused to conform or to pretend to and in the names that appeared again and again on the lists of recusants, and who were heavily fined until their households faced poverty. The pressures increased when Parliament won the Civil War, though by this time the Protestant cause had become split by factionalism. After a short-lived veneer of Puritanism, the Valley indulged in the complexities and became a varied mosaic of beliefs. When Charles II was restored, in 1660, the ecclesiastical wheel of fortune turned again and the orthodox became the subversive. Anglican clergy and bishops returned to power and the Puritans were evicted. One cannot resist the image of an encounter on some dark Nidderdale lane between a Puritan dissenter and a Jesuit, each one furtively flitting between supporters. Would they have passed, unspeaking, on different sides of the track or else have exchanged awful grimaces and gestures of hate? Or might they have engaged in silent combat, each frightened that a grunt, crack, cry or gasp might attract outside attention?

The dissenters, Presbyterians, took root in the lofty fastnesses of Greenhow, in a young community hardened by the lead mining life and the struggle to eke out a farming existence in a place of the bleakest beauty that had but three seasons to its year. At the end of the seventeenth century, when official attitudes had mollified slightly, a house in the new village was converted into a meeting house.

The purest colours were added to the religious palate with the arrival, in that century, of the 'Quakers'. Their burning convictions apart, they were largely simple but stolid people, working hard in their farm and cottage economies. Though they were theological poles apart, the Quakers, like the early Cistercians long before, fitted very comfortably into the Valley. Both were attracted into austere, lonely and soulful places by the quest for spirituality and both arrived with great zeal that was later tempered by life's realities. The white monks, however, were rigidly marshalled and disciplined, while the Quakers or 'Seekers' spoke spontaneously when they thought they might have become conduits for a sacred truth.

Intolerance within the Protestant community remained rife; an impulse to enlighten an Anglican congregation at Pateley Bridge in 1654 was nearly the downfall of the Quaker Edward Haley. He was dragged out of the building and kicked so badly about the body and head that he almost died. A century later, Pateley's reception for unorthodox ideas had not greatly improved. In 1752, the Wharfedale weaver turned Methodist preacher Thomas Lee, was the victim of a mob that was encouraged by the local curate, James Pattison. Lee was stoned and splattered with mud on his arrival but, having a head wound dressed, he recovered and preached outside the village. During the following year, the mob dogged his footsteps and on one occasion he was dragged from his horse, badly beaten and rolled into an open sewer. When his wife came to tend to him, she, too, was attacked and beaten. Nevertheless, once bathed and changed, the redoubtable preacher rode to Greenhow and preached to a large Wesleyan congregation.

The early zeal and quiet intransigence of the Quakers marked them out for persecution and their renunciation of the militant aspects of statehood assured their victimisation (this was not confined to pre-industrial periods: the inspirational twentieth-century writer on the history and landscape of the Yorkshire Dales, Dr Arthur Raistrick, was interned for his Quaker pacifism). It took courage to join the Quaker ranks and take part in their illegal gatherings, but between Pateley Bridge and Killinghall numerous brave people could be found. Thomas Taylor had preached in Hartwith in the mid-seventeenth century and Hardcastle Garth became a little focus for the Friends. After the establishment offered a measure of toleration in 1689, licensed meeting houses were founded at Dacre and Hardcastle Garth, both with burial grounds, and soon in other townships, too. Several religious movements in the Valley began in purity, but that of the Seekers remained so. With its introspection and love for silence, this was never likely to be a religion with mass appeal. While Presbyterian meetings took place in Hartwith and Greenhow, it was Methodism, arriving in Nidderdale in the middle of the eighteenth century on the very eve of the Industrial Revolution, that could appeal to the diverse masses of mill and rural workers and all social groups from the middle class downwards.

The results of the sale of monastic lands, so feared by the pilgrims at the time of the Dissolution, in some places vindicated the alarms. The Byland estates were bought by Sir John Yorke, but though he had southern connections, his dynasty became rooted in Ramsgill and was aligned with the Catholic nobility of Nidderdale (and, along with middle-ranking gentry like the Nortons, he pursued a remorseless vendetta over hunting rights with the great Cliffords of Skipton Castle). The fate of the Fountains estates was more in line with popular predictions, the purchaser being the exceedingly rich London merchant, Sir Richard Gresham. A process of division and sub-division then followed, as the estates were fragmented, sold and sold on. By the time that the process had worked down the hierarchy, many tenants in the Valley were the owners of their own farms.

Were anyone to have been seeking a villain who would epitomise all the worst fears of the pilgrims they might have found him in Sir Stephen Proctor. He bought a large portion of the Fountains estates from Gresham in 1597 and proceeded building Fountains Hall. He then engaged in a number of disputes and lawsuits with other landowners and claimed ownership of the commons and lead mines of Bewerley. Members of the family were active in exploring new smelting technologies for lead and iron, but were mainly noted in the Valley for their remorseless persecution and betrayal of Catholics. Given the Catholic inclination of the other leading families, Fountains Hall can scarcely have been a hub for local social activity.

Now, as the seventeenth century advanced, the space and freedom that the Black Death had created had all but been consumed. There were more aspiring tenants than holdings and more households than homes. New homes were being built and old ones were being rebuilt. This was not the arrival of the Great Rebuilding that had transformed and renovated the villages of southern England in Tudor times. That would not really break on the Dales until the eighteenth century. Houses were being built in the Valley in traditional ways, but they were *better* houses.

****

Tom and his brother-in-law were wandering through a remnant of the ancient wood pasture, scrutinising each tree with care. There was a regulation that banned the taking of timber, other than browse and light poles, for fuel. However, there was an older rule that allowed tenants the right to take timber for house-building, and this is what they were seeking to do. One neglected pollard looked promising: it had a gently arcing bough, much thicker than a man's thigh, which maintained its smooth curve for a good eight cubits. Tom climbed up on Arthur's shoulders and the saw was passed up; after much sawing, sweating, bad language and expressions of contrition, the bough lay among the sparse tussocks, looking much bigger than it had when on the tree. There was no point in leading useless twigs and branches back home, so they lopped off the browse for the cattle and trimmed off all the side growth. The naked bough was then propped on some bulging tree roots and iron wedges were hammered in at intervals along the long side of the curve. Each tap on a wedge widened the split until, with a rasping groan, the bough split to form a mirrored pair of blades. They would form a gable end of the new house.

The house-builders sighed with relief to see the bough divide in the intended manner, but this was the easy part. The hard part would be to find three other blade-yielding boughs of very similar form. These blades would be arranged like a bridal arch at a wedding, to define the ends and three bays of the house. Back at the farm, they cornered the nag and slipped a halter over her head; she was taken out to the felling place and harnessed to drag the two blades back to the building site, their trailing

Pateley has an idyllic setting, though its population could sometimes be intolerant and cruel towards religions dissenters.

tips ploughing a double furrow through the dust. Then the search for the other curving boughs began. The tree-studded hedgerows that had gone up in the reigns of Henry and Elizabeth were too young to produce such massive timbers, but Tom recalled an old oak pollard growing on a woodbank that was more promising. Its neighbour produced another pair of blades and the final pair came from a stag-headed tree on an ancient boundary hedgerow.

   At the chosen site, some wain-loads of boulder rubble had been led in from the riverbed and from a derelict field wall. A few rough courses were set in a shallow trench and these would raise the oaken sill beams at the base of the house above the level of the damp rising from the ground, thus preserving the timbers. The timbers were smoothed with an adze and used green: seasoning took far too long. The village cartwright-cum-joiner was called in and he cut cross-halving joints at the apex of each pair of blades. Next, he drilled thumb-wide holes through the joints with his auger and then anchored the joints with wooden pegs driven through the holes. Now, each pair had the splayed form of a letter 'A', but with slightly convex sides. The feet of each A-frame were then set on large, flat-topped padstones placed in the wall rubble at the corners and the ends of the intended bays.

The next part was tricky, for the four pairs of linked blades had to be set upright like a tunnel of croquet hoops to form the basic structure of the house. Light timbers were nailed on to provide temporary supports and then the structure of the roof ridge beam, purlins, wall plates and windbraces were added to create a rigid framework of timber. Walls were formed of a wickerwork of woven coppice rods plastered with mud mixed with cattle dung and animal hair. (In some houses, the coursed rubble was raised to form a complete wall, though in many Valley dwellings, the timber framework would sooner or later be encased in grit rubble walling to conceal the timbers and give the illusion of a stone structure. The last few surviving timber-framed houses in the Valley stand undetected by passers by, inside their stone cases.)

In terms of roofing, there were various possibilities: ling from the moors, turf, slabs of fissile sandstone, grain straw or reeds. Reed beds at the river margins could be harvested and would produce a more durable thatch. In our case, however, the stackyard was bursting with wheat straw. In those days, the crop grew almost man-high, while hand-reaping meant that the straw was not battered by great mechanical cutters. Armfuls of straw were brushed straight and bundled together. Then they were secured to the thin laths that spanned the rafters of the new roof- and as extra bundles were added, these were pegged down with staples made from hazel rods from the coppices. Floors in the Valley were sometimes made from pounded shale rubble, with stone flags appearing in the better houses, though an earthen floor may have been given a dark smooth crust from applications of ox blood. Once complete, the floor was strewn with rushes, which could gather dirt and later be swept out and replaced. The work finished, Tom and his wife, Ellen, now had a modest house perfumed by fresh straw, bark and oak sap. It was at least partly a homemade home, but one suitable for a small tenant and better than most cottagers enjoyed.

✳✳✳✳✳✳✳✳✳✳✳✳✳✳✳✳✳✳✳✳✳✳✳✳

The houses that were being built in the Valley at the close of the Middle Ages and for a while after were essentially medieval in construction. They were generally somewhat bigger than the medieval prototypes and incorporated superior materials, as well as welcome innovations like chimney stacks and sleeping lofts. They were, in effect, intermediate between the medieval hovels and the stone-built products of the Great Rebuilding that were to come. The cruck-building technique, just described, was quite different from that used in the larger box-framed dwellings seen in most other parts of England and in local towns like Knaresborough and Ripon. People judged and measured their houses according to the number of crucks or post pairs they contained, for each cruck or 'crock' defined the end of a bay, so that a house of, say, five pairs of crucks, had four bays. In the first example given below, the distinction between pairs of posts and 'crockes' suggest a difference between larger, post built or 'box-framed' buildings and the lower-grade cruck houses.

A survey of houses in Clint and Scarah, made for the lord of the manor in 1635, provides details of the dwellings of this period. Francis Hey was one of the most substantial tenants, for he had:

> … *one howse of 7 pare of postse, with a kitchin, hall, 3 parlours, 4 chambers, I kilne [kiln], and steep fatt [vat], 1 othere chamber, 1 flower [floor? threshing floor?], 2 barnes, the one of 4 pare of postes, the other 2 pare of crockes, a little stable, and a swine cote [pigsty], some of these buylinges [buildings] have slate [i.e. sandstone flag roofs] and are in good repair, a garden paled [fenced] around.*
> *The whole tenement, all halfe valewe,* [Ingilby had consented to take his rent at half rate] *will amount unto £22.9s.0d.*

William Reynard was occupying a much more modest property in the cruck-built style. It is impossible to imagine how he could have lived on the agricultural production of his tiny holding. This is how he was listed:

> House with barn in the west end of 3 pairs of crocks, parlour chamber and oven house in good repair £1 12s.0d.
>
> *He holds 3a-2r-22p of land* [a little over a hectare]

He must have had some other source of income, and this makes us wonder about his relationship to William Raynardson, who also occupied a traditional house that still had a 'hall' as its main room, in medieval fashion. William Raynardson clearly had a second string to his bow – his smithy:

On[e] hall howse, a kitchin, 4 parlours, 4 chambers, one stable, one smithie, a barn and a kiln, all of crockes, in good repair, 6 aple trees.

£0.13s.4d

This must be the William Raynardson who we met earlier as a younger man in trouble with the manor court for his encroachments on the common, and then for his fencing of enclosed land. If his smithing took up a good proportion of his time, he may not have been a man to tangle with.

One name that catches the eye in this context is that of Christopher Loftus. There was a Lofthouse locality in Clint, where he lived, but the name indicates somebody who occupied a house with an elevated sleeping shelf or loft (it also produced the Lofthouse village name in Upper Nidderdale). This feature is not mentioned in the description of his house, though we are told that his oxhouse or byre needed to be thatched.

A minority of the houses were in need of re-thatching and there is a reference to the need to repair walls, as with Anthony Verity's abode, which was in '*…want of some thack and waleing*' or Widow Thomson's home, '*… decayed in walles and thack*'. These will have been walls of the old wattle and daub construction rather than of stone. There is also evidence that houses of the traditional cruck-framed type were still being built in 1635, for Edward Wells had '*… one howse latly buylded, of 2 pare of crockes*'. Other homes must have been standing so long that their great oak beams were rotting, for William Craven's post-built house had '*… the great tymberys in great decay…*'. We see that chimneys became commonplace in humble houses in the seventeenth century, for in 1650 Thomas Pearson had had his chimneys for long enough to be ordered to repair them by the manor court of Ripley.

A problem of the old timber-framed tradition concerned building houses of greater width. The limitations on the size of timbers meant that it was easy to add on extra bays and increase a building lengthwise *ad infinitum*, but one could not broaden it. Houses tended to increase by gaining new ranges or cross wings at right angles to the original, giving rise to 'L', 'E' or square 'C'-shaped plans. This appears to have been the case with Robert Bransby's house, roofed both in sand-stone and thatch, which seems to have terminated in a cross wing:

One howse and kitchin, 2 parlours, I buttry, 3 chambers of 4 paire of postes with a crose end, part slate and part thacked, in good repaire, a stable and laith [laithe=barn] *of crockes, a laith of crockes in Marle Pitt Close* [presumably by the old Abbot of Fountains' marl pits between Ripley and Nidd], *in good repaire, this is valued as demane* [demesne land]

In medieval England generally, a holding of a virgate or around 30 acres (about 12ha) was normal for the better-off families of villeins. Today, a farm of 30 acres in the Valley would scarcely be considered viable. In the early seventeenth century, Valley people were being dragged away from the old semi-sufficient farm lifestyles into more commercial conditions, and so larger farms were sought. Yet it is plain that in Clint and Scarah there were numerous tenants paying rents on holdings of 6 acres (about 2.4ha.) or less. They included at least four widows, but also workmen, and the only tenable conclusion is that we are encountering small holders with more than one occupation. William Raynardson, William Atkinson and John Ward all had smithing workshops and Ward's house contained another shop of some kind. Thomas Holdsworth also had a shop in his house as well as a kilnhouse and a small orchard. Several properties had apple orchards and there may have been some commercial cider-making going on.

Clear answers to our questions were provided by the inventories compiled when Valley people died, for until about 1740 inventories of a deceased person's goods, compiled by local assessors, accompanied their will. Probate inventories provide remarkable insights into the possessions of people of this time and how the contents of their houses were organised.

James Kilvington of Clint died in May 1678 and his clothes and the contents of his purse were valued at £1 16s. On his landholding he had nine cows and calves worth £34; four two-year-old beasts (cattle) worth £8; seven yearling calves worth £3; a mare, a 'nag' and a yearling foal, valued at £12; £2 worth of old hay; a 'stamp' of rye and a stamp of peas, with an acre of hard corn and an acre of ware corn worth £3 in his fields. When the assessors went into his main room or 'house' they found two tables and frames (these will have been like the trestle tables used at village shows today) worth 16s; three chairs, one form (a bench) and three buffet stools worth 6s. There was also a great mass of equipment associated with cheese-making, as well as the cooking and table gear: one cheese trough; four skeels (tubs); one flasket, and one cranweit (an iron pot stand, I believe), worth 7s; twelve shelves; forty-five milk bowls; five cheesevats and two sinks, worth £1 3s; three brass kettles; four pans; one chafing dish (warming pot); one ladle, and one candlestick, worth £1 10s. Then, arranged around the fire or hanging from the ceiling, were: two spits; one pair of racks; two pairs of tongs and two reckans (wall hooks), worth 4s; beef and bacon worth 7s, and twenty pieces of pewter, worth £1.

Adjoining the 'house' was a room recorded as a parlour, and this contained one cupboard; one ark (chest), and one table and frame, worth £1 10s; one bedstead with its bedding worth £3 3s; 34 yards of hemp and linen cloth worth £1 10s; two churns, four tubs, two barrels and one bottle, worth 5s. Next to the parlour was a room that was just recorded as a 'chamber' and this contained three beds and bedding, grouped with four cheeses that happened to be there in a valuation of £4 5s; there were also four pillowbears (pillowslips), five pairs of sheets and four napkins, worth £1 6s.

Finally, there was the 'house end', which must have been a barn linked to the end of the house, and this contained two ploughs; one harrow, and a yoke and team worth 15s; a cart and gear worth £2 and cushions and other 'husl' (household-ments), worth 10s. The total possessions were valued at £102 13s, though like many of his neighbours in the Valley, James had considerable borrowings, a debt of £16 10s as well as owing 1½ years of back rent to his landlord, amounting to £52 10s.

These inventories and wills are quite revealing; for example we know that modest homesteads in the Valley were being glazed in 1634 because Thomas Edeson of Whipley Moorside, near Ripley, left his son '… all the glass in the windows'. Multiple occupations had arrived and were making it possible for households to survive on tiny holdings and still to meet their rents. Most households were practising at least two out of farming/smallholding; woollen cloth weaving; linen weaving; and cheese-making. The emphasis varied from household to household, and the family of widower John Dixon, neighbours of the Edesons, inherited the following when John died and was buried at Ripley in 1634:

> To my son Thomas Dixon, one cow, colour red, one whie (young cow), colour black and crimule (?) headed (crumple-horned?), one cupboard, one bed, one arke, one table and brickes, one coffer. To my sons Thomas and John, 2 gimmer hogs (young ewes) equally between them; to my son John one coult (colt) of 2 years old, colour gray, one loom and all gear belonging it, some timber in the laithe at the hie (high?) house and one cloak lately made, colour blue; the residue to my son John and daughter Margaret, I make them my executors

> Witnesses: Thomas Thompson, John Raynard, Robert Joy, Edward Wells.

> Inventory: 4 cows £8.13s.4d.; 3 heifers, 1 bull, worth £4.13s.4d.; 4 stirks (yearling cattle), 1 calf worth £3.6s.8d.; 3 horses, worth £4.10s; 13 sheep, worth £2.10s.; hay, worth 10s.; 1 cart; 1 loom, 2 pairs great shears for cloth 5s.; 1 spinning wheel; 38 lea hemp and some wool 5s.6d.; 6 yds. Hemp cloth (linen); 4 yards linsy woolsey (a coarse mixed cloth), 3 quarters white hersey [no value given for these].

It is plain from the inventory that the Dixons were small farmers who were involved with all the spinning and weaving processes associated with linen or

This barn is one of the last remaining thatched buildings in the Valley. Some surviving houses with very steeply pitched roofs were designed to carry roofs of thatch. They could seldom support replacements in the form of local roofing flags, but when thin sheets of Welsh slate were brought in by the railway, their thatch will have been replaced.

hemp cloth and a variety of woollen cloths, from spinning to cutting the finished cloths. On the other hand, Christopher Joy of Clint, who died in 1624, and who may have been the father or uncle of the witness named above, appears only to have had a spinning wheel when he died in 1624.

Thomas Edison of Clint, who died in 1607, was listed as a yeoman and tanner. It is quite possible that he was associated with the 'bark house' site first commemorated in a field name recorded in 1523, *Barkhowsegarth*, lying by Ripley Beck and park. Oak bark was gathered and stored in these houses for use in the tanning industry. His will shows that he owned sufficient cattle and sheep to be regarded as a small farmer rather than a smallholder. As noted, his will also shows that he had left his windows to his son, Thomas, and these were probably the same windows that another Thomas had willed to *his* son. He also left to his daughter, Jane, 18 lb (8.2kg) of wool and a spinning wheel. When his known occupations are added up, we have: tanner; leatherworker (perhaps shoemaker), owning a handcart for the relevant gear; farmer; and spinner of woollen yarn. He may have done other things, too.

Such multiple occupations intensified the domestic chaos in times when rooms were yet to gain their specialist designations as bathrooms, bedrooms, sitting rooms and the like. It is only fair to remember that Valley people with four or five rooms in their houses, plus a lean-to barn against the lower gable end, were not so far removed from the medieval occupants of long-houses, where the only division was between the family and their milk cow or sheep. Still, it is plain from the inventories that the ubiquitous home brewing, which provided the only safe-ish drinking liquid; cheese-making, for home consumption or for sale; spinning and weaving, often for a variety of yarns and cloths, were dispersed around the home in near-random fashion.

Dairying was particularly likely to crop up in unexpected places, while in the Kilvington house the greatest concentration of beds was shared with four cheeses. William Hardcastle of Whipley Lane had a brandreth (cooking gridiron) and bakestone in his bedroom, though his namesake and close neighbour, who died three months later, seems to have moved his loom and all its gear into a 'working house'. Lest this should convey an illusion of orderliness, they shared the space with a cheese trough, cheese press and householdments that were, for whatever reasons, here rather than in the 'milk house' with the churn, vats and barrels. In William Shaw's house in Clint, in 1674, one room that contained a bed also housed seven pairs of wain and cart naves (hubs), some salt beef and a salted hog, amongst other things. He had a parlour that also contained a bed, as well as two churns, two tubs, an iron bakestone, a grate, a spinning wheel, and sundry other items.

It can safely be said that these Valley homes of the seventeenth century looked just about as unlike a Laura Ashley cottage interior as one can possibly imagine. Were we able to stay with one of these households, there would be no knowing who might come strolling through our 'bedroom' on their way to somewhere else, or what we might trip over when we got out of bed. Farming never ends at the farmhouse door, but in these cases, the multiple occupations and the essential home brewing, butchery and salting and dairying simply filled every house with piles of useful clutter. And if there was a loose consensus about the functions of milk houses and brew houses, anything could be found almost anywhere. (Having written this, there surely must be an error in the transcription that locates, '… *manure, reckon, 3 hens and 6 chickens with a total value of 6s.2d.*' in the *parlour* of William Coates' house at Burnt Yates?)

The chapel at the lead mining village of Greenhow Hill, where the miners' devotion to Methodism superseded an earlier Presbyterian tradition.

While new dwellings were appearing in most localities, there were winners and losers in the pattern of settlement. The medieval pioneering settlement of Birthwaite seems still to have endured early in the seventeenth century, for in May 1607 the Ripley manor court laid a 'pain', '... *that the inhabitantes of Birthwait shall appoynt which is the right course of the water which commeth of Birthwait Greene, and cause to rune down same*'. The drainage from the village green was a regular source of annoyance, and one can still recognise the ditch and green, the latter much diminished by lane widening. However, the little village seems to have perished during the decades that followed. Today, all we find are some very strongly developed house platform earthworks on the western side of the lane.

Elsewhere, there was growth. Early lead mining seems to have been a little-regulated process and the miners may have been part-timers who walked in across great distances, and they may have mined in slack farming seasons. As the easier veins were worked out, mining became more capital intensive and expensive drainage pumps became more important as the industry went underground. The industry became increasingly professional – and this involved the recruiting and settlement of a permanent workforce.

The origins of Greenhow Hill, which, reaching up to an altitude of 1,350ft (about 411m), claims to be the loftiest village in England, are found in a legal agreement of 1613, which was made in settlement of one of Sir Stephen Proctor's numerous disputes with his Nidderdale neighbours. It provided for the building of on-site cottages for lead miners, and these would have common rights of pasture for their livestock – and there would also be grazings provided for the draught oxen and horses employed by the mines. The resultant settlement is more reminiscent of a Celtic straggle than a planned English village. Its appearance was completely transformed in the 1980s, about a century after the decay of lead working in the Pennines, when the mainly dilapidated and redundant cottage/farmsteads were sold and experienced very thoroughgoing facelifts.

The medieval period was being left further and further behind. So, too, was its defining feature, the feudal system. People in the Valley were experiencing some new freedoms. The Roman religious monopoly had gone, and a selection of new religions was available. Meanwhile, the development of cottage industries and multiple occupations marked an end of the era of the feudal tenant, whose life was hidebound by the manorial calendar of work. However, freedom of choice brought persecution for those whose choices of worship did not coincide with those of the prevailing dynasty, and greater independence at work was bought at the price of a divorce from all the customs, checks, balances and safety nets of the caring feudal community. For those with families and consciences to support, life in the new, enlightened world would have been hard. Even so, anxieties that were endured in settings festooned with shimmering leaves, serenaded by birdsong and where the meadows, reed beds, lanes and coppices were ever a-twitch with wildlife, must have been so much easier to bear. There was not a household in the Valley that did not have both sanctuary and a wildlife sanctuary directly outside their door. On each little journey to work, shopping trip or errand the spirit was soothed and expanded by the input from the eyes and ears. Now, we need relaxation strategies to help us to recover from our trips.

CHAPTER 11

TWO STEPS TO TODAY

(1700 − *c.* 1850)

The Valley was stretched out like a slumbering hound. Soon it would twitch, stir, scratch and set off with the rest of the pack in a new direction. This trail of 'progress,' it was said, would lead away from discomforts and impositions, so following it seemed so right. Before progress vanished in its own vacuity, its followers would be stripped of their identities and the meaningfulness that made them whole people. Very few may have been able to see beyond the next improvement, pay-packet or profit and one cannot say how many knew the importance of the bond between people and land. Not many minds could discriminate between progress and change. So often, progress was simply something that somebody wanted to do for his or her own particular ends. Strangely, those who had the least, the squatters on the Forest commons, seemed to be far less wedded to progress than those with a few bags of copper, silver and gold to invest. How strange. Was there something that only these dolts and wastrels knew?

Progress, for those who sought it, involved improving the conditions for manufacturing. It also involved rationalising the rural population − which in turn involved getting rid of a great many of them and winkling most of the remainder out of their cottage workshops and installing them in mills.

All the opportunities and potential freedoms that the plagues of the fourteenth and fifteenth century had created had been squandered. Once again, the Valley contained more people than it could comfortably hold. Lords of manors agonised over whether to evict squatters from their commons or to take small rents from them and turn them into lawful tenants. The great Forest of Knaresborough remained extant for most of the eighteenth century, and its dusty, over-grazed, dung-hungry commons were magnets for a mass of wretches, who advanced from its margins like maggots on a rotting joint.

The countryside was burdened with landless households, and amongst the landless there was a minority of feckless and disorderly people, and within that minority, a much smaller minority of dangerous ruffians. However, we must realise that history was written by the haves, rather than by the have-nots. The accounts of the day emphasise the irresponsibility of the squatter and rural pauper. They do not point out that money could be made by getting rid of these people, and that the profit motive lay at the heart of the vilification of largely defenceless souls. This implication that poverty is in itself a sin permeates most of the commentaries, not least those of an official nature. This is what a *General View of the Agriculture of the West Riding* (the county boundaries shifted in 1974) recorded of our region in 1794:

> This waste [Forest common] in its open state yielded the inhabitants fuel, and pasturage for their sheep, horses, and stock of young cattle; and some opulent yeomanry profited exceedingly thereby; but to the necessitous cottager and indigent farmer, it was productive of more inconvenience than advantage – if not to themselves at least to the public at large, who were by that means deprived in a great measure of the exertions of the farmer, and the labour of the cottager and their families; for it afforded their families little milk, yet they would attempt to keep a horse and a flock of sheep. The first enabled them to stroll about the country in idleness, and the second, in the course of every three or four years, were so reduced by rot, and other diseases, that upon the whole they yielded no profit. ... [However, once they were deprived of the use of the common,] The poor cottager and his family exchanged their indolence for active industry, and obtained extravagant wages; and hundreds were induced to offer their labour from distant quarters....

Like much establishment propaganda, this is deceitful gobbledegook. The reader is invited to believe that commoners were inconvenienced because they were enabled to keep cows and produce some milk, though this little milk was enough, apparently, to purchase flocks and horses! Then they chose to go riding around while their sheep perished from foot rot (why not sell the sheep before they got the rot and buy some more?). These shiftless activities had prevented the cottagers from earning extravagant wages (though how could the wages remain extravagant with hundreds flocking to offer their labour? The hopeful masses would have driven wages down. Such wages had never existed). Having rendered hundreds of thousands homeless in England, people of a better sort needed palatable explanations for what they had done. These did not have to make much sense.

The environmental pressures were real enough. A map of the Forest of Knaresborough that was drawn in 1767 showed the commons stippled with a rash of encroachments that advanced on its edges or radiated from its villages and hamlets, with a cluster swarmed around the honeypot of Harrogate's developing medicinal wells. During the first half of the century, illegal encroachments on the common had been made at an average rate of about seven per year, and squatter cottages had been built at a rate of well over two per year. The establishment's response to this problem was to apply Parliamentary Enclosure, well established as a means of privatising common land elsewhere in England, to the Forest. Previous attempts had failed, and the marking of boundaries in 1767 and the launching of a proposal to enclose the Forest in the following year sent waves of alarm surging through the poorer communities. Protest meetings were held, but the complainers might as well have stayed at home. At last, the wealthy and the worthy had a tool that would prise the landless from their cottage perches.

Grainge, the antiquarian, may have been recording some persisting grudges when he wrote a century afterwards that:

> In 1770, an act was obtained to divide and inclose this extensive waste, and the powers thereof committed to no less than five commissioners, and three surveyors, all, or most of them unequal to the undertaking, from whom both delay and expense were incurred. After four years had elapsed, an amendment of this act became necessary, which was obtained in 1774. ... In 1775, the commissioners made out a description of their intended allotments, and in or about the year 1778, they executed their award.

This was a most unusual situation, for normally Enclosure operated on an individual parish basis (as it did in some neighbouring parishes) but here the entire Forest, containing about 25,000 square miles (about 65,000 sq.km) of commons alone, was the subject. The results, however, were as elsewhere. People were given compacted holdings that notionally equated to their shares in the lost commons, shared ploughlands and meadows. In effect, the cottagers and squatters without rights on the common received nothing and had to leave, while the smaller farmers were not properly compensated for all the bounties of the commons and often found the cost of the obligation to wall or hedge their new farms quite crippling. Those who had encroached on the common were given the chance to regularise their positions by leasing their lands from the Crown – but often survival was meshed into the lost commoning system, with its shares in turf for burning, bracken, for stock bedding, walling stone, sand, firewood, rabbits and so on. Harrogate got its 200 acres (81ha) of Stray at this time, still one of the finest spreads of green urban common to be found. Otherwise, those who benefited were the bigger landowners and substantial tenants who could meet the costs of Enclosure and take over the holdings of bankrupt neighbours.

The process may not have been just, but it was the single most important land-scape-shaping process for many parts of the Valley, especially for the more lofty places. Households who reckoned to have done well from Enclosure set out, con-fidently, to improve their newly consolidated farms. The fieldscape was now an orderly patchwork rather than a rag basket of holdings. Those rejoicing in their new, compacted holdings would often leave their village or hamlet communities to set up shop at the hubs of their farms. This launched a spate of house-build-ing to add to the frenzy of walling and hedge-planting occasioned by Enclosure. Moreover, the Commissioner's plan included new, rationalised country roads that darted like little grey needles to the Forest boundaries.

Much ink is spilt in ill-informed writing about Olde Worlde English country-side. In the Yorkshire Dales, many of the most evocative scenes are almost pure creations of the eighteenth century and of Parliamentary Enclosure: the geo-metrical field walls; the stone laithe houses; the neat but myopic Enclosure roads (seeing no further than the area boundary); and the straight walls that so cruelly slice the ancient common like sabre slashes across the faces of the poor. All human life is there. They may not be as old as the marketing managers in their offices might like, but there are no more areas of charismatic countryside in England than those created in the northern uplands in the decades around 1800. Those in charge of planning should set aside their phoney GIS computer programmes and learn properly to understand these real landscapes – and how to protect them.

✶✶✶✶✶✶✶✶✶✶✶✶✶✶✶✶✶✶✶✶✶✶✶✶

Nathaniel had his back to his home. It was both new and ramshackle, and at just nineteen he felt much the same. Inside, the baby was squalling and the cow was dry. Behind him laid several other small and technically illegal enclosures, each with its tatty homestead, mongrel farm dog and, apparently, squalling babes. In front, stretched the open acres of the commons, sprinkled like a poppy-seed bun, with cattle and sheep, with the odd horse here and there. In some parts of the Valley, organised communities jealously regulated the number of 'gates' to their common and so controlled the number of animals that each person with rights to the grazings could let in. Here, it was hard to persuade a penniless cottager that the extra sheep or two that he put on would cause much harm to the vast pastures. The washed-out look to the sward, myriad wild flowers, the puffs of dust raised by scampering beasts, the yellow speckling of ragwort and the threadbare, crumbling nature of the turf all told of overgrazing. Nathan looked out and saw the bracken where he could cut pig bedding and, further up, the peat beds where he got his fuel. The common might not look much but it promised survival, albeit survival of a deprived and miserable kind. It let you farm badly and hungrily for quite a long time.

Figures were moving across his field of view. Two strangers in tall hats. One had a cluster of hazel rods under his arm; the other carried poles and a measuring chain. While he gazed, they slowly moved across his field of view, gradually making triangles as they went. Surveyors. This was it, then. They were preparing the Enclosure of the Forest commons. When it was done, he knew there was no way he could afford to lease back his holding from the Crown. For a couple of years he was able to hang on by working in a walling gang, one of several that arrived with Enclosure, as they materialised boundaries for the new holdings. Mile upon mile of angular walls dropped a net-like maze across the old open horizons. Quarrying, digging foundation trenches, stringing lines, grabbing the right stones, fillings of stone chips, throughs, capstones, scuffed hands – then it was all done.

It was almost twenty years later. The child had died before she could be put to work and the wife was living at her sister's and earning coppers by carding wool. The medieval layout of Leeds was still recognisable, the main street, The Briggate, being crossed like a 'T' by The Headrow, the row of houses at the head of the vill. But there had been real changes. The mills had been increasing throughout the century and the coming of the Leeds and Liverpool canal and the building of canal warehouses around the time that the common was enclosed had accelerated the changes. Nathan was hobbling back to his room in borrowed clogs. His ancient farm boots were hanging around his neck by their laces. He could not afford to have them soled yet and if he left them in the rooming house then someone would steal them (there were tales of boots being stewed and eaten). He must get back: it was his turn to share part of the bed until the next shift arrived.

A fragment of an old song from his Valley days fluttered into his head:

Home, boys home,
Home I'd like to be.
Home far away in the North country,
Where the oak and the ash and the bonny rowan tree
Are all a-growing greener in my own country.

He recalled how the old farmers said 'rowan' as in 'mekkin' a gurt row' rather than as in 'rowing a bo-at'. He couldn't remember when he had last been close to a real tree. There were a few stunted, sooty ones in the toft hedges just over to the west of The Headrow, but not like the trees in the Valley.

Still under forty, he was an old man. Lint coated his lungs and made him wheeze. He was more than half deaf from the clatter of the frames and the crashing of the shuttles, which rent the mill air like cannonballs over a battlefield. Things would not get any better. Sad, broken people were streaming into the town in ever-greater numbers – drawn to work at Gott's, Marshall's and many other mushrooming mills. Labour was cheap; Enclosure might have been made for the mill-owner. It brought the village, pleading, to his door. The housing was shameful and getting worse and the first slums of back-to-backs would soon spring up beside their stinking alleys.

A bit from a tattered news sheet was skipping over the mess in the gutter. He snatched at it. There was a list of sailings. One fancy name caught his eye, the *Orlando*, due to sail from Liverpool under Capt. James Laughton bound for New York: an American merchant ship, brand new, it said, a 3-master of 300 tons. He could almost sniff the sea air and feel the salt spray purifying his lungs. How clean the sea must be! How much longer would he have to work to earn their fares? He looked down at the Leeds & Liverpool Canal and imagined following the black, sluggish water until it came to life again and turned silver and blue. Way away to the west, he followed it in his mind, till it reached the spot where the *Orlando* was berthed. How much longer to work if he just crept away on his own …?

✳✳✳✳✳✳✳✳✳✳✳✳✳✳✳✳✳✳✳✳✳✳✳✳

The transformations of the Valley landscape wrought by Parliamentary Enclosure were profound, but the influence of the greater landowners was felt outside the Enclosed areas as well. It was in the eighteenth century that the last areas of ancient wood pasture, the tree-studded grazings that had covered so much of the Norman and earlier countryside, were swept away. In 1733, Sir John Ingilby sold to Ambrose Edwards Esq, a timber merchant of Durham:

> … one hundred and thirty oak trees which is now numbered and markt in thirteen parcels standing growing and being upon or within the Pasture belonging to the farm at [Scarah] Banks late in possession of Richard Lanbothaw as Tennant there … and also thirty oak trees more which is set out in three parcels standing growing and being in or within one plowing close and pasture joining to the Plowing Close …

Geometrical patterns of Parliamentary Enclosure fields overlay an Iron Age field network beside Blayshaw Gill.

For these 160 doubtless old and twisted pollards, Sir John received £350. This being wood pasture, its gnarled trees will have been of limited value as planks, but the oak bark was a significant resource of the tanning industry. Arrangements were made for barking the trees and for stacking the bark in a bark house. On these occasions, it was also thought important to clear up all the felling debris, so as to keep the ground dry and open for ploughing. Here, and in many other places, the last remnants of the most traditional areas of countryside were swiftly removed, never to appear again.

Many of the springs or coppices that had multiplied during the Middle Ages were still at work, though the demand for home-grown oak was declining. In the decades leading up to the First World War, numerous ancient woods in the Valley were coniferised. The old hardwoods were clear felled and the woods were replanted with conifers, which produced softwood timber for use around the estate, and with beeches. Beeches shaded out the under-storey and woods of mixed Scots pine/larch and beech were considered ideal for the mass extermination of pheasants that became a leading social activity on the larger estates.

The houses, too, were changing. The revamped, improved, and yet archaic long-houses described in the previous chapter were being superseded by stone-built laithe houses (meaning 'barn-houses'). The long-awaited Great Rebuilding broke across the Dales at the very time that Enclosure was transforming the fieldscapes.

The evolution of the laithe house is uncertain, though the design first appeared in a few of the more affluent farmsteads around 1650. The laithe house, two rooms deep and fully two storeys high, both taller and wider than the old post and cruck homesteads, provided favoured tenants and freeholders with housing of a style unimagined by earlier generations. More and more members of the rural farming classes aspired to occupy these stone farmhouses that shared their long roofs with a barn/byre that was otherwise separate.

The stone laithe houses set the norm for rural expectations until the 1870s. By then, farm houses were being built as freestanding buildings that were quite detached from their farm buildings. To prevent unpleasant seepages into the farmhouse, the barn or byre of the laithe house was placed on the downslope end of the building. Laithe houses typically echo the Georgian fashion for a symmetrical façade, though symmetrically organised rooms and windows can scarcely have been of much practical value in an agricultural household. These stone farmsteads are very numerous in the Valley; they housed families who had done tolerably well from Enclosure and who were taking over their new holdings, and they superseded generations of farmsteads/cottage workshops of antiquated design. Though built largely or partly by 'professional' journeyman builders (who were often also themselves farmers and dealers in livestock, land or property) the laithe houses were distinctive of the Dales and West Riding and, with their projecting 'kneelers' retaining the coping stones, walls of the local grit and sandstone flag roofs, they were the last creations of the vernacular building tradition.

A laithe house in the high country at Greenhow.

Industrialisation was about making profit and people could not profit if unable to shift their goods. For centuries, the Valley had timed its pulse to local roads that did not work very well and, sometimes, did not work at all. There had only ever been one properly engineered road, the Old Road of the Romans, and that had not really been maintained. It was still the main link between York and Lancashire, though there were various stretches where two small carts could not pass. Road repairs and bridges depended upon the generosity and civic consciousness of local people and institutions: a precarious dependence.

The kingdom had stumbled across a solution to such problems in the form of the turnpike, a well-built road financed by investors who recouped their investment and took their profits from tolls levied on road users. With the middle of the century just past and the Industrial Revolution about to break, an eruption of turnpike-building activity, sponsored by the local gentry and by the manufacturing interests of the rising or aspiring mill towns, transformed travel in the Valley, where packhorses had hitherto reigned almost supreme. In 1752, a turnpike linking Leeds, Harrogate and Ripon was driven across the commons of the Forest of Knaresborough to take advantage of the old bridge linking Killinghall and Ripley. Scarcely a year had passed before another turnpike, this time connecting Bradford, Harrogate and points beyond, linked to the first turnpike just before it descended the Valley side, heading northwards towards the bridge. In the middle years of this decade, the building of a turnpike, over-ambitiously, between Wetherby and Grassington via Knaresborough and Pateley Bridge, resulted in a turnpike that ran along the north side of the Valley and intersected the merged turnpike near Ripley.

The provision of new, commercial roads resulted in the closing of some useful old routes. When the Forest of Knaresborough was enclosed, a turnpike between Knaresborough and Skipton was created to replace the ancient salt-trading track that had traversed the commons. To prevent wily travellers from slipping around the ticket stalls, the lane still known as Chain Bar Lane was – yes – barred by a chain. The old track using stepping stones at Glasshouses was similarly closed.

✱✱✱✱✱✱✱✱✱✱✱✱✱✱✱✱✱✱✱✱✱✱✱

The practice of actually charging people to travel taxed the geographical ingenuity of the Valley people to the limit. Adam paused on the plateau edge just to the east of Burnt Yates. He and the old pit steward had loaded three packhorses with coal at the little pits at Birstwith. He had then backtracked to the rickety bridge on the old packhorse road between Fountains' former granges at Brimham and Kilnsey (the new pack horse bridge, New Bridge, would be built there in 1822), and had followed this medieval road up to the turnpike. He was caked in coal dust and sore after one of his German ponies slipped on the steep, cobbled track and fell on him. Now he was pondering: ½*d* per laden horse carrying coal. That made 1½*d*.

Ahead, by the Thornton Beck and on the western edge of Ripley township, stood the Scarah tollbooth. He might have been able to get around it by heading down Whipley Lane and emerging, uncharged, in Ripley market. However, that useful little byway had been closed by the turnpike trustees, otherwise he would have taken it in the first place. How about a cross-country diversion through the fields? This depended on finding gates in the right places and evading irate farmers. He supposed one could do a big loop round by Bishop Thornton, but that would use more energy than 1½*d*-worth of oats could replace, and probably land them on another turnpike. He just could not bring himself to ease the coins from his purse. He called at a farmstead, below. Would they like to buy some coal? No, they got all the turf they needed from the moor. And so, he headed grimly for destiny and the ticket window of Scarah tollbooth. With a degree of torment that only another Dalesman could imagine, he paid 1½*d* for walking down the new road. Worse, there was another booth on Nidd common. He wondered if the River Nidd was low enough for the ponies to walk around it, unobserved, below the bank on its shingle and boulders.

The Georgian era and bracketing decades witnessed the building of superior stone barns, like this one at Birstwith, with a cart access and distinctive projecting kneelers.

Little bridges, like this one at Thornthwaite, belonged to the era of the pack horse.

✳✳✳✳✳✳✳✳✳✳✳✳✳✳✳✳✳✳✳✳✳✳✳

As well as imposing anguish on the local population, the turnpikes resoundingly affected life and landscape. Suddenly, places like the linen town of Knaresborough, the emerging canal mill town of Skipton, the road hub of Wetherby, the declined medieval textile centre of Ripon and the brazen new health resort of Harrogate could be visited with certainty. Broken axles, sprung spokes, split naves, flash floods, collapsed bridges and rut-entombed wheels really need no longer figure in the calculations. It was quite reasonable to expect to arrive in a place, even one a dozen or more miles away, without having to indulge in any crisis management. Moreover, one arrived far more quickly than before. Seedy little markets that were visited only by a few mounted local farmers would suddenly attract wagons and carriages from far away. Dingy ale houses tapped the rocketing traffic and became coaching inns. Visitors appeared unexpectedly on the doorstep. People travelled to look at things: houses, parks, rock formations, ancient trees – all became worth the risk and effort of the journey. Pieces of cloth all reached the cloth halls predictably, without adventures, and far more quickly than before. Salt, iron, lime and tar all found their way smartly to farmhouse doors, while eggs, chicks, bacon, cheese and butter were shipped no less smartly away.

Perhaps the strangest of the turnpike experiences was that of Killinghall. A township of Ripley parish, it nestled amongst the Forest commons and was a manor of minor Forest gentry, the Pulleyns, who had furnished the Valley with priests. The place had fallen on hard times, and about the start of the eighteenth century, Thomas Pulleyn, rejoicing in the office of High Sheriff of Yorkshire, had abandoned the family seat and moved to Carleton Hall in Cleveland. The hall crumbled, and in 1832, the antiquarian, Hargrove, wrote that the manor house:

> … with some other stately building formerly at this place, have been suffered to decay, and out of their materials, farm houses and their offices are erected: heaps of ruins covered with grass mark the place where two of these mansions stood.

Perhaps the only remaining impressive feature of the locality was the sixteenth-century stone bridge across the Nidd, whose 'lofty and high built' character had, in 1725, impressed the author, diarist and spy, Daniel Defoe, far more than the perilous roads that then approached it.

The Killinghall of the mid-eighteenth century had lost most of any village-like coherence it may once have had. It consisted of a few farmsteads dotted loosely around the old manor site and a straggling tail of farms strung along the common

The bridge at Killinghall was praised by Defoe, who damned the roads that served it.

New bridge at Birstwith – a traditional pack-horse bridge in design but not built until 1822, the successor to various ill-fated timber bridges.

edge. From their locations there, tenants would have been able to put their beasts out directly on the waste. The Enclosure of all the Forest commons eliminated the advantages of farming life perched on the edge of the common, but on the other hand, the converging turnpikes had introduced the bustle of commerce. Consequently, after Enclosure, Killinghall reformed as a 'Y'-shaped settlement, with the farmsteads and cottages now located beside the new turnpikes. A few farmsteads from the earlier straggle can still be seen surviving but stranded, lined along the vanished edge of the lost common.

Further up the Valley, the turnpike from Knaresborough to Pateley Bridge had passed through the youthful Burnt Yates and then swung out across the wild country of Brimham Moor. Had its planners taken a little time to reflect, they would have chosen, instead, to stick much closer to the river, and so pick up a chain of developing industrial hamlets drawing their energy from the brisk river. In 1826, this new line was adopted (above Low Winsley one can find the traces of an old road that the new turnpike must have rendered redundant). This revised turnpike allowed, among other things, the development of New York Mill, one of the biggest of the flax mills, and gave several other ventures (culminating in the making of parachute lines) their links to the wider world.

Soon, the middle section of the Valley would become puddled with mill ponds, striped silver by goits or leets and punctuated by mill wheels. This shale and grit Dale had an advantage over its limestone neighbours: its water did not seep away through fissures in the thirsty rock. True, the river was more subject than the placid southern watercourses to extravagant moods and violent floods that could wreak havoc. Over the centuries, people had learned to indulge and deceive rather than to provoke the river. Medieval corn mills and fulling mills found ways of taming water power. Problems could be avoided by not dipping a precious wheel directly in the mercurial river itself but by using systems or holding ponds, sluices and goits, and by setting overshot, undershot or breastshot wheels in artificial channels where water, diverted from upstream, approached the mill in a more reliable and deferential manner.

The Industrial Revolution in the Valley, which gained momentum ('gathering steam' came later) after about 1760, involved doing familiar things rather differently. Sheep and the spinning and weaving of their wool had been known since distant prehistoric times; the Nidd waters and its tributary becks had turned wheels since before the Norman Conquest, and flax had been worked in Valley homesteads since the close of the Middle Ages. The great changes concerned the volume and organisation of production. The Revolution sucked the industries out of their cosy cottage perches and disgorged them into the mills that lined up along the Valley bottom. The Revolution changed commerce, manufacturing and the social hierarchies built on them, but a semi-industrial culture slipped easily into the Valley. Most of the vocabulary of industry was here already. The Puritans, Presbyterians and Quakers had broken the ground of dissent so that later Non-conformists, like the Wesleyans, could easily take root and prosper. Their chapels sometimes had older meeting houses for neighbours. Meanwhile, the lead mines were expanding on the rough slopes to the west of Pateley Bridge and of Lofthouse – they and their polluting smelt mills with their poison-puffing underground flues and their ravenous appetites for fuel. Land improvement was the fashion and more wood-drying kilns and coal diggings were needed to fire the lime kilns that promised sweeter soils. While all this was happening, a rising demand for gritstone, not least for mills and industrial housing, was turning quarrying into a serious commercial activity.

With the Revolution less than a century old, seven flax mills had been established along the 3 miles of the Valley between Glasshouses and Dacre Banks, with another by the small beck at Fringill and three on the little Thornton Beck around Shaw Mills. Birstwith was different, for it had a cotton mill. Here, the industrial legacy, with the great stepped waterfall below the old river barrier, is perhaps the most spectacular of remains to be seen in the Valley. After the close of the Middle Ages, in 1596, a grain mill was moved about a mile upstream from the tiny Tang Beck, near Hampsthwaite, to the locality known as 'Wreaks'. In the 1790s, a partnership, Arthington & Blessard, established a cotton mill that dwarfed this neighbouring flour mill. Possibly the dam and goit layout of the existing mill were enlarged to serve the textile mill which, by 1803, was employing 150 workers.

The mill passed into the ownership of a Mr Willet and in 1805, a Keighley industrialist, John Greenwood, bought the enterprise. Greenwood purchased almost all the land that he could see from the hall to become his estate; he rebuilt the stone dam staircase from stone quarried from Black Wood on his new estate, and he or his predecessors must also have straightened the river, both above and below the dam. The waterfall just predated the nearby bridge, a publicly funded project of 1811. Perhaps the most interesting historical aspect of his cotton mill was the early date of the gas works built to serve it: 1820. He also bought a large house just below the crest on the south Valley side and, like several Lancashire mill owners, he came east to set himself up as a gentleman and found a dynasty. Wesleyan worship was not only for the poor; Greenwood had a new chapel on the Darley road, which became a school in 1855. Three years earlier, his house had been reborn as a mansion, Swarcliffe Hall (now Grosvenor School), and in 1857 the village had been given its steepled church. The dynasty became sufficiently acceptable to produce an officer caste and the persistence of the family influence was demonstrated during the Second World War, when the grain mill was enlarged and workers were instructed to pour streams of sooty water over the fresh rendering so that its brightness would not offend the eyes of the residents of the somewhat distant hall. The question of whether it might beckon the Luftwaffe seems to have had a lower priority.

Foster Beck Mill, near Pateley Bridge, engaged in the spinning of heavy yarns for a century up to its closure in 1966. The water wheel was installed in 1904.

Though the gentrification of the owners proceeded, Yorkshire cotton mills were not prospering. Lancashire had a damper climate, more favourable for cotton-making, while squire-like considerations did not divert owners from the crushing exploitation of their workers there. The cotton shortages caused by the Civil War blockade of the slave-owning states proved fatal to the declining factory, and the Birstwith cotton mill closed in 1864, though grain milling survived. In the middle of the twentieth century, water could still be diverted into the mill-stream or goit by raising the river level, which was done by swinging up massive wooden boards aligned along the top of the waterfall.

Though a Victorian antiquarian credited John Greenwood with, '... acquiring the whole village, which he rebuilt and improved in every way – indeed the place may be said to have been created by him, as he reclaimed it from hill side and moor ...', in fact there had been no preceding village of Birstwith. Two clusters of estate cottages had been built, but there was no mill village as such. People walked down to work from their cottages and failing farmsteads on the slopes and plateaux above.

✼✼✼✼✼✼✼✼✼✼✼✼✼✼✼✼✼

This time, very early in the nineteenth century, it was not the doffers or spinners that had come down the grassy path from Clapham Green to the mill gate in the Valley bottom, but the mothers. There they were, with their sagging shawls heavy from the drizzle, some in work boots, some slipping in alder clogs and some barefoot. They might be damned as rioters, but it was the overseer that they were after. Some had sticks, some were tearing up clods and turf. 'Ayup maister, a've got summat f' thi!' shouted one mother. The real master seldom came near the mill, and it was his overseer that they were after.

The river had been running strongly and the mill had been working long shifts, accordingly. Now it was 8 p.m. and the light was failing fast. The children had pattered from their homes in the dark at around 5.30 a.m., clutching their skimpy snacks, stumbling and slithering down over rock-strewn tracks and sliding on invisible cow pats. Down they went, the child streams merging, towards the glow of the coal boiler and the flicker of tallow. Then they could hear the swish of the wheel and the murmurs from the water channels. For much of the year, they only saw their homes in daylight on Sundays, when rest was the only joyful experience amongst the Sabbath grey.

Too many of the under ten-year-olds had been coming home with bruises, and too often. It was only at weekends, when the non-mill-working mothers saw their children in daylight, that the extent of the strapping was apparent. The overseer had seen, as clearly as anyone could, the wretchedness of employment in the mill. His position was all that saved him from constant exhaustion and humiliation. He was terrified that if he failed to deliver levels of production that would match those of the latest mills in the erupting towns then he would be demoted to tending the clattering frames. And so he compensated for his ineptitude by driving the cotton workers and by strapping the mites who slaved their childhood away for 1*s* 6*d* a week, less than a quarter of adult rates.

The mothers had come down before and so they knew some of his escape routes. A figure slipped from the shadows by the door, but it was only the doffin mistress, in charge of the little tots who loaded the bobbins on the frames. Then they saw him creeping up the other side of Elton Spring wood and the chase was on. (Some years later, in 1832, a cotton mill worker, John Hannam, testified to a House of Commons Committee about conditions in Wreaks Mill at Birstwith. He told of child beating and of shifts that could stretch for fourteen or even sixteen hours, or of being sent home in little more than half that time if the river was low and slow to build up a head of water above the dam. What the rural mills lacked in modernity was somewhat compensated by the relative ease with which their workforces could be exploited.)

The artificial waterfall at Birstwith.

While the mothers, struggling with their long skirts, dashed, tripped and shuffled after the fleeing overseer, a nine-year-old girl sank down on a tree stump in the wood and gulped the moist air. She had wheals on her bony shoulders that were turning from red to mauve; the rest of her was pale – the sort of pallor that only a shortage of vitamins, protein and vegetables and a diet centred on skimmed milk and oatmeal could achieve. She had worked for more than twelve hours, with just a forty-minute break. Her eyes were like targets, with dark outer rings and narrow reddened rims around the white and watery blue; her little voice was already husky from the lint in the air. Her sleep-starved eyes roved among the trees.

She thought she saw a boy sliding silently between the ash trunks. He was tanned, thick-set and his eyes were lively and shining. His jerkin seemed to be of deerskin and he carried a bow. There were feathers in his hair and wolf teeth in his necklace. He looked such a strange boy; he didn't stoop, his nose was clean and dry, his movements were fast and certain and his whole being seemed to delight in being a part of the wood and Valley setting. A flickering life force seemed to dance between him and the trees and rocks around him: they rejoiced in their association. His arrows, tipped with glinting little flints, looked like real ones – she wished her brother could see them. Perhaps he'd let Sam have a go with his bow? Oh, of course, poor Sam was dead.

As she watched, he gave a false pigeon call, tensioned his bow and then seemed to drift in and out of reality, his image rippling like a pond. She thought she had slept for a moment, but then he was very close and facing her, radiant with good health in a way she had never seen. 'Tell me about progress', she thought he said. She had heard of *Pilgrim's Progress*; she heard on the day she was smacked for sleeping in chapel. Otherwise, 'progress' was only a word that Maister ever used. 'Progress', 'production' and 'profit': those were Maister's words. Then the boy was gone and mother had taken her skinny hand; it rested like a cold fish tail in the big, chapped paw. They went back up Elton Bank and some people were sobbing. The overseer was out of sight, but tomorrow he would be back.

✱✱✱✱✱✱✱✱✱✱✱✱✱✱✱✱✱✱✱

While Valley people were discovering just how ruthless the profit motive could be, the settlements were changing. Hamlets were the ancient homes of Valley people, but many of them seem to have perished in the crises of the Middle Ages. However, when Jeffrey drew his *Atlas of Yorkshire* of 1772, at the very time that

Enclosure was being imposed on the Forest, he showed that a wealth of hamlets still persisted in the Valley. They clustered on the higher ground rather than the Valley bottom and bore largely forgotten names, like Hugh Green, Cragg End, Padsides or Clapham Green. The Industrial Revolution in the Valley changed the traditional pattern, partly by drawing people out of their cottage industries and smallholdings in hamlets and farmsteads, and partly by generating the energy that allowed larger villages to grow beside the new mills.

Darley was just a string of little hamlets, including Darley Head, Darley and Holme, arranged beside greens that clustered along a Valley road like well-spaced beads on a string. Then a flax mill was founded on Fringill Beck, east of Darley, in 1830, while to the west of Darley Head, a corn mill and a bobbin mill were established on another beck. Between these industrial nuclei, facilities for the workers were established: a Wesleyan chapel in 1829, a Primitive Methodist chapel in 1841, a school in 1846 and a church in 1849, with the railway station opening nearby in 1862. Industry created the concentrations of workers that favoured investment in industrial housing, the new communities caused the growth of village facilities, and the emergence of all these produced Darley, a new addition to the village fold.

The section of the Valley between Dacre and Pateley Bridge displays the intensity of the changes, with villages crystalising along the new 1826 turnpike. Places like Low Laithe, Smelthouses, Wilsill and Glasshouses seem well rooted, yet they are

The industial village of Glasshouses, where a corn mill was converted to spin flax in 1812 and where seventy-three mill workers were employed in 1832. It closed in 1972.

largely the relatively recent products of river energy, entrepreneurial ambition and indigenous labour. Their flax spinning, twine and rope-making and bobbin-making origins all derived from the Industrial Revolution, with little pre-existing hamlets sometimes being the nuclei around which settlement would condense.

In parts of the Valley such as this, on the great wall-strapped and enclosed commons, along the turnpikes and around the laithe houses and their domains, we are reminded that Nidderdale resonates to the accents, projects and themes of the Georgian era. This does not make the panoramas any less worthy or interesting, just more immediate.

The new villages were partly populated by people who were reluctantly obliged to forsake the freedoms of home employment for the tyranny of the overseer. Woollen textiles had developed around Leeds, Bradford and Halifax, while industry in the Valley was dominated, though not monopolised, by the flax spinning mills. Still, the small stockmen-cum-clothmakers must have shuddered whenever they went past the factories and heard the machinery clattering and churning, for it was the death knell of the small operator that was being sounded. Linen proved rather intransigent towards mechanisation, but by the middle of the nineteenth century a capable power loom was introduced. Industry became a thing of the mills. Once commonplace in the Valley, the handloom weavers had become unusual by the 1870s. By this time, the Industrial Revolution was a good century old and the Valley had been transformed by it. With the passing of another century, rope and twine maintained a toehold at New York Mill, but otherwise industry had forsaken the rivers and was actively forsaking the coalfields, too. Today, it is hard to imagine just how much of an industrial region the Valley almost recently was.

The cruelty of the overseers and the wretchedness of all toilers on twelve-hour shifts, those whose weekends began at 5 p.m. on Saturdays, were quickly forgotten, as were the lessons to be learned from the experience. What the Revolution did do was to leave the Valley with a fascinating and diverse working population. To explore Nidderdale in the early years of the new Elizabethan era was not like a trip through, say, rural Norfolk or Devon, where agricultural talk and accents were universal. While the farmers whose forbears survived or prospered from Enclosure have tended to stand rather apart from the village populations, in the villages themselves one would meet estate workers, quarrymen, joiners, keepers and water bailiffs, poachers, Foresters, roadmen, gangers on the railway, coal carters, flour millers, cheese-makers, twine mill workers: a much richer selection of people than most backwaters can offer. The industrial experience gave an extra dimension to the Valley people.

CHAPTER 12

THE LAST GRAINS OF SAND

(1850 – PRESENT)

Time had woven many wonders there. It had produced a countryside mosaic where the legacies of many different ages snuggled together in scenic perfection: meadow to coppice, pasture to moor, lane to hedgerow and farmstead to corn. The landscape of the Valley was probably at its most beautiful early in the nineteenth century, as the spreading lichens mellowed the bare stones in the interloping Enclosure walls and before the quarries gaped, the reservoirs rose and the old woods were coniferised. There were quite a few details yet to be added to the scene before the engines of gentle scenic evolution were shut down.

As it existed in late Georgian times, the landscape of the Valley was a most remarkable construction: an intricate fabrication that had been 10,000 years in the making. To speak of it as 'scenery' would be as inadequate as describing one of Turner's works as 'a pattern of colours'. It was so many things. A succession of beautiful passages of countryside, it certainly was. But it was also, for those who would painstakingly learn to crack its code, a historical text that recorded life and landscape past as well as present. It embodied and encoded the life stories of those who had lived there. Each one has left some sort of mark, however tiny, whether it be the picked-bare lead seam that trips you on the moor, the footings of a roadside cottage in a failed and grassed-over hamlet or the strident barn conversion with flashing patio doors where the cart access used to be. These legacies and epitaphs do not lie in one plane: they are layered. We may look, say, across a vista with an eighteenth-century fieldscape, complete with its period farmsteads, roads and walls. Yet surging gently through, like a boulder in a sea swell, there may be the outlines of a squatter cottage from the lost common, a scatter of inscribed and

Valley countryside, like this area around the Fountains abbey grange at Bewerley, was composed of layer upon layer of past activity.

ornamented stones from a derelict monastic grange or intertwining hollows that were parts of a braided prehistoric trackway.

The document that is landscape was written and overwritten by many hands and on countless occasions. All the authors have much to tell us, though few of us have time to listen. Most people struggle to understand even the current scene and the fear, for all those who have troubled to learn the code, is that before civilisation is restored, the modern cult of unabashed ignorance and greed will have obliterated the whole creation. There will be nothing left but massive foreign 4x4s charging their thirsty ways across eviscerated areas of countryside: across countrysides composed of nothing but new signposts telling the dim how to go for walks. Across countrysides of barn conversions and of pony paddocks; countrysides of the spies and the spied upon. Countrysides of strangers who do not even know the old names of the places on their very doorsteps.

The Valley had existed as a backwater that, periodically, was almost uniquely favoured with portholes on the great events of the past. The Industrial Revolution had cast out a line that bound our backwater more tightly to the national mainstream. Yet even in Victorian times, one could still step out of the thunder of a mill stocked with up-to-the-minute machines and enter a world in which the Puritan weaver or Jacobean smallholder would have been quite at home. Now we can look back on Victorian Nidderdale, and though it no longer exists in living memory, it may still not seem so far away. Yet when we realise that in those days the pine martin, known locally as the 'fomud', still roamed the Dale and salmon would sometimes glide upstream as far as a weir at Killinghall, then it does seem long ago. Time and distance are flighty; they can ''ave us foxed' (or 'davered') as the old Valley people would say.

A powerful theme of aristocratic recreation (usually synonymous with slaughter) permeated the history of the Valley. Saxons had probably hunted in game parks at the Valley head and the Normans certainly put the bloodsports on a more organised basis. The old hunting parks at Haya, Haverah, Dob Park, Bilton, Brimham, Fountains and Ripley employed lawn, grove and wood pasture landscapes that could easily be tweaked and tickled-up to become landscape parks. Studley Royal park originated at the end of the Middle Ages as some sort of association between farming and deer park, but it was developed to become one of the finest surviving water gardens. John Aislabie, serving as his own landscape architect (with time to spare after his disgrace in the South Sea Bubble affair and expulsion from Parliament in 1721) was the designer. A mansion of the sixteenth century was rebuilt in the fashionable Palladian style and work on the garden was launched in 1718. It proceeded to John's death in 1742 and was continued by John's son, Willam. For years, the Aislabies had cast envious eyes on the neighbouring estate of Fountains Abbey. In 1767, a sale was agreed and William was able to include the ruins of Fountains in the view – ruins that were doubly interesting for being real rather than an architect's confection. With its avenues directed on Ripon Minster, its geometrical ponds and its lake, this was a work of heavy landscape engineering. Not everyone was impressed. In 1772, the Revd William Gilpin, perhaps sniping at the amateur origins of the designs, wrote of the canal and moon ponds that he saw: '… it is hard to say, whether nature has done more to embellish Studley; or art to deform it. Much indeed is below criticism. But even, where the rules of more genuine taste have been adopted, they are for the most part unhappily misapplied'. (The art of the calculated insult was perfected in the eighteenth century and has never since been surpassed.)

The lordly tastes for deer parks and landscaping had cost hundreds of English villages their lives, though medieval Owlcotes, entombed in Ripley park, might have been emptied to populate the new village before the park's creation. With the dawning of the nineteenth century, the rising humanitarian values must surely have made further depopulations impossible. Not in Yorkshire. Not in the Valley.

Nidd was the most uneventful and stable of villages. It had remained more or less the same size for almost 1,000 years: thirty-two households in 1290; thirty-six or more in 1323; about thirty in 1379, though only seventeen recorded families

Part of the parkland at Fountains and Studley Royal.

in 1666. It had known nothing of the excitement of life in its neighbours: the royal patronage of Hampsthwaite, the revolutionary eventfulness of Ripley, the disaster of Cayton or the phoenix-like existence of Killinghall. It had suffered from the Scottish raids, but was less devastated than other villages in the Valley by the plague. Nidd was a double line of dwellings, with the Town Street weaving between the lines and running northward to the junction with the Old Road, where its old church stood. This was a simple nave and chancel building, with no tower, only a little belfry with two bells. It may have been rebuilt in the fourteenth century, after the Scottish raids, and will have been packed by the sixty worshippers said to have used the old building.

The Trappes had taken over Nidd at the start of the seventeenth century, but they sank under their burden of debts and their estates were auctioned two centuries later. Their papers included a map, dated 1818, that suggested a large bite had been taken from the east side of Nidd village in creating a small park for the hall. This could account for the drop in population of thirty-four between the 1811 and 1821 censuses, though Jeffery's map of 1772 suggests the clearance had already been made. Benjamin Rawson, a Bradford merchant, bought the estate in 1825, and revived the depopulations. He extended the park westward and he shunned the ancient Town Street and built a serpentine carriageway to approach his hall. He ran it through a furlong of the old village fields and knocked down a couple of intruding dwellings where it crossed on a bridge above the Town Street. His second enlargement of the park, in the mid-1840s, was the most destructive, for it wiped out most of the homes remaining on either side of the old village street. There was nothing left to be destroyed by his third and final enlargement. The final insult occurred when the old roadbed of the Town Street was dug up and its course greatly deepened. It had remained a right of way and the creation of a steep-sided cutting saved the occupants of the hall the discomfort and unpleasantness of seeing ordinary people moving about their business when they scanned the vistas of their new park.

That a community could be ruthlessly evicted, wholly or largely in the nineteenth century, and mainly in the Railway Age, will strike many as remarkable. By English standards, it was – but let us not forget the Victorian clearances on Skye and humanitarian disasters wrought by the creation of 'deer forests' in the Scottish Highlands later in the century. The people of Nidd having been got rid off, benevolence could begin without the inconvenience of a community to think about. Elizabeth Rawson, who had embraced the emparking of the village, set herself up as the benefactress of what little was left. The ancient church – what a wonderful window on rustic medieval worship it must have been – was demolished and rebuilt on a much grander scale in 1865. (Shame about the congregation.) Her estate passed to the Butlers, the Viscounts Mountgarret, who picked over the bones of the dead community. An inn, formerly The Ass in a Band-Box (the name was a reference to Napoleon's ambitions to invade England), had stood outside the old village, where the tail of the Town Street had met the Knaresborough turnpike. The 14th Viscount thought it beneath his aristocratic dignity to have an inn on his estate, so in 1903 he pulled it down and put up a shop and a pair of cottages instead. Almshouses, a school for girls and a home for waifs and strays were acceptable, and were set up accordingly, but near the turnpike, not on the old village site.

Patronage had also transformed Ripley, though without demolition and eviction as its prerequisites. Here, Sir William Ingilby was the patron: slightly dotty but rather more agreeable than his neighbours to the east. Failing, rather sadly, to hold on to land that would become the centre of fast-growing Harrogate, he nevertheless had wealth from some Lincolnshire estates to underwrite his schemes. In the years running up to 1830, he rebuilt Ripley as a stone village in a manner owing something to the Tudor and something to Alsace Lorraine and what he had seen on his holidays. Model villages were appearing all over the place, not least in Yorkshire. They gave their patrons the appearance of caring for their tenants, while also gracing the approaches to their halls. Lest any Ripley dependants should forget whose they were, the Ingilby and Amcotts crests could be seen cast into the iron fireplaces in their new bedrooms. Whatever the motives of patronage may have been, the

retainers and estate workers must have benefited from the comprehensive rebuilding of their village. They may not have complained about the endowment of three
inns, the Oak, the Star and the Boar's Head, though muttering may have been heard
when Sir William banned Sunday drinking and the three landlords quit in protest.
Then they had to wait till 1990 for their next drink in Ripley.

However, what fascinates me the most is the fact that the Ripley that was pulled
down must surely have contained something of the 'new' Ripley of the fourteenth
century. Thorpe had seen the old village and in 1866 he wrote that it had consisted
mostly of two-storey dwellings, with sunken ground floors and with roofs of thatch.
Above, there were windows in the gable walls, while the houses were often built of
lathe and plaster on a lower storey of masonry. Apparently, a row of enormous but
decayed elms lined the track to the original church site. Had Sir William and his
successors restrained their enthusiasm for change, it seems likely that Ripley might
well have become Yorkshire's best village of medieval dwellings. As it is, only the
medieval layout and bits of the castle remain.

While Nidd was coming down and Ripley was going up, another of the old villages, Clint, was subsiding slowly into oblivion. This village of medieval Foresters
and assarters of the greenwood had survived the Middle Ages, but during the
nineteenth century it just faded away. There was no monstrous landlord involved,
and probably no single cause. We last met it as a place full of smallholders, small
farmers, cloth-makers and flax spinners. The devastation of cottage industries by
the new, riverside mills must have played a part. So many in Clint had relied
on multiple occupations. Also, Clint's old high street was now a backwater and
the Knaresborough-Pateley Bridge turnpike was carrying the commercial traffic. Thus, the growth, in the same township, of Burnt Yates must also have had
an effect. During the eighteenth century, the village, which had run westwards
towards the (ruined) Beckwith manor, contracted into a hamlet on the flanks of
the eastern end of the old green. Before the nineteenth century was over, only
one house from the old village remained (it still does). Then, in the century that
followed, history gave a strange twist to events and a string of houses was built to
capture the view across the Dale. They more or less follow the line of medieval
houses on the northern edge of the green – but surely more by coincidence than
by design. There are thousands of lost villages in England, but not many that have
been lost *and* found.

Change was at work on the lower part of the Valley that rolled down into
Village England, while at its upland end, transformation was also running strongly.
'T'owd man' (as the old lead miners were known) was being shown the door. In
1875-85 the industry was in freefall. Globalisation had come to the Dales; cheaper
lead could be imported, mining settlements in Swaledale, Arkengarthdale and on

Cottages in the rebuilt village of Ripley.

The cross base at Clint may formerly have guarded the boundary of monastic land. After being moved it was used, as were many other convenient places, to advertise the business of a Knaresborough draper.

Part of the site of the deserted settlement of Clint. The tree nearest the camera stands in a dip which is the trough of the old High Street.

Greenhow Hill imploded. In the desolate bars in shrinking upland settlements, those still left to 'sup' may have imagined that the sky itself had fragmented and fallen on their heads as the symbols of upland employment, the pick, the droving dog and the pack pony, all seemed to shatter at once. But plenty of life remained in the uplands yet: water and moors were now much valued.

Grouse shooting rather crept up on the Valley, but suddenly it was there, beckoning royalty, luring in prime ministers, and various others of the richer and sillier kinds. (Meanwhile, a less friendly face was being shown to the new, rambling breed who, escaping from the steaming, smoke-hung towns, searched for air that was pure, and sights uplifting). In order to become fashionable, grouse shooting had to be regarded as a suitable activity for people of 'the better sort'. But much more was needed than a manipulation of its image. Technology had to create guns that would allow shooters of modest ability to mow down the birds in great numbers and it had also to provide the means to allow people who habitually lunched and dined too well to reach the moors without inconvenience. (Very little had been written about the landscapes created by grouse shooting until Andrew Done, my research student, wrote an excellent MA on the subject.)

The burning or 'swaling' of patches of old, woody heather was not the invention of grouse shooting, but had been done since at least medieval times in order to produce a 'soft bite' of new growth for sheep grazing the upland commons.

For many years, grouse shooting was the preserve of a few hardy sharp-shooters, mainly fit and active Dalesmen who were prepared to walk up to the moors and hit the departing birds on the wing with a musket ball from a flintlock. In the 1790s, the Duke of Devonshire was content to sell tickets that admitted would-be grouse shooters to his moors. This was not a pastime for the country house set, and as H. Alken commented in 1821, 'The pursuit of moor-game is not to be classed with those gentle exercises which afford gratification, without fatigue to the sportsman; on the contrary it is one of the most laborious and fatiguing exertions which can be taken with the gun …' However, as the century advanced, and the status of a gentleman came, increasingly, to be measured by his prowess in the slaughter of wildlife, it was appreciated that killing grouse posed various manly challenges. The activity gradually became formalised, allowing top guns to compete for the biggest bags. As the shooting took root, so the moors, mostly privatised under Parliamentary Enclosure, became increasingly exclusive and unwelcoming. Particularly unwelcome were the last representatives of 't'owd man', for the lead miners were talented poachers and could, in the 1820s, get up to 10s a brace for the birds in the nearby blossoming spa town of Harrogate.

Meanwhile and step by step, improvements to the transport system made it possible for the most corpulent of aristocrats or mill owners to be trundled up to the moors. The turnpikes made swift and relatively smooth coach travel possible, with overnight stops at inviting coaching inns. Then, the railways opened our northern moors to southern shooters. There were even grouse-shooting specials

The old Pump Room in Harrogate, where the rise of the spa industry paralleled and complemented the fashion for grouse shooting.

with horse boxes and flats for carriages. Pateley Bridge got its branch line in 1862, from whence a light railway reached Lofthouse in 1907. Shooting scarcely began before boxes of dead birds were being whizzed back south on the network to the big hotels, with the masters of the main stations receiving appropriate gifts to expedite the transit.

These transport revolutions allowed the rich to see the birds, but not necessarily to kill them. Shooting had to be made easier. Breech-loading shotguns that fired cartridges were brought to England by a London gunsmith, George Daw, in 1861, choked bores were introduced in 1874 and hammerless versions appeared in 1875. Now, it was almost as hard to miss as it was to hit, especially as the new smokeless charges left clear views for loosing-off the second barrel. Very few remained who were so myopic or gout-ridden as to feel debarred from the great social gatherings on the moors (with great matters, from international diplomacy to insider dealing, being decided, it was a risk *not* to be there). However, the new killing power threatened the grouse with extinction if the traditional pattern of 'walked up' shooting over dogs persisted. And so a new form of driven or 'battue' shooting was developed. Members of the shooting party were half-concealed in butts and the birds were driven towards them, giving more difficult, fast, head-on and passing shots. The changes will have been welcomed in some hard-pressed upland communities, for it gave employment as beaters to estate workers in addition to the permanent keepers, as well as the possibility of good tips for those who got winged. Local hotels, carriagemen, stores and casual workers also stood to gain. At first, Enclosure stone walls sometimes served as impromptu butts, though a variety of semi-circular, square, sunken and other forms were purpose-built and sited in relation to the prevailing winds that governed the directions of beating.

What had once been a minority pursuit for informal or ticket-buying marksmen who roamed the desolate, often un-Enclosed commons behind a couple of pointers, had become a socially essential activity of the establishment and aristocracy. An unsavoury grossness tainted the activity when the proprietors of the moors and those lauded as sharpshooters set out to kill as many little birds as they possibly could. It seems, dimly, to have been imagined that the twitching heaps of feathers were gauges of virility and status. On 30 August 1888, Lord Walsingham set off for Blubberhouses Moor with four of the best breech-loading guns and two beaters and faced twenty drives, during which he killed 1,070 birds. On the other side of the Valley, Lord de Grey launched a remorseless vendetta against the grouse population of Dallowgill Moor. Between 1867 and 1895 he killed 47,468 grouse and even more pheasants and partridge, while completely escaping any retaliation by the enemy. One has to wonder how the British empire lasted as long as it did.

Red grouse, the focus of much attention in the days of the country-house parties.

During its heyday in the half-century or so preceding the Great War, grouse shooting created its own landscape of shooting lodges, shooting houses, lunch huts, butts and carriageways. It injected some employment into settlements that were hit by the decline of traditional industries – and yet again, it gave the Valley its porthole on the ways of some of the most powerful and influential of people. While not wishing to share the company or their activity, I could not deny that the shooting was beneficial to the environment. In the Valley, the grouse moors are largely unnatural; for centuries, the pasturing of sheep on the upland commons helped to perpetuate the heather, but while some grouse shooting persists here, the consequences of neglect are widely apparent. In some lower places, rowan and birch are successfully attempting to re-establish a more natural landscape, while as one goes higher, bracken and then rough grasses are making inroads into the dappled, 'camouflage jacket' patterns of heather and swaling. The withdrawal of sheep from the grouse moors in Victorian times was a misguided practice and the low level of support for sheep discourages their return. The picture is not one-sided, for the keepers waged unholy war against threatened predators, like hen harriers, buzzards, short-eared owls and merlin, and some still covertly do.

In the same era when death duties sent shudders through the grouse-shooting ranks, a new and much more plebeian activity rocked the Valley uplands. Ironically, it was perhaps as unfortunate for conservation as the rompings of the elite had been beneficial. Progress had lured industry down to the riverside watermills and then the coalfields sucked most of it out. Huge conurbations had grown to the south, and they were extremely thirsty. People living in the Valley in Victorian times knew of Bradford – it was said to be a hell amongst hells. They had become aware of the reddening in the winter sky to the south, and had realised it was not the winter sunset, but Bradford's lights reflecting on the cloud base. Each year, they grew brighter and more widely spread. Then, Bradford would creep much closer.

Leeds had slaked its thirst from Wharfedale, so now the gaze of Bradford settled on the Valley: Parliament coughed out the necessary legislation in 1890. The wilful Nidd, full of youthful frolics, was dammed at Gouthwaite and tamed. Its days of gorging on run off streaming down from the fells and then careering down the Valley, to the consternation of millers and the terror of their workers, were over. Placid and controlled, it sulked and spread behind the dam – a dam that owed much to the toil of Scottish workers, many of them being quite the reverse of the stereotype of the profane, hard-drinking navvy. Then the way was clear for two dams to be built in the upper fastnesses below the river's source, at Scar and Angram, from which an aqueduct of 31½ miles (50.5km) could divert the Valley's water to the mill taps, sink pumps and street fountains of Bradford. In 1901, the aqueduct was finished; three years later, work began on Angram reservoir and continued until the First World War had been over for a year. When the flow began, peat-stained Valley water went sloshing through the darkness in a tunnel under Greenhow Hill, beneath a landscape vacated by t'owd man, and then across country over chains of bridges to Chellow reservoir.

At Scar House, work began in 1921, and the work was no fleeting episode of bustle, but a great campaign, with Nature's landscape as its adversary. It lasted until 1936. A special road and light railway hauled materials from the standard-gauge branch line terminus at Pateley Bridge, up and up, to a location which seethed with activity. In normal times, even shepherds might have felt lonely there. A quarry was opened on the northern fell side and it disgorged its stone into the dam until the local topography itself was remodelled. From the bottom of its foundations to its crest, the dam had a height of 194ft (around 59m). Not only were there workers, labourers and craftsmen from a spectrum of trades, but also their families – and an entire settlement was built to house them all.

A village, Scar Village, came into being right beside the great works, with ranks of hostels to house the single workers and sixty-two family bungalows – all provided with the services such as had yet to reach some rural villages that were many centuries older. There was a school, a shop, a church and a public hall. Life here had the most peculiar qualities; such projects were being undertaken in Siberia at this time, but they at least partly involved slave labour. In the USA, the dams of the Bonneville Power Administration were also being engineered by massive work forces in semi-wilderness settings, though much New Deal social policy was involved, rather than the somewhat one-sided civic objectives of an industrial town. In the uppermost reaches of the Valley, and in climates that sometimes seemed sub-arctic, families were raised and grew up. There was a

Gouthwaite reservoir, built in 1893-1901 at the expense of valuable Valley-bottom meadow land.

far broader spectrum of life than would ever be seen in an all-male work camp. There were Methodist housewives who enforced abstinence on their families and lay preachers in search of an audience. There were also navvies who traded sweat for ale, women who slaved for the communal ideal, and there were drunks fighting through the journey back from the pubs in Pateley Bridge.

Not many children of fitters or concrete workers could stroll from their homes to picnic among flora left over from the Ice Age. There were parties for the children, socials for their parents and, not infrequently, there were funerals. From the recollections of some who survived, life in Scar Village does not seem to have been an unpleasant experience. Hot and cold running water, hospitals, a billiard room, a library, tennis court, football field and, not least, a fish and chip shop: these were not the facilities on an ordinary navvy camp. With its air tumbling down from Great and Little Whernside, freshly across from the high Pennines, Scar Village must certainly have been far healthier and more wholesome than were the lives of most of the recipients of the Valley's water.

The story of the reservoirs did not begin or end with the turning of a tap in Bradford. Between 1856 and 1866, water consumption in Leeds rose from 1,596,000 gallons per day to 4,407,241 gallons and the eyes of the municipality settled on the little Washburn valley. A chain of reservoirs was completed: Lindley Wood in 1875, Swinsty in 1876 and Fewston in 1879. Until it was inundated, the small village of Little Timble housed sixty-three people in just nine houses, but as the waters of Swinsty rose, it was gradually deserted. Confidence in the brave new world of the industrial engineer may have been dented when the slopes flanking the reservoirs became unstable, causing the village of Fewston to sub-side. Permission for a fourth reservoir, Thruscross, had been granted by the Act of 1867, though the axe took almost a century to fall. In 1965, work was undertaken to start Thruscross and to end the hamlet of West End. Now, it can only be visited in times of extreme drought, when the field walls, the footings of buildings and the little hump-backed bridge emerge, briefly, into daylight. The great mill towns had already contributed to the decline of the cotton, hemp and flax milling by the little communities of the Washburn valley; drowning their settlements added the note of finality.

The railway that had so greatly assisted the reservoir building at the head of the Dale had a complicated history. Had history taken a different course, as it so easily could have done, the branch line in Pateley Bridge would have been an early and important example, visited by railway buffs in their thousands. In the event, build-ing was long delayed and the track was lifted after just a century of use. A looping line from Leeds to Thirsk had reached Nidd Bridge station in 1848, when the final touches were still being made to the costly park at Nidd. Thus, it might be said that the feudal world and the modern world met at the fence that separated the new park and the new railway.

In an age of railway mania, the gaping Valley and the potential bridgehead at Nidd represented an irresistible opportunity. Parliamentary approval to run a railway up the valley from the Nidd that would ship Valley products out, import products at hugely reduced prices and do away with the makeshift horse buses to Nidd was gained in 1849. Valley opinion was divided. The 'progressive' inter-ests of manufacturing, mining and estate management had predictable views, but the Revd Sir Henry John Ingilby of Ripley took a more ambivalent and traditional outlook. He did not like to have his estate sliced by the track, but the modern age had arrived, with compulsory purchase as an instrument. He swallowed his resentment and, in old patrician spirit, agreed to cut the first sod. In 1862, a train puffed and tooted not so far from his doorstep to herald the first Age of the Train. In 1951, the passenger service closed and all I can remember of the passenger journey as a small child is that there was a fallen tree trunk near Killinghall that looked very vaguely like a lion – not a fact to trouble future generations of historians very much. In 1964, with its centenary only just behind it, the railway closed completely.

In railway building, as on so many other occasions, a core of skills and experience already existed in the Valley. Useful stones, mainly in the forms of hard, coarse grits and tough flagstones, were abundant. Centuries of experience in small-scale quarrying for walling stone and local buildings left a legacy of quarries. Many were located on commons and situated at the crest of valley sides, so that blocks could be wedged-off a hard cap rock and easily sledged down hill to their places of use. Mining for lead produced more specialised skills, while quarrying offered alternative employment for part-time miners. In the upper Valley, coal was mined near Lofthouse and Middlesmoor and small farmers, miners and quarrymen lived cheek by jowl – sometimes they were combined in one person. When the railway came in 1862, it helped the export of the hard flags from Bishopside and the durable step- and paving-stones of Scot Gate Ash and Guisecliff. For a while, the steam cranes clanked and the stone saws whined as they converted the blocks into kerbs, steps and the slabs that pave platforms. However, quarrying could not compensate for the collapse of lead mining and the twentieth century was still young when it began a slow decline.

Since the arrival of the turnpikes, accelerating change had been guiding the course of landscape change. Valley people danced to the tunes of outsiders and the national drive to industrialise dominated local affairs. Even so, the Valley retained a rural appearance. Very few views were dominated by industry, which was usually hidden by dips and spurs and masked by trees. Meanwhile, in the countryside, tradition and stability were still well-represented. Multiple occupations persisted until quite recent times, giving extra dimensions to individual experience and to the character of the Valley itself.

The fascinating settlement of Middlesmoor is an example. Its presumed origins as a monastic grange is well known and its Church of St Chad, a pre-Conquest-style dedication, was built in 1484 and rebuilt in 1866, but where had its Norman font and its ancient cross dedicated to the seventh-century missionary bishop come from? If the origins of the village are puzzling, its people knew where *they* were from. However, any map of Victorian employment would have been covered in overlapping layers. There were small farmers who did a bit of quarrying and quarrymen who farmed in a small way. People who dug stone or farmed might also build, while those who dug for stone at one time might dig for lead at another, and then for coal. The coppices across the Valley gave work to those who cut the fuel and dried it in kilns. The rise of grouse shooting on nearby moors, like, Dallowgill and Masham, provided employment as beaters. Meanwhile, the growth of the governmental infrastructure, with jobs for postmen, roadmen and so on gave some consolation for the winding down of cottage industries. Innkeepers could also be smallholders and, once again, the whole picture is reminiscent of the multiple occupations practiced by members of Scottish crofting communities throughout the century that followed.

If the railway assisted the stone and water industries, it sounded the death knell for many coaching and horse bus services, as well as for a Scottish droving trade that extended back into the medieval period.

****

Finlay took a last look at Kirkby Malzeard. He was returning to the Highlands and would not come this way again. He would go back to his glen, though it was no longer home. A late clearance by a laird who had given up his struggle to extract money from the paupers who passed as his clan tenants had seen the latter packed-off on a Yankee clipper. The black cattle that had set off from the Grampian glens many months before had been passed on to rest and fatten before their final journey. Sold at a 'tryst' in Falkirk, they had traversed the high plateaux of the Southern Uplands and followed the Pennines southwards. Onwards they had gone – but not so fast as to trot off their meat – feeding at stances on the high ground and at lofty pastures by the inns where the drovers drank and slept. The rounded backs of fells that swelled like basking whales were open and welcoming, unlike the cramped lanes and jealously guarded fields of the lowlands. Then down through Masham and Winksley they had gone, skirting the ruins of Fountains. The last time he saw their black and now bony backs was when they were sold on and being driven away by some other dogs to be fattened in a Midlands vale: then off to Smithfield Market, whatever that was …but those times were all over.

Before the day was old, he had gained the high ground. He was happy to be back on the old droving trail, where the track was grooved by countless iron-shod hooves of the driven cattle and the boulders were scoured and polished by these metal shoes. Ahead, he could see the emerald patches in the sombre tones of moor, bog and coarse pasture. These were the fertile stances where, for year after year, the grazing cattle had been folded. In the summer, darker, damper patches on the uplands would yield moor-silk (cotton grass) for the sheep to munch with such joy as a sheep can muster. Soon, swaling for the shooting interest would dapple the uplands in black, mauve and green, but Finlay and his kind would be gone by then. He was slightly uneasy, for at Dead Man's Hill, at the head of the Valley, a gruesome find had been made. Over a century ago, in 1728, three headless bodies had been dug from the peat. They were presumed to be tinkers and countrymen of his (though might they not have been Iron Age sacrificial victims?).

His droving journeys had taken him through England rather than among the English. As the railway system had extended its tentacles and lassoed the trade, Highlands drovers had become ever less familiar, so he had abandoned the 'outlandish' plaid for lowland garb. Often, he regretted the change, for now he had to carry a separate blanket to sleep under. He was little bothered about clan tartans; they were something largely concocted by Walter Scott and the Edinburgh crowd. But he did still have a withered sprig of myrtle in his bonnet; his great grandfather and others of the clan had worn such at Culloden. It was good to know who you were. He was also becoming bilingual – each time that he returned to the glen there were fewer of his own people left to converse with (in this way he anticipated the Dalesfolk by a century or so).

Once on the upland trail, the dogs became more frisky. No longer furtive, their ears rose and they bounced skittishly against his legs or sent the grouse scattering on whirring wings. Their legacy to the Dales would be a great population of border collies, some long-haired and black and white, others smooth, mottled-grey and with mixed eyes of blue and brown. All the farmers wanted them and he sometimes thought that he would do better to sell Scotch dogs than Scottish cattle.

Finlay turned for a parting glance at the lowlands. He did not like the young stone walls that came slashing up the fell sides, snatching land into one ownership, devouring commons and threatening the freedom of the high trackways. In the bottoms of the narrow plains, the silver streams bulged like constricted arteries wherever the milldams choked their flow. Soon, the ponds would seem like raindrops compared to the reservoirs that would displace whole communities and inundate their farms.

Not everything had changed. Those faint stripes on the hill flank were windrows, where a thin late crop of hay drying in rows expressed some farmer's prayer for a droughty spell before the autumn rains set in. The teasel combs, spinning wheels and looms may have been driven from the farmsteads, but much of what the farm produced was still consumed around the kitchen table. When the lamb-ravaged wool grew again, the ewes were still being immersed in the same sheep-washing place in the same chilly stream; later, the blacksmith-made iron shears still separated sheep and fleece. To Finlay, the English were certainly foreigners, though the Dalesfolk of the farmsteads and cottages reminded him very much of the Lowland Scots who were, to him, foreigners, too. He turned to face the track. Already the Lancashire mills were staining the skies of the Dales. To see things with great clarity, a cleansing north wind was needed. Now it washed down, steeped in the scent of peat, loch and firth; his stride lengthened in anticipation. Many miles away, he thought he saw a grey streamer quivering like wool caught on a nail. It was too low down for moor burning. Might some barn be alight – or was it moving? Might this be that railway that had slammed the door on his trade?

✳✳✳✳✳✳✳✳✳✳✳✳✳✳✳✳✳

Change had buffeted the farmers of the Valley, but as people they were still closer to their Tudor forbears than to ourselves. Were we able to visit the Valley in Victorian times we might see a farmer/shepherd leaning on the wall at the gate of his fold. Two or three dogs could be milling around like backstreet rascals, desperate for something to nip and chase. They could be Scotch dogs, either the shaggy black and white or the smooth-haired, wall-eyed type, though other forms were still kept on farms, one like a rough-haired slate and tan terrier with a loud bark and the other, a strong, slender black and tan dog with a smooth coat.

The shepherd is concentrating closely on the sheep as they pass through the gate, his stick idly but expertly controlling their escape. As we approach, he seems to be mouthing gibberish: '*Yain; tain; eddero; peddero; pitts; tayter; later; overro; coverro; dix; yain-dix; tain-dix; eddero-dix; peddero-dix, bumfitt.*' These, in fact, are the old sheep-counting numerals, one to fifteen, that were formerly employed in Nidderdale. How old? Well, there are plain similarities with the sheep-counting numbers that were used in Wales, and across the uplands, suggesting that the systems go back to a distant, common (Celtic?), tradition. Pastoral farming is expanding in the Valley, particularly towards its head, where the perpetual struggle to raise oat crops is being abandoned in many fields.

The sheep are of a local, Nidderdale breed, produced by crossing a Scotch ewe with a Leicester tup or 'mug', though in earlier Victorian times pure Scotch flocks were normal. In time, the more complicatedly cross-bred Mashams and 'mules' will take over the better pastures, leaving the uplands to Scottish black face, Dalesbred and Swaledale strains. Today, the introduction of continental breeds has produced a complex mosaic of flocks and cross-breeds. Similarly, in the second half of the twentieth century, the big, black and white, dual-purpose Friesian cattle seemed to be an essential part of the Nidderdale countryside, though in the middle of the century, stately brown and white Ayrshire cattle and the beef and dairy shorthorn strains, compact and often mottled roan or blue, seemed rooted in the scene. In the seventeenth century, however, the longhorns, with their intimidating head gear, ruled the roost, though now they are hard to see outside western movies. Towards the end of the eighteenth century, a cross between the longhorns of the Dales and shorthorn cattle, developed in Durham and eastern Yorkshire, became popular, though cattle brought down from Scotland were also seen. About 1882, Lucas wrote, 'Nidderdale is now one large grazing field. Not only are there young shorthorns nursed here, but vast flocks of sheep are reared on the moors'.

If our Valley farmer were to take us home, as well he might, we would enter a setting that would have been much more comprehensible to a countryman of Cromwell's day, or even an Elizabethan one. There is still a scorching bakestone sitting on an iron frame or branderi. A kale pot in which a pie is cooking bakes among the smouldering peat of the hearth, and though the room is no longer lit by candles of rush steeped in melted fat, the stone flag floor is still scoured with sand ground down by a large, flat stone. The girl's clogs give a hollow clatter as they cross the room. She has dairying work to do; the butter churn and the cheese press still intrude upon the living space. Guests would always be offered a bite. It might be hasty pudding, made from oatmeal – meal now probably brought in from Scotland via one of the numerous stores that each village manages to support. The meal was boiled smooth and served hot, with a choice of milk or treacle as an accompaniment. There might be tiffany cakes, named after the hair sieve used to separate the flour from the bran, or perhaps dough baked in a stone wall-oven on a fire of woody heather stalks.

But if we should stay too long on the long settle near the hearth, could we ever be persuaded to return to our own world?

And then it was over. The ending began to accelerate a little after 1947 and the passing of the Town and Country Planning Act that would help 'conserve the best in the landscape'. Some time in the 1970s, the cultural door slammed shut and the old Valley people found themselves on the outside, looking in. There was no Secretary of State to protect the culture and language. While the Welsh and the Gaelic communities in the wests of Scotland and Ireland were thought precious and worthy of protection, the Dalesfolk, with their nigh comparable cultural identities, received not a morsel of recognition. In the limestone dales, the landscape, at least, was valued, in some measure, by the creation of the Yorkshire Dales National Park. In the gritstone Valley, however, the water interest was too deeply entrenched. Nidderdale was left out of the National Park, tantamount to serving Christmas cake without currants or cheese.

So now just the pictures remain:

It is early May and I am eight years old. I went down with pneumonia at the start of the year but last week I got out of bed and began to learn to walk again. At first, even the attempt to stand made me vomit. Now I mean business. I swing open the big door with its maroon paint: the cast-iron boot-scraper I last saw in January snow is still out there in attendance. On shaky, white legs I head up the bank by the red-brick council houses on Collin Bank. In the field to my left are the two oaks, relics from a hedgerow that vanished centuries ago. I have pinged them with arrows, but they never seem to mind.

Behind the council houses there is a dappled and secretive little wood where long-tailed tits build cushiony nests like balls of tufted wool. There are other birds in there that would set today's watchers all a-twitch. It is a place of slopes and shadows, the last fragment of a much larger medieval wood. Now it all begins to bite – the brilliant clarity of the air borne down on a northerly flow. The crystal fluidity of the birdsong arriving like darts from all directions. And the colours of spring: the near-psychedelic brilliance of the blues and greens. All these explode on a mind deadened by months of gazing at faded brown wallpaper. I have looked at landscape, but never seen it before – never seen a countryside throb with the pulse of life. (1990s: much of the wood is cut down, but they name the new housing estate after the wood that was cut down so that it could be built. Am I strange, or is that rather sick?)

Two years on. A goods train rumbles by on the embankment right outside my window. Look up the line, and soon the world turns inside out, for the embankment becomes a cutting. As the wafts of steam thin on the swell of the flanking field I can see rabbits scuttling and nibbling at its edge. Soon, I am up where they were and I carry on going by using the stones of a tumbledown wall as stepping stones through the nettle patches. Summer holidays have reached the village school: six whole weeks; not quite eternity, but almost. There are now inklings in this young mind that landscape is not just a thing to play in but something that can envelop you with its own sensuous vocabulary. I skip down and across the cutting and soon I am on the huge slab steps of the waterfall. The sun is up and the algae strands left straggling above the waterline are baking into a crisp, khaki cake. That is the strongest smell, acrid, like greens spilled on a hotplate, but there are many other scents, too. There is also the last of the cool of night fluttering away in a breeze around the stocking tops, the burning on the back of the neck as the sun takes charge, and the dew seeping in through canvas pumps. The Valley is claiming me with each sight, scent and touch.

It never really let me go. I was at its funeral and it will be at mine.

I am thirteen, and every evening I trespass on the resting railway line with my two sheepdogs. Walking restores some order to the life of a gauche country boy who cannot really cope with grammar school. A cheap

Friesian cattle characterised the Valley fieldscape in the second half of the twentieth century.

cherry wood pipe in my pocket signals a kind of growing up, though, thankfully, ethics will soon triumph over the urge to hunt and the gun will be put aside forever. Just before reaching the rail bridge outside Hampsthwaite station I whistle a short note to the dogs and turn. The blazing orb of the setting sun bursts full in my face. It gilds the bowl of sky around it and carpets my home-place in molten light. Long shadows seem to reach out towards me like nature's fingers. Without any need for conscious deliberation, a thought of immense power is born in my head: 'I can never leave this place'.

But even the farmers' sons found it hard to stay in the Valley and there would be no work here for ex-sixth formers. 'I'll get a job in Wood's mill' I vow, 'if that is what it takes, then I'll do it'. But six years later, I left like all the rest. It took twenty-five years to get back, and when I did, the real Valley people had almost all gone and their homeland was a husk.

I am just nineteen; out of school and out of work. Desperate to do something, I get an evening job pushing a rotary floor-polishing machine in the US base at Menwith Hill. Down in the dug-outs there are automatic pistols in holsters hanging on the back of chairs and secret papers of all kinds scattered around. There is still some innocence abroad,

The churchyard at Birstwith.

for I have no vetting though half my pals are in CND. Thirty more years pass and I am attending a meeting of Birstwith parish council to argue some conservational case or other. There has been an 'application' to extend facilities at the American base. The chairman holds up a plan, but neither the public nor their elected representatives are permitted to comment a single word on proposals for our parish. Humiliation adopts the form of silence. Is this the democracy that we are urged to fight and die for? So then we, natives and off-comers alike, knew that the Valley was no longer ours. It has become the dominion of a power whose people know nothing about us.

It is the mid-1900s, and the snow that is starting to fall will be of a strange, buttery kind that I have never driven on before. I leave York at 4.30 p.m. and within an hour I am at Knaresborough, though now the snow is falling hard. Sometime after 8 p.m., I abandon the car on New Park hill with 7 miles to walk. After all the sticking and lurching and spinning, it is a relief to be out and walking. Every few minutes, a vehicle passes me, but these are always the big, thirsty off-roaders that the strangers drive (though never off-road). Three people die in the blizzards that night. I wonder, how many times were they, too, spattered and left to trudge, ever more desperately, homeward?

Struggling on, I thought of the old times, when any snowfall of note would bring out the grey Fergies and the Fordson Majors without anyone needing to ask for help. 'Ayup!' might be all the driver said to you, but he towed you out of the ditch anyway. With snow caking my eyebrows I realised that my homeland had become a foreign country. Right on midnight I reached my house. No longer was it a home, for homes stand in homelands.

2004 is at an end. I go with my boy, Kieran, to listen to *Magna Carta*, formed and led by Chris from Hampsthwaite, an old school friend. They are playing and recording in the little Wharfedale theatre in Grassington. We take our seats at the back and look around. Something feels strange, almost eerie, but I can't tell what it is. I scan the audience and then it hits me. These are not the off-comers, not strangers, not the off-roaders or the pony-pullers. These are the Valley people. For just a cruelly short time, home's door has been opened; light bursts out.

The local doctor reads a monologue about the plight of the Dalesfolk – it leaves me both sad and happy: happy to discover that I am not the only mourner at the funeral. But we are all saddened. We miss our kind. We exchange some greetings and hear the accent coming back, then some of the old words. And then the clan fragments into the December blackness leaving its last members to weave their ways round pony paddocks, past second homes hacked from barns and by the corpses of farmsteads without farmers. The lights that there are glare brighter, but there are not nearly so many of them as before.

I stand, a child, on Cundall's Lane and look to the south.

So *small*, but safely cradled by the Valley.

The years have gone and I am in the churchyard at Birstwith. There lie Mum and Dad, and over there, Nan and the Granddad I never knew.

All around me, *my* people are scattered like fallen leaves; can they know how much I miss them? There is Joe, my schoolmate, so bright and hopeful till the night he was run down. There, Mick and little Tony, who also died too soon. There is Jackson, who organised things around the church, and Gilbey, who fixed our bikes.

My People – I can almost hear your voices whispering. I can't bear that I am forgetting the old Nidderdale words, with their drawl and double vowels, and how we used to say them. I mouth a few, but the accent is all wrong; like a fiddle or a motor, language has to be used otherwise it just will not work. Yes, they even took our language from us. Did they cart it away in their pony trailers?

Down below my feet, the bones and the boards are returning to the earth. Churchyard yews send down their roots, snaking and searching among the soil. Thus, the elements from the earth build branches and twigs where the birds can perch – can perch till they, too, come back to the ground.

Meanwhile, the cleansing rain replenishes the damaged river in streams naturally stained with peat, iron and ochre. I look down across the Valley. Those monstrous metal sheds will soon be gone. Despite all that has been done, the pulse of life is still beating. See how the Valley trembles with defiant life! To all who will listen, it whispers its message, 'All is one, all is one, otter, trout, peat beck and alder, all one.'

The nettles, the hips and haws and the ash keys: all are waiting, patiently waiting, for time is as nothing. The seeds and spores and spawn of life will still be here when the wrecking is over.

For 10,000 years or more, the Dale-born men and women have released their bodies to the Valley earth. Molecules to the trees, atoms to the grass.

Such *tiny* fragments of people.

So *huge* a valley.

Then they became part of the Valley and its bigness was shared.

They are the Valley and the Valley is them: all *is* one, TRIUMPHANT.

REFERENCES

The main books and articles used in researching this text were as follows:

Bishop, T.A.M., 'The Norman settlement of Yorkshire' in Carus-Wilson, E.M. (ed), *Essays in Economic History*, vol.II, 1962.

Chandler, J. (ed*), John Leland's Itinerary*, Sutton Publishing, 1993.

Chibnall, M., *The Ecclesiastical History of Orderic Vitalis*, Oxford University Press, Oxford, 1969.

Done, A. and Muir, R., 'The landscape history of grouse shooting in the Yorkshire Dales', *Rural History* **12**, no 2, pp. 195-210.

Fisher, J., *The History and Antiquities of Masham and Mashamshire*, Simpkin Marshall and Co., London, 1865.

Gelling, M., *Place-names in the Landscape*, Dent, London, 1984.

Grainge, W., *The History and Topography of Harrogate and the Forest of Knaresborough*, John Russell Smith, London, 1871.

Hargrove, E., *The History of the Castle, Town, and Forest of Knaresborough*, Hargrove and Sons, Knaresborough, 1809.

Jennings, B. (ed) *A History of Nidderdale*, 2nd edn, Advertiser Press, Huddersfieldd, 1983

Jennings, B. (ed), *A History of Harrogate and Knaresborough*, Advertiser Press, Huddesfield.

Jennings, B., *Yorkshire Monasteries*, Smith Settle, Otley, 1999.

Jones, G.R.J., 'The multiple estate as a model framework for tracing early stages in the evolution of a rural settlement' in Dussart, F. (ed), *L'Habitat et les paysages ruraux d'Europe*, Université de Liège, Liège, 1971.

Jones, G.R.J., 'Multiple estates and early settlement' in P.H.Sawyer (ed), *English Medieval Settlement*, Edward Arnold, London, 1979.

Lancaster, W.T. *The Early History of Ripley and the Ingilby Family*, John Whitehead, Leeds and London, 1918.

Michelmore, D.J.H., (ed), *The Fountains Abbey Lease Book*, Y.A.S. Record Series vol **cxl**, 1981.

Muir, R., 'Village evolution in the Yorkshire Dales', *Northern History*, **35**, 1998, pp.1-16.

Muir, R., 'The villages of Nidderdale', *Landscape History*, **20**, 1998, pp.62-82.

Muir, R. 'Pollards in Nidderdale: a landscape history', *Rural History*, 11 (2000), pp.95-111.

Muir, R., *Landscape Detective*, Macclesfield, 2001.

Muir, R. and Amos, J., 'Nidd: the death of a village', *The Local Historian*, **28**, no. 4, 1998 pp.208-216.

Palliser, D.M., 'Domesday Book and the Harrying of the North', *Northern History*, **29** (1993) pp.1-23.

Parker, G., *Studley Royal and Fountains Abbey*, George Parker and Co., Ripon, 1890.

Pennant, T., *A Tour [in 1773] From Alston Moor to Harrogate and Brimham Crags*, John Scott, London, 1804.

Sheeran, G., *Landscape Gardens in West Yorkshire*, Wakefield Historical Publications, Wakefield, 1990.

Speight, H., *Nidderdale and the Garden of the Nidd, a Yorkshire Rhineland*, Elliot Stock, London, 1894.

Thorpe, J., *Ripley: its History and Antiquities*, Whitaker, London, 1866.

Tinsley, H., 'The former woodland of the Nidderdale Moors (Yorkshire) and the role of early man in its decline', *Journal of Ecology*, **63**, 1975, pp. 1-26.

Township of Clint-cum-Hamlets, Women's Institute of Burnt Yates, Ebor Press, York, 1982.

Whitaker, T.D., *History and Antiquities of Craven*, Joseph Dodgson, Leeds, 1878.

INDEX

References to illustrations are in bold.

Aldborough, 11, 59, 72-73, 77, 81-82, **84**, 119, 130, 183, **185**
Alnwick, 154, 159
Amotherby, 166
Armathwaite, 102
Angram, 240
Appletreewick, 73
Bainbridge, 72
Bank Slack, 65-66
Bewerley, 108, 111, 115, 140, 142, 181, 198, **230**
Bilton, 106, 122, 123, 231
Birk Gill, 188
Birstwith, 10, 13, **28**, 111, 122, 173-174, **175**, 217, **218**, 222, 224-**225**, **250**-251
Birthwaite, 151-152, 193, 207
Bishopside,
Bishop Thornton, 111, 183, 185, 218
Blayshaw Gill, **215**
Blubberhouses Moor, 238
Bolton Priory, 142, 154-155
Boroughbridge, 47, 59, **84**, 157, 183, **185**, 188
Bouthwaite, 179, 181
Bradford, 25, 217, 228, 232, 239-241
Braisty Woods, 177
Brearton, 111

Bridlington, 187
Brimham, 37, 38, 46, 115, 122, 127, 142, 163, 178, 180, 190, 217, 221, 231
Brimham Rocks, **29**, 30, 38, **39**
Brough, 72
Brough on Humber, 64
Burnt Yates, 206, 217, 221, 234
Byland Abbey, 114-115, 142, **182**, 184, 197
Cana, 46
Carlisle, 156
Castlerigg, **41**
Catterick, 88
Cayton, 111, 115-**116**, 118, 141, 232
Cheddar Gorge, 27
Clapham Green, 224, 227
Clint, 65-**66**, 73-74, 117, 122, 128, 139, 141, 147-148, 158, 163, 171, **174**, 191, 201-203, 205-206, 234, **235-236**
Coldingham, 92
Coverham Abbey, 188
Cragg End, 227
Dacre, 87, 108, 111, 114-115, 127, 140, 142, 176, 197, 222, 227
Dallowgill Moor, 238, 243
Darley, 8, 223, 227, **125**
Dead Man's Hill, 224
Devil's Arrows, **44**, 47, **50**, 59-**60**, 93

Dob Park, 122, 231
Doncaster, 71, 188
Dunbar, 156
Edinburgh, 155, 245
Elslack, 72
Felliscliffe, 106
Fewston, 65, 159, 242
Flamborough, 25, 36
Flask, 166
Follifoot, 126
Foster Beck Mill, **223**
Fountains Abbey, 112-**114**, 115-118, 141-146, 151, 165, 169-170, 175-176, **178**, 180-181, 184-185, 187, 197, 202, 217, 231, **232**, 244
Fountains Earth, 114
Fountains Hall, 197-198
Fringill, 222
Fulford, 105
Glasshouses, 217, 222, **227**
Godwinscales, 11, 165
Gouthwaite, **109**, 240, **241**
Grassington, 179, 217, 251
Greenhow Hill, 73, 81, 181, 183, 196-197, **207**, 208, **216**, 236, 240
Guisecliff, 181, 243
Hadrian's Wall, 72
Halifax, 228

Hampsthwaite, 10, 72, **76**, 115, 118, 121-122, 128, 130, **131**, 132, 136-137, 141, 147-**149**, 158-161, 174, 185, 190, 222, 232, 249, 251

Hardcastle, 197

Harrogate, 211, 217, 219, 233, **237**

Hartwith, 115, 197

Haverah, 122-124, 231

Haya, 122-124, 173, 231

Hayshaw Bank, 73

Herleshow, 113-115

Hexham, 91

High Ash Head Moor, 27

Holme, 227

Hugh Green, 227

Hutton Moor, 46

Hutton Wandesley, 166

Ilkley, 72-73, 82

Ingleborough, 39, 60, 64-**65**

Iona, 89-91

Jervaulx Abbey, 187

Keighley, 223

Kettlesing, 173

Kilburn, 60

Killinghall, 60, 106, 110-111 118, 123, 128, 147, 158, 163, 173, 197, 217, **220**-221, 231-232, 242

Kilnsey, 170, 217

Kirkby Malzeard, 111, 114, 122, 140, **141**, 190, 244

Knaresborough, 10, 47, 82, 95, 106, 108, 117, 119-124, 130-134, 139, 147, 157-160, 172-173, 183, 188-189, 201, 209, 211, 217, 219, 221, 233-234, 250

Knaresborough, Forest of, 122, 172, 209, 211, 217

Knowlton, 45

Ladybridge, 48

Lancaster, 72, 77

Langdale, 36, **40**, 41

Laver, River, 47

Lead Wath, 181, **184**

Leeds, 88, 213-214, 217, 228, 240-242

Lincoln, 72, 183

Lindisfarne, 89-90

Lindley Wood, 242

Liverpool, 213-214

Lizard, The, 40

Lofthouse, 143, 146, 179, 181, 202, 222, 238, 243

London, 165, 183, 188

Long Marston, 188

Long Preston, 72

Low Laithe, 227

Malham, 170

Malton, 72

Marston Moor, 189

Masham, 140, 187-188, 243-244

Melrose, 90

Menwith Hill, 249

Middleham, 159, 188

Middlesmoor, **83**, 140, **141**, 243

Mount Hekla, 52

Myton, 157

Newcastle, 159

Newton, 117

New York Mill, 221, 228

Nidd, 95, 108, 110, 117, 130, 133-134, 147, 160-161, 166, 191, 218, 231-234, 242

Nidd Bridge, 242

Northallerton, 106

Nun Monkton, 95, 160

Nunwick, 46

Oundle, 93

Owlcotes, 118, 147, 149, 151-152, 168, 231

Padsides, 227

Pannal, 159

Pateley Bridge, **55**, 140-**142**, 147, 157, 159, **179**, 183, 196-197, 217, 221-**223**, 227, 234, 238, 240-242

Pen-y-Ghent, 39

Pike o' Stickle, **40**

Plumpton, 47, 106, 110, 154

Pontefract, 123

Priddy, 45

Ramsgill, 140, 181-**182**, 190, 197

Ribchester, 77

Richmond, 157, 159

Rievaulx, 27, 157, 187

Ripley, 8, 10, 95, 108, 110-111, 115, 117, 122, 128, 130, 132-133, 141, 147-148, 158-159, 163, 165, **166**, **167**, 168, 172, 174, 183, 189, **190**, 191, 193-195, 202, 204, 207, 217-218, 220, 231-**235**, 242

Ripley Beck, 47, 84, 93, 95, 205

Ripon, 61, 90, **92**, 93, 95, 111, 117, 134, 140, 147, 183, 188, 190, 195, 201, 217, 219, 231

Rochester, 183

Rossett, 106

Roulston Scar, 59-61, 63-64, 66

Rowden, 118

Scara Bridge, 147

Scarah, 47, 118, 194, 201, 203, 214, 218

Scar House, 240

Scar Village, 240-241

Scorton, 45

Scot Gate Ash, 243

Scotton, 111, 132

Scriven, 108

Shaw Mills, 222

Sheffield, 71

Skelldale, 111

Skell, River, 47, 90, 93, 112, **114**, 144

Skipton, 155, 188, 197, 217, 219

Smelthouses, 227

South Stainley, 106, 111

Spittle Ings, 102

Spofforth, 106

Stamford Bridge, 105

Stanwick, 70-**71**

Stirling, 155-156

Stonebeck Down, 114

Studley, 141, 231-**232**

Summerbridge, 97

Sutton Bank, 59, 61

Swale, River, 42, 45, 68

Swinsty, 242

Tadcaster, 88

Tang Beck, 106, 222

Tenter Hill, 183

Thirsk, 106, 222

Thornborough, 44-45, 49, 67, 87, 93

Thornthwaite, 141, 185, **219**

Thorpe Underwood, 176

Thruscross, 242

Timble, 106, 111

Ure, River, 42-43, **44**, 45, 47, 49, 51, **60**, 61, 68, 72, 82, 90, 93, 183, 188

Warsill, 127, 178

Wath, 99, 102, 194

West End, 201, 242

West Tanfield, 172

Wetherby, 217, 219

Wharfe, River, 68, 82

Whipley, 106, 110-111, 118, 148

Whitby, 61, 90, 95

Wilsill, 227

Winksley, 224

Winsley, 115

Woodale, 102

Yarmer Head, 47

York, 71, 73, 75, 77, 89, 91, 93, 95-97, 104, 106, 117, 138, 159, 183, 188, 193, 217, 25